SPORT FOR DEVELOPMENT

What game are we playing?

Fred Coalter

Routledge
Taylor & Francis Group

LONDON AND NEW YORK

First published 2013
by Routledge
2 Park Square, Milton Park, Abingdon, Oxon OX14 4RN

Simultaneously published in the USA and Canada
by Routledge
711 Third Avenue, New York, NY 10017

Routledge is an imprint of the Taylor & Francis Group, an informa business

British Library Cataloguing in Publication Data
A catalogue record for this book is available from the British Library

Library of Congress Cataloging in Publication Data
Sport for development : what game are we playing? / edited by Fred Coalter.
p. cm.
1. Sports and state. 2. Sports--International cooperation. 3. International
organization. 4. Internaitonal relations. I. Coalter, Fred.
GV706.35.S653 2013
306.4'83--dc23
2012043407

ISBN: 978-0-415-56702-2 (hbk)
ISBN: 978-0-415-56703-9 (pbk)
ISBN: 978-0-203-86125-7 (ebk)

Typeset in Bembo
by Taylor & Francis Books

Printed and bound in Great Britain by MPG Printgroup

Dedication
To the optimists of the will: Alka S, Bob M, David T,
Henry M, Manna B, Matthew S, Priyanka S, Sheetal S,
Trevor P and Vicki.

CONTENTS

ACKNOWLEDGEMENTS

In a book that reflects on my experiences over the past six years and visits to sport-for-development programmes in 11 countries and three continents it is not possible to acknowledge all those who have contributed to my learning and development.

However, starting close to home, I would like to thank Annemarie Elsom for her constancy and support throughout a difficult but rewarding journey of discovery. Thanks are also due to Peter Argall for commissioning the work reported in Chapter 7 and for his patience, support and lunch. John Taylor for his invaluable contribution to the design and implementation of the surveys reported in Chapters 4, 5 and 6 and for his unstinting work on our statistical journey. Steve Dowers for his belt and braces advice and support on many aspects of statistics, interpretation and computer repairs. (Thanks to Derek Casey, who knows the nature of his contribution.) Thanks also to Simon Whitmore and Joshua Wells at Routledge for their support and patience.

Thanks are also due to all those in The Kids' League, Praajak, Elimu, Michezo na Mazoezi (EMIMA), Kamwokya Christian Caring Community (KCCC), Sport Coaches Outreach (SCORE) and Magic Bus for their commitment and staying the course – I hope that they gained as much as I did. I would also like to thank both Magic Bus and the Mathare Youth Sport Association (MYSA) for permitting me to continue to learn with them, although I am not sure that they will agree with all my analysis and conclusions.

I am also grateful to Sage for permission to include material from "'There's loads of relationships here". Developing a programme theory for sport-for-change programme', International Review for the Sociology of Sport. June 5, 2012 as doi:10.1177/1012690212446143.

1

INTRODUCTION

'Fred ... you have not spoken for a long time'

The comment was made by Alka Sesha, one of the founders of Magic Bus. My uncharacteristic silence was caused by the shock of my first visit to Dharavi, the Mumbai slum that subsequently featured in the film *Slumdog Millionaire*. As part of a project to develop a monitoring and evaluation manual I had arrived in India having visited the Mathare slum in Nairobi – one of the largest and poorest slums in Africa, with a population of about 500,000 people living in an area of two kilometres by 300 metres (1.2 miles by 0.2 miles). It is a maze of low, rusted iron-sheeting roofs with mud walls. Housing is wholly inadequate, with most houses measuring about eight feet by six feet and holding up to ten people. Few houses have running water, open gutters of sewage run throughout, the road infrastructure is extremely poor, refuse and litter dominate the area and the local authority provides few services. My visit to Mathare shocked me deeply, but it did not prepare me for Dharavi. In my report to my funders (UK Sport) I stated:

> My expression when we visited Dharavi was that we had 'descended into hell' – it was like the last stages of the journey up the river in the film *Apocalypse Now*. The people live in indescribable conditions, with an average household of five in 15–20 square metres, they are packed extremely close together with very narrow pathways providing access. These pathways are so close there is little light and no privacy, or space for children to play. It is estimated that 25 to 35 per cent of children work six–seven hours per day in zari factories/garbage picking/selling utensils.

The day before I had visited an illegal settlement called Bombay Port Trust (BPT) where Magic Bus also works. I reported that

... it is almost impossible to describe the conditions in these areas – the closest I can get is that BPT is like a post-holocaust environment, dominated by metal salvaging, metal dust and extremely polluted water, in which children swim. It has few public health and educational facilities and it is estimated that about 20 per cent of the children work five–eight hours per day in leather factories, garages and stealing iron/steel/scrap materials from disused factories and old ships, sometimes being killed in the process. There is little open space and the children mostly 'play' in narrow lanes between a dense collection of tiny huts, made of a mixture of cardboard, corrugated iron, tarpaulin and plastic. The lanes are not wide enough for two people to pass easily and the huts are so close together there is very little light – the images of Dickensian England appear luxurious compared to this.

In such circumstances my concerns with finding ways to measure the impact on individuals of participation in sport-for-development programmes seemed utterly trivial. Perhaps it was a failure of my imagination, but I was unable to understand how participation in such programmes would lead to what is so casually and loosely termed 'development'. This term is promulgated by sports evangelists and conceptual entrepreneurs, usually with little consideration given to its inherently ambiguous, contentious and contested character (Black, 2010), or the moral implications of the promises implied via the loose use of the term.

These experiences and others in a camp for internally displaced people in Northern Uganda, the Kamwokya slum in Kampala with very high rates of HIV infection, a post-conflict sports programme in Liberia, a programme in rural Senegal, a programme for street children in Malawi, an organisation working with railway children in Kolkata and a refuge for battered children in Cape Town all served to raise a concern about *displacement of scope* (Wagner, 1964). This refers to the process of wrongly generalising potential micro level effects to the meso and macro levels. In part it relates to long-standing debates within social science about the relationship between structure and action, between the individual and the social or even between values, attitudes, intentions and behaviour. Or more politically, Weiss' (1993: 105) concern that:

We mount limited-focus programs to cope with broad-gauge problems. We devote limited resources to long-standing and stubborn problems. Above all we concentrate attention on changing the attitudes and behaviour of target groups without concomitant attention to the institutional structures and social arrangements that tend to keep them "target groups".

The issues relating to the meaning of 'development' and displacement of scope – to what extent do any sporting impacts on individuals go beyond the touchline? – underpin the concerns of this book. However, before we can address such issues, a more basic issue remains unresolved – do such programmes lead to changes in individuals and, if so, how and to what extent? For some time I have been concerned to 'de-reify' sport (Crabbe, 2000; Coalter, 2006, 2007) and the monitoring and evaluation manual was developed to support a collaborative and *process-oriented* approach. It was based on the important distinction between necessary conditions (i.e. participation in a sports programme) and *sufficient conditions* – what type of sports, social relationships, processes and experiences lead to what type of impacts for whom, in what contexts and to what extent can these meaningfully be regarded as 'development'? It proposed a broad typology of programmes – sport, plus sport and sport plus – to suggest that 'sport', however defined, was usually only one component of such programmes and its contribution to the impact of programmes varied widely. Rather than families of programmes – sport-for-development – the concerns should be with *families of mechanisms* (Coalter, 2007). Coakley (1998) and others contend that sport is a site for, but not cause of, socialisation experiences (Witt and Crompton, 1997; Crabbe, 2000; Fox, 2000; Hartmann and Kwauk, 2011). This perspective, combined with Pawson's (2006) realist perspective, leads to a concentration on middle-range mechanisms and the development of programme theories – the components, mechanisms, relationships and sequences of cause and effect that are *presumed* to lead to desired impacts – the issue of subsequent *outcomes* raises much more complex issues (see Chapters 3 and 7).

However, in the research reported in this book (Coalter and Taylor, 2010) a more fundamental issue emerged – the dangers of an environmental determinism that assumes that deprived communities inevitably produce deficient people who can be perceived, via a deficit model, to be in need of 'development' through sport. This seems to be a necessary legitimating for much sports evangelism but, as we will see in Chapters 4, 5 and 6, such assumptions may need to be reconsidered.

The issues of the nature of 'development', assumptions about participants and their 'development needs', sufficient conditions and programme mechanisms, the nature of impacts, their relationship with outcomes and issues of displacement of scope inform this book and are dealt with in detail in various chapters. I make no claims to the resolution of such issues, but simply wish to contribute to, or provoke, a debate. Sadly such a debate seems not to be welcomed at many of the conferences, or congregations, of sports evangelists that seem to be dominated by forms of 'incestuous amplification' in which sceptics are barely tolerated and agnostics and atheists banished. A policy area that cannot accept sceptics and agnostics is doomed to remain undeveloped, even in its apparent attempts to contribute to 'development'.

While I have tendencies towards atheism, I remain a sceptic for reasons outlined in the next section.

Sport-for-development: pessimism of the intellect, optimism of the will

This is the title that I wanted for this book but the publishers refused, feeling that it would not attract sufficient customers on Amazon – too obtuse or overly intellectual. It is a paraphrase of Gramsci's advice to radicals. He argued that the challenge of modernity was to live without illusions and without becoming disillusioned and in that context he stated that 'I'm a pessimist because of intelligence, but an optimist because of will' (Letter from Prison, 19 December 1929, in Gramsci, 1994). This represents a succinct summary of the dilemmas that I have faced since my visits to Mathare, Dharavi and Bombay Port Trust and I am privileged to continue to work closely with the Mathare Youth Sport Association and Magic Bus. As I have said, my view of the complexity and depth of the social, cultural and economic problems that characterised these communities was that they were not only beyond comprehension – certainly beyond my ability to describe accurately to someone who has not experienced them – but also beyond solution.

In this context I have strong intellectual and moral reservations about many of the claims made by sport-for-development evangelists and conceptual entrepreneurs. First, I regard scepticism as a core element of academic practice (Portes, 2000) and to view research simply as an ideological partner that proves 'success' (Koss in van Kampen, 2003) is to reduce the role of social science to confirming what we already think that we know to be the case. Such attitudes towards the nature and role of research contain substantial dangers for young academics seeking to establish an academic career in this area. In this regard I agree with Emler (2001a: 3) that 'we should be suspicious of any convenient convergence of self-serving interests with the greater good'. Second, many of the claims of the conceptual entrepreneurs of sport-for-development are not supported by robust research evidence, or even coherent theory-based explanations. In fact, despite rather odd claims that sport-for-development is a 'new field' in its 'formative stage' (Kay, 2009: 1177; Woodcock et al, 2012), substantial bodies of research evidence exist that raise significant questions about many of the claims made for the presumed impact of sports participation on individuals, with even more fundamental questions asked about subsequent behavioural outcomes (Coalter, 2007; Value of Sport Monitor, nd). It seems contradictory, or at least paradoxical, to claim that this is a new area of research, yet base its claims for legitimacy on long-standing ideologies of, and assertions about, sport. Third, there are few areas of social intervention that can claim anything approaching total success in all contexts with all participants and there are few areas of social science where research findings are unproblematically supportive of the type of generalisations found in sport-for-development rhetoric (Coalter, 2007). (These issues are explored in Chapter 3.)

However, Kruse (2006: 8) refers to the widespread existence of strong beliefs 'based on an intuitive certainty and experience that there is a positive link between sport and development'. Such faith provides impressive motivation – an optimism of the will – for many *practitioners* who deliver programmes. I have been privileged to meet some of the most committed, selfless and optimistic people that I have ever met, working in unimaginably difficult circumstances with limited resources. My reactions are succinctly summarised by Black (2010: 121) who states that

> there is much to admire about the enthusiasm, idealism and 'can-do' zeal of many of those caught up in it. Their preoccupation with development practice – with the imperative of 'making a difference' in the lives of poor, marginalized and often conflict-affected communities globally – is also both admirable and inevitable ... development as a field of study indissolubly links theoretical

reflection on issues of justice, equity and social change with the imperative of action.

Craib (1984) argues that social theorists are working in three dimensions simultaneously: the *cognitive dimension* seeks to establish objective knowledge about the social world; the *affective dimension* is one in which elements of theories embody the experience and feeling of the theorist; the *normative dimension* refers to the fact that any theory of the way that the world is, is also based on assumptions about the way the world ought to be. It seems to me that too often the cognitive element is greatly compromised in sport-for-development.

Consequently, it is the intellectual and emotional tension between the essential requirement for academic scepticism and the practitioners' optimism of the will that informs this book and is the source of the personal tensions that I felt when writing it. While I follow my academic training and personal intellectual preferences by expressing substantial scepticism about the grandiose claims of the self-interested conceptual entrepreneurs, I am constantly aware of the enormous optimism of the will of the many admirable practitioners with whom I have the privilege to continue to work.

The sport-for-development impact study

The empirical data that forms the basis of Chapters 4, 5 and some of 6 are derived from a major research project funded by Comic Relief and UK Sport and managed by International Development through Sport (IDS) (Coalter and Taylor, 2010). It sought to test the hypothesis that 'sport contributes to the personal development and well-being of disadvantaged children and young people and brings wider benefits to the community'. Because of resource constraints and conceptual and logistical issues, it was decided not to address the complex and vague issue of 'wider community benefits'. In addition, it sought to:

- build a body of evidence and good practice around the use of sport and development;
- enable participating organisations to develop their M&E methodology.

Comic Relief and UK Sport each chose five projects – loosely divided into *plus sport* and *sport plus*, although the choice was largely pragmatic and based on availability. Plus sport organisations are defined as social development organisations whose core concerns are with issues such as conflict resolution, homelessness and children at risk. Sport was either part of their programme, or they were encouraged to introduce it as part of this project – a relatively unsuccessful tactic based on a rather superficial view of sport. Sport plus organisations are those whose core activity is sport, which is used and adapted in various ways to achieve certain 'development' objectives, such as HIV and AIDS education or female 'empowerment'. Subsequently, after initial visits, four organisations were omitted for a variety of reasons and the research collected data from six organisations (more detail can be found in Coalter and Taylor, 2010):

- The Kids' League. A sport plus organisation working with internally displaced young people in northern Uganda and providing mixed-sex, open-access, six–seven week football/netball programmes for 12–15 year olds. A before-and-after survey of participants was undertaken.
- Praajak. A plus sport social development agency based in Kolkata (India) working with 'railway children' – young people who run away from home to work on the railways. It held three all-male outdoor physical activity camps over 20 months and a before-and-after survey of participants was undertaken.
- Magic Bus. A sport plus organisation working in the slums of Mumbai (India), providing a range of age-related programmes, including the Voyager programme for 14–16 year olds. Two before-and-after surveys were conducted: (i) with participants in the Voyager programme; (ii) with participants in the peer-leader training programme.
- Elimu, Michezo na Mazoezi (EMIMA) in Dar-es-salaam (Tanzania). A sport plus organisation providing an after-school and weekend programme that uses sport and other activities to develop life skills and raise awareness of HIV and AIDS. Two sets of data were collected: (i) a survey of participants and non-participants; (ii) a before-and-after survey of participants in the Girls' Empowerment Programme, although respondents had been taking part in the programme for at least four months.
- Kamwokya Christian Caring Community (KCCC). A sport plus organisation in Kampala that is a faith and community-based NGO seeking to improve the quality of life in an impoverished area and deal with issues of HIV and AIDS. A before-and-after survey was undertaken with participants in the All Star Sports Academy (which holds weekend soccer clinics) and the Treasure Life Centre, which provides recreational and competitive netball plus education and training activities, although participants had been taking part in the programmes for some time. In addition, a survey of non-participants was undertaken to enable comparisons with the KCCC data.
- Sport Coaches Outreach (SCORE) is a South African NGO that aims to empower individuals and develop communities through sport and recreation. In-depth interviews were undertaken with female and male community sports leaders to explore the impact of their training and aspects of their work.

Surveys: a neo-colonialist conspiracy?

As we will see in Chapter 3, the survey method is subject to radical criticism by a number of liberation methodologists in sport-for-development, who view the approach as part of a neo-colonialist epistemological conspiracy to marginalise local voices. However, I accept Hammersley's (1995: 19) position that research is a practical activity and that 'philosophy must be not be seen as superordinate to empirical research [which] cannot be governed in any strict way by methodological theory'. The need for pragmatism in often very difficult circumstances is illustrated by the work of Burnett (2001) in South Africa and Woodcock, Cronin and Forde (2012) in Kenya, which will be referred to later.

Both self-completion and interviewer-administered questionnaires were used for the majority of the data collection for several practical reasons:

- Unashamedly we wanted to quantify the nature and distribution of the impacts of participation in the programmes, rather than rely on inevitably selective and non-representative ad hominem stories and case studies, which tend to represent 'evidence' for the conceptual entrepreneurs – what Hartmann and Kwauk (2011: 286) refer to as 'heartfelt narratives'. The before-and-after and, in two cases, comparative approaches make an original, if admittedly limited, contribution to the evaluation of the impact of participation in such programmes.
- The use of questionnaires and the collection of quantitative data permitted some degree of inter-programme comparability, a central part of the project and one that would have been extremely difficult to achieve via qualitative data.
- The project aimed to contribute to the development of organisational M&E expertise. This was best achieved by attempting to develop the intellectual and technical aspects of questionnaire and survey design, survey implementation and subsequent quantitative data analysis and reporting, as each organisation produced its own report to the clients. However, as anyone who has taught research methods will understand, developing such expertise in such a short period of time with people with widely differing experience via limited workshops proved to be challenging.
- Such an approach reduced greatly the strong possibility of social desirability bias related to qualitative data collection by programme providers. However, we were not able wholly to avoid this.
- The need to provide technical support and assistance via email over approximately 18 months meant that the design of questionnaires and the implementation of surveys was the optimal logistical approach.
- The lack of research expertise and a lack of understanding of the programme theories underpinning programmes meant that qualitative data gathering via in-depth interviews was impractical. Where this was attempted, via the training of inexperienced personnel, the results were limited, with little in-depth exploration of meaning or process and indications of social desirability bias (Coalter and Taylor, 2010).

Types of surveys

There are three possible approaches:

(i) The 'gold standard' is randomly allocated participant and non-participant groups in which before-and-after surveys are conducted to assess the relative impact of sports participation. For logistical and resource reasons this was not possible.

(ii) The main method adopted for this project was a before-and-after survey of participants in a sport-for-development programme, with any changes assumed to be a function of participation in the programme, if not 'sport'. However, in some circumstances, especially the EMIMA second survey and KCCC, the participants had been taking part in the programme for some time and these cannot be regarded as true before-and-after studies. Woodcock *et al.* (2012:379) acknowledge that this is a widespread drawback in such environments because 'the collection of baseline data from projects with a rolling recruitment is problematic, since coaches or leaders would need to administer questionnaires for new recruits at almost every session, disrupting activities for the rest of the group'.

(iii) A cross-sectional comparison between roughly matched samples of participants and non-participants selected from broadly similar communities. We adopted this approach for EMIMA and KCCC, with participants who had been in the programmes for periods of between four months and two years. The hypothesis is that participants who have been in sport-for-development programmes for some time will differ in significant ways from non-participants – otherwise what is the rationale? One limitation of this approach is that it may tell us little about the impact of the programmes on participants. For example, if we find no difference between the two groups this *might* reflect the fact that those who took part in sport-for-development projects were initially 'deficient' and that participation has improved their scores on a number of factors. If we do find a difference it might be explained by self-selection – those who choose to participate in sport-for-development programmes are different from non-participants. However, the data indicate that this is unlikely and such an approach provides useful and thought-provoking comparisons.

How was it done?

The approach was to assist in the development of expertise in questionnaire design, survey method and data analysis – contributing to the development of organisational M&E capacity and expertise. The process was as follows:

- I visited all programmes for four–five days to understand the nature of the environment, the programme, the desired programme impacts and outcomes and the research expertise.
- During these visits workshops were held to explore approaches based on the broad notion of a programme theory, the assumptions that underpinned the programmes and the desired impacts and how these related to realistic impacts. Defining and measuring impacts unrelated to programme processes is pointless and sets organisations up for failure. This was a concern of some of the projects, but when addressed with the clients it was agreed that if programmes were able to explain 'failure' and learn for this then funding would continue. Here we see a key feature of a programme theory approach in which the understanding of failure is a valuable learning process and not something to be hidden.
- All questionnaires were designed in collaboration with programme personnel and contained two broad elements – the core questions required to permit cross-programme comparisons and issues specific to the programme and context.

All organisations were provided with copies of a wide range of questionnaires and permitted to choose the issues and formulations that best suited their requirements. The relevance of the core questions was discussed and agreed. This resulted in some variation and reduced the degree of comparability. Ongoing email and telephone support was provided throughout – the questionnaires took several iterations before they could be used!

- After the completion of the data collection all organisations came together in a data analysis and interpretation workshop so that experiences and interpretations could be shared before they completed their reports to the clients.

All of the above took place with minimal interference by the funders, in part because the research was as exploratory for them as anyone else. A framework for understanding the potential diversity of the relationship between researchers and funders, rather than deriving them from first principles, is provided in Chapter 3.

Age and development

Many concepts implicit in the notions of 'personal development and well-being', such as perceived self-efficacy, self-esteem, gender attitudes and moral reasoning, assume a particular stage of emotional and cognitive development. For example, developmental psychologists suggest that it is not until the early teenage years that young people begin to develop an abstract adult intelligence, begin to reason beyond their own experience, think hypothetically and begin to anticipate achievement and consequences. Such traits are associated with the ability to reflect meaningfully on oneself and one's abilities and this is required to address subjective and experiential issues of perceived self-efficacy and self-esteem. Although the precise timing of such development phases may vary between cultures and circumstances, we initially decided to survey only those aged 14 and over. However, in some cases in order to achieve reasonable sample sizes we reluctantly have had to include respondents as young as 12. A more general sociological reason for concentrating on these age groups is that it is during this period when young people are developing into adults and making decisions based on self-evaluation, values and attitudes that will impact on adult behaviours and choices, including sexual behaviour.

Some reflections on well-meaning ambition

A key assumption was that the organisations and personnel would be relatively stable over the period of the project and beyond. This was necessary for the successful completion of the project, but also underpinned the desire to contribute to the development of organisational M&E philosophy and capacity. However, this proved to be a dubious assumption and in some organisations there was a lack of staff continuity, with those involved in the initial training and development work leaving at various stages in the project. This resulted in the need for training of new personnel, a lack of continuity and a lack of robust development of organisational capacity.

Second, although the attitude varied between organisations, some adopted a rather pragmatic approach to what seemed to be regarded simply as another project funded by important strategic funders. Here the approach was one of conformity to funding agreements to collect data and on occasion this seemed to be privileged over the methodological requirements of robust research – strong advice was ignored. The opportunities for organisational development and capacity building were not grasped by all – although lack of continuity was always going to make this difficult. Those who had previously committed resources to M&E benefitted most and were most likely to continue with the work. However, this was a small minority.

Third, the development of a robust and valid approach to monitoring and evaluation required an ability to outline a broad programme theory describing the assumptions about the nature of participants, the relationship between programme processes and participant responses and resulting impacts. Without this there is a clear danger of seeking to measure impacts that programmes would not deliver and thereby defining the programmes as ineffective. One programme provider in Liberia informed me that the key desired outcome of the programme was 'peace', but could not explain to me how this was to be defined or achieved. Another in Malawi suggested, with no discernible irony, that sport's contribution to the reduction of HIV and AIDS was that football players were too tired to have sex. We will deal with the problems involved in the definition of realistic and valid impacts and outcomes in Chapter 3. Here it is raised simply to note the widespread strength of the mythopoeic view of sport and the substantial difficulties involved in getting programme providers to think about it in terms of social processes and experiences that might lead to a relatively precise set of measureable impacts – for many it was simply 'sport'. As will be suggested throughout the book, without the programme providers having some theory of behaviour change it is very difficult to develop a legitimate and valid approach to M&E and contribute to increased programme effectiveness – especially if one wants to avoid accusations of neo-colonial epistemological oppression (see Chapter 3).

Such issues raise important questions about the extent to which a robust M&E philosophy and practice can be embedded in under-funded and relatively unstable organisations.

The structure of the book

Chapter 2 questions the extent to which sport-for-development can be regarded as a 'new field' when its legitimacy is based on traditional ideologies and policy rationales that emphasise the supposedly developmental nature of sport. It is suggested that essentialist views of 'sport' and untheorised notions of 'development' combine to produce unexamined issues of displacement of scope (Wagner, 1964), in which potential micro-level impacts are wrongly generalised to the meso and macro levels. This conceptual ambiguity and the mythopoeic nature of sport underpin forms of sports evangelism. This has lead to the emergence of conceptual entrepreneurs pro-mulgating ideas about the supposed 'power' of sport via self-reinforcing processes of incestuous amplification, in which sceptics are not welcome. The chapter explores the development of the sport-for-development 'movement' (Kidd, 2008) and the diversity of programmes and organisations included under this vague and weakly theorised banner. It is suggested that, although the rhetoric of sport as a human right has provided some rhetorical legitimation for sport-for-development initiatives, the increase in interest reflects changes in the aid paradigm and an increased concern with civil society organisations and social and human capital. It is argued that the marginal status of sport-for-development and generic aspects of policy processes lead to over-inflated promises, a displacement of scope, the ignoring of material, economic and cultural contexts and the encouragement of mission drift by aid-dependent sports organisations. If sport-for-development is to make a contribution to wider processes of development there is a need to de-reify both 'sport' and 'development' and to view research and evaluation in terms of local programme and broader theoretical development, rather than the legitimation of international organisations and conceptual entrepreneurs.

Chapter 3 explores the political and intellectual context within which sport-for-development research is conducted. It suggests that sport-for-development is a rather extreme example of the fact that evaluation is a rational exercise that takes place in a political context (Weiss, 1993). Evidence is only one, often minor, factor involved in policy-making processes. Further, such processes produce 'commonsense' and vague claims about impacts and outcomes that present complex problems of definition and measurement and relatively standard issues of social science methodology are often ignored. There is a danger of research being compromised or even debased if its function is seen as simply confirming political and ideological positions and sustaining strategic alliances. This is made even more difficult by diffuse notions of 'development' and essentialist views of sport – even critics seem to retain a basic belief in certain inherent properties of sport. This leads to a lack of consideration of the significance of types of provision, context, relationships, rules, experiences, types of participants, the varying significance of sport in *plus sport* and *sport plus* programmes and the complex relationships between values, attitudes, intentions and behaviour. In addition, a brand of 'liberation methodology' has emerged that questions the very nature and purpose of research. Issues of ontology, epistemology, methodology and methods are combined in abstract ways and mixed with diffuse notions of politics, power, liberation and research ethics (or even manners) to designate the type of quantitative research reported in this book as being unavoidably part of neo-colonialist hegemonic repression and contributing to the reproduction of unequal power relations. The desire to confront perceived oppression leads to epistemological and methodological over-reach and the over-attribution of symbolic and political importance to what are marginal policy and academic areas. Much of these supposedly geopolitical arguments seem to be little more than an age-old debate about the relative merits of the essentially complementary approaches of quantitative and qualitative research. The chapter proposes a collaborative theory-based approach to evaluation, with its concerns with mechanisms and the development of middle-range theories. It is suggested that this addresses some of the more reasonable methodological concerns of the liberationists.

Chapter 4 explores one approach to defining and measuring the contribution of sport-for-development to personal development – perceived self-efficacy. This was chosen because social learning theories and models of behaviour change place perceived self-efficacy at their centre. Further, Pajares (2002: 1) argues that 'self-efficacy beliefs touch virtually every aspect of people's lives'. The chapter explores theories of perceived self-efficacy, how it can be strengthened and the implications for sport. It draws on generic research on self-efficacy to warn against overly individualised views of perceived self-efficacy and resilience and the need to recognise that it is better to change the odds than to try to resource individuals to beat the odds (Ungar, 2006). The chapter then draws on survey data from samples of participants in three sport-for-development programmes in East Africa and India to explore the nature of participants and the impact of participation (see below for more details of the surveys). The key finding is that, contrary to an implicit assumption in universalising sport-for-development rhetoric, the young people had a relatively normal distribution of perceived self-efficacy – how else would they survive, or decide that they could join a sports programme? Second, although there were increases in the average scores in two of the samples, the key finding related to the varied impact on participants. Although there was a broad tendency for those with below average perceived self-efficacy to increase their scores, substantial proportions *decreased* their self-evaluations. The impact of participation varied and was not uni-directional – participation in different programmes in different contexts affected different people (and sexes) in different ways. In a comparison between participants and non-participants in two East African programmes there were no consistent statistically significant differences, with the participants in the sport-for-development programme remaining broadly representative of the communities from which they were drawn. Although the data indicate general *tendencies,* the variations between the programmes indicate that, not surprisingly, there is no simple and predictable 'sport-for-development effect' – would we expect a universal 'education effect' or a 'crime prevention effect'?

Chapter 5 uses the propositions of the hierarchical competence-based model of the development of self-esteem (Sonstroem and Morgan, 1989; Harter, 1999) to explore the nature and relevance of self-esteem to personal development and the potential of sport-for-development programmes to develop or strengthen self-esteem. The review of research indicates that impacts are contingent, with the development of self-esteem depending on the nature of the participants, the social climate of the programme and the extent to which physical activity or sport is regarded as important to self-definition. Research also questions the status of self-esteem as a social vaccine and indicates that many of the claims about its positive impacts are not rooted in robust evidence (Emler, 2001a). In fact it is argued that high self-esteem, especially when not rooted in positive achievements, can be the source of problems. The chapter then draws on survey data from samples of participants in five sport-for-development programmes in East Africa and India to explore the nature of participants and the impact of participation (see below for more details of the surveys). As with perceived self-efficacy, the key finding is that the groups could not be regarded as uniformly deficient. Contrary to an implicit assumption in universalising sport-for-development rhetoric, the young people had a largely normal distribution of self-esteem, although there were cultural and contextual differences — especially between the East African and Indian samples. As with perceived self-efficacy, the average scores increased in all samples, although only one was statistically significantly. As with perceived self-efficacy, there was a broad tendency for those with below average scores to increase their scores and some with scores above average to *decrease* their self-evaluations. Overall, there were no significant differences in the degree of change between males and females. Once again, despite some general trends, the data indicate the contingent nature of impacts in such diverse programmes. The nature and strength of relationships between the degree of change in perceived self-efficacy and self-esteem was contingent and varied between programmes, cultures and by sex. The explanation for some of these differences may lie in programme processes, social climates and participants' priorities.

Chapter 6 explores issues related to a core rationale for sport-for-development programmes — that they can contribute to the reduction of the incidence of HIV and AIDS. It raises questions about often unexamined assumptions about generalised low levels of awareness and the issue of the definition of at-risk groups and the need for a sophisticated understanding of the nature and distribution of risks. It is argued that the presumption that increased knowledge will reduce risk-taking behaviour is not supported by health-related research. However, the emphasis by some sport-for-development programmes is also on strengthening perceived self-efficacy, although discussions of self-efficacy remain vague and often seem to be confused with notions of expressed intention. A critical review is provided of one of the few systematic studies of sport-for-development and HIV and questions are posed about its validity, reliability and its conclusions about peer-education and reduced risk. Peer leaders are viewed as symbolically central to sport-for-development and as highly effective in disseminating HIV and AIDS education, with their use supported by a number of theories of education and learning. However, research suggests that peer educators are often the main beneficiaries of peer-led programmes and that this does not necessarily transfer into effective pedagogic practice. Further, health education researchers have identified a range of potential disadvantages, including identifying appropriate and effective peer leaders, providing relevant training and support, ensuring consistency and quality of delivery and issues relating to their status and legitimacy in communities. As in other areas of sport-for-development, researchers raise issues about displacement of scope by criticising the overly individualised nature of such approaches, the lack of targeting of high-risk groups, and the ignoring of the wider social and traditional cultural contexts in which sexual activity takes place, which often involve violence and the exploitation of women. Survey data are used to raise issues about the relative effectiveness of sport-for-development programmes and to illustrate that attitudes are complex and inconsistent, consensus is rare on significant cultural and moral issues and that there was no consistent 'programme effect'. The chapter concludes by suggesting that sport-for-development will always be a minor player in this league.

Chapter 7 reports on research on the effectiveness of UK sports-based interventions that sought to address issues of gang membership, racism, at-risk youth and a rather ill-defined notion of 'conflict' (Coalter, 2011). Based on extensive in-depth interviews with participants – but making no claims for a liberation methodology – the chapter illustrates the varying centrality of sport in such programmes and explores the nature of participants' experiences and perceptions of the programme elements that had the greatest impact on their values, attitudes and behaviour. The analysis draws on a number of youth work programme theories about how such programmes might work and emphasises the centrality of social relationships between leaders and participants and the development of respect, trust and reciprocity as a basis for potential attitude and behaviour change. The interview data and previous research are used to develop an *indicative* programme theory, which illustrates that, where change occurs, it is most likely to occur via systems of social relationships most characteristic of sport-plus programmes.

Chapter 8 explores the implications of the increasing emphasis on the strengthening of civil society, the United Nations' (2005b) turn to sport as 'an important sector in civil society' and the potential contribution of sport to the development of social capital. The chapter reviews theories of social capital and suggests that current research relating to sport-for-development tends to be rather descriptive and lacking in analytical rigour. A case study of the Mathare Youth Sport Association is used to explore the extent to which certain elements of sport-for-development *organisations*, rather than 'sport', can contribute to the development of certain types of social capital (bonding, bridging and linking). It also illustrates the potential limitations of overly romanticised, communitarian views based on limited and untheorised notions of bonding social capital and points to its similarity with the 'economy of affection' (Hyden, 1983) and the negative implications for development. The potentially different social capitals and outcomes associated with connected and isolated clubs (Seippel, 2006) are explored. The chapter concludes by arguing that there is an urgent need for more theoretically informed and analytically robust empirical research to understand the relationships between forms of sport, forms of organisation, types of social capital and forms of development, or the extent to which such relationships can exist.

Chapter 9 presents the conclusions and argues that the often self-serving claims that sport-for-development is 'new' can be contested. Such claims serve to ignore a range of potentially relevant sports research and, even more importantly, to narrow the definition of relevant research. It is proposed that, rather than an accumulation of descriptive studies of the impacts of sport-for-development projects – outcome research is much more difficult – there is a need to adopt an approach based on programme theories and families of mechanisms. This should enable the development of middle-range theories about how such programmes are presumed to, or actually, work and provide a more secure basis for generalisation. It is argued that while all social science contains a tension between cognitive, affective and normative dimensions, the latter two are predominant in sport-for-development to the detriment of the former. It is also argued that the widespread assumption that deprived communities necessarily produce deficient people needs to be reconsidered, with a need for a much greater specificity than is implied by universalising, if politically correct, slogans such as the Global South. The need for greater specificity also relates to the urgent need to address issues of displacement of scope, the nature of relationships between *possible* programme impacts and broader individual and social outcomes and their relationship to 'development'. This also relates to issues of social capitals and the clear need for greater analytical and theoretical clarity in the use of such concepts, recognising that social capitals are not always for the public good. Because the impacts of programmes are contingent on a wide range of factors it is unrealistic to speak of a 'sport-for-development effect', despite its rhetorical appeal. Finally, it is argued that even among those attracted by the potential of sport-for-development there is a need to embrace the traditional scepticism of sociology, if not the pessimism of Gramsci.

Surveys: technical details

Survey data are presented in Chapters 4 and 5. In order to make these chapters as readable as possible the necessary technical details are included here.

Data sets and the Statistical Package for the Social Sciences (SPSS)

SPSS data files were created by project staff and sent to the team at the University of Stirling. Separate files were obtained for the before and the after surveys and merged. The data were processed using SPSS version 18.

To obtain valid comparisons of before and after findings, only matched data were compared (i.e. where the participant returned both a before and after questionnaire). The sample sizes for each project and the final matched sample size are shown in Table 1.1.

Two additional data sets were used. A 'control' group of non-participants in KCCC (n: 46) was used to compare data from the KCCC first survey; another data set of EMIMA participants and non-participants was compared.

TABLE 1.1

Project	Before survey sample size	After survey sample size	Matched sample size
EMIMA	60	35	35
KCCC	58	50	46
Magic Bus: Voyagers	46	46	45
Magic Bus: Peer Leaders	18	17	17
Praajak: Railway Children	72	46	38
The Kids' League	125	117	117

Statistical testing

Checking for strength of relationships

The study sought to examine the strength of relationships between different variables e.g. perceived self-efficacy and self-esteem, or change in self-efficacy and self-esteem. Also, the analysis sought to predict one variable from another. This analysis was achieved through the use of correlation and regression analysis.

Correlation

The *correlation coefficient* tells us the extent to which there is a relationship between both measures and the strength of any relationship. A score of 1 would mean that there is a perfect positive correlation between the two measures – an increase in one being associated with a proportionally related increase in the other. A score of 0 indicates that there is no tendency for the one variable to increase or decrease as the other variable changes. The variations in value of the variable may be dependent on other variables not considered, or may be wholly random. To compare the strength of association between variables, the non-parametric Spearman's correlation coefficient (r_s) was used. This test was used because self-efficacy and self-esteem measures do not meet all the criteria for interval data i.e. a meaningful continuous scale of measurement such that equal differences between values in the scale genuinely correspond to real differences between the quantities that the scale measures.

Regression

Multiple regression was used to assess the relative impacts of different variables on changes between the before and the after surveys.

Testing differences

The *significance test* takes into account issues such as sample size and the probability that the measured relationship is a product of chance. For example, this might say that there is a 20 per cent probability that the measured relationship is by chance ($p = .200$). Usually a probability of 5 per cent or less ($p = <.05$) is considered statistically significant.

To assess the extent of difference in findings, a range of non-parametric tests was used. Such tests were used because the scoring systems for perceived self-efficacy and self-esteem do not generate interval data. Further, the data were not all normally distributed. This means that the results were not as robust as those produced by parametric tests, but the non-parametric tests were more appropriate.

Two related samples test

To assess if there was a statistically significant *difference* between the before and after mean scores for self-efficacy and self-esteem, the Wilcoxon signed-rank tests was used.

This is appropriate where the results come from the same participants (i.e. before and after scores).

Two independent samples test

For the comparison between participant and non-participants in KCCC and EMIMA, the Mann-Whitney U test was used. This test is appropriate for two independent samples (i.e. comparing results from different groups).

All the tests were undertaken using SPSS version 18.

2

SPORT-FOR-DEVELOPMENT

Limited focus programmes and broad gauge problems

Is it really new?

It is claimed that sport-for-development is a 'new field' in its 'formative stage' (Kay, 2009: 1177) and that there is an 'evidence gap' (Woodcock *et al.*, 2012: 370). It is clear that at an ideological and policy level, sport-for-development has some of the characteristics of an emerging, if still disparate, new 'movement' (Kidd, 2008; Giulianotti, 2011; Darnell, 2007). However, at the level of practice and implementation – at the level of programme mechanisms, which are one of the concerns of this book – the claims to 'newness' are at least contestable. In part this is because the legitimacy of sport-for-development is derived from the fact that it is *not* new.

Public support and funding for sport have always been based on some vague and ill-defined notion of 'development'. Like most social policies, the public promotion of sport has been characterised by an essential duality – extending social rights of citizenship, while also emphasising a range of wider individual and collective benefits presumed to be associated with participation in sport – what economists refer to as externalities (Coalter, 2007). For example, sport has consistently been regarded as 'character building' – not only capable of developing certain personal and social skills, but also moral personality traits such as discipline, honesty, integrity, generosity and trustworthiness (President's Council on Physical Fitness and Sports, 2006). More widely, it has consistently been promoted in schools and via civil society organisations as contributing to improved educational performance, reduction in anti-social behaviour and crime and contributing to social cohesion (Coalter, 2007). Such supposed properties were even used by colonial administrations seeking to create 'a universal Tom Brown: loyal brave, truthful, a gentleman and, if possible, a Christian' (Mangan, 1998: 18 quoted in Giulianotti, 2004). The attraction of the supposed ability of participation in sport to contribute to the development of individuals and groups has also been strengthened by its construction as a 'neutral' social space where all citizens, or so-called 'sports people', meet as equals in an environment regarded as an 'unambiguously wholesome and healthy activity in both a physical and moral sense' (Smith and Waddington, 2004: 281).

Therefore, claims made for sport in the rhetoric of sport-for-development are based firmly on long-standing traditional assertions about the nature and contribution of sport. For example, the following statement by the United Nations (2005b: v) has a rather odd nineteenth-century rational recreation feel about it:

> By its very nature sport is about participation. It is about inclusion and citizenship. Sport brings individuals and communities together, highlighting commonalties and bridging cultural or ethnic divides. Sport provides a forum to learn skills such as discipline, confidence and leadership and it teaches core principles such as tolerance, cooperation and respect. Sport teaches the value of effort and how to manage victory, as well as defeat.

The essentialist and universalising reference to the 'very nature' of sport implies a strong continuity with previous practice, rather than a wholly new area of policy and research. This point is made because one of the striking aspects about this area is the wide-spread ignoring of a very large body of research evidence that, at the very least, raises questions about many of the claimed impacts and outcomes (President's Council on Physical Fitness and Sports, 2006; Coalter, 2007). Certainly there is a relative failure to build on this extensive body of method and theory, much of which goes well beyond limited sports research to include more generic areas such as theories of behaviour change and the psychology of learning. Perhaps even more importantly the research indicates the fallacy of generalised essentialist views of 'sport' – a collective noun that hides more than it reveals. In relation to sport-for-development, Saavedra (2007: 4) warns of the dangers of regarding sport in an abstracted 'de-historicised' and 'de-politicised' manner and Crabbe (2000) argues for the need to 'de-centre' and de-reify sport.

Displacement of scope

Such issues are compounded when the amorphous notion of sport is combined with the amorphous notion of 'development' – Black (2010: 122) refers to 'the inherently contentious and contested character of this ubiquitous concept' and Hartmann and Kwauk (2011: 286) refer to it as 'deeply complicated and poly-vocal'. Here we are faced with the issue of displacement of scope (Wagner, 1964). This refers to the process of wrongly generalising micro-level effects to the macro. This in part relates to old debates within social science about the relationship between structure and action, between the individual and the social or even between values, attitudes and behaviour. As the detail of this debate is well known we will not repeat it here. However, it is worth noting that Wagner (1964: 582) suggests that

> the problem of differentiated scope is inherent in the tremendous range of sociological subject matter itself. In other words, it imposes not only theoretical but also methodological tasks upon sociologists who are concerned with the micro-macro-sociological continuum as a whole.

In a way this is analogous to seeking to deal with the tremendous range of issues encapsulated in the summative term 'development'. Like sport, the term 'development' conceals much more than it reveals and contains mostly unanswered questions about the nature and extent of relations between the micro level (e.g. the *possible* impact on the individual of participating in a sport-for-development programme), the meso level of organisations, institutions and communities and the macro level of economy, government and a globalised world. Other than the quantitative work of Burnett (2006) in South Africa and the qualitative work by Driscoll and Wood (1999) and Tonts (2005) in Australia there are few attempts to research the nature of any relationships between the micro and the meso levels (this will be dealt with in detail in Chapter 8) and fewer attempts to theorise the relationships between these levels. In this regard Black (2010: 122) comments that in 'its contemporary manifestation, the SDP [sport-for-development-and-peace] emphasis on practice has come, for the most part, at the expense of critical and theoretically-informed reflection'.

The vague use of the term 'development' and the significant issues relating to displacement of scope relate to Weiss's (1993: 103) concern that many social interventions fail because they are 'fragmented, one-service-at-a-time programs, dissociated from people's total patterns of living'. For example, in the area of sport-for-development and HIV prevention, Jeanes (2011) questions the targeting of young people as if their health behaviour is played out within a social vacuum.

Perhaps one reason for the relative lack of engagement with such questions may be that many academics are concerned with strategic socio-political analyses and deciphering the 'meaning' of sport-for-development as a component of some form of neo-colonialism, or part of exploitative Global North/Global South relationships, or its symbolic importance in carrying neo-liberal messages of individualism and individualised models of 'development' (Giulianotti, 2004, 2011; Lindsey and Grattan, 2012; Darnell and Hayhurst, 2012). For example, Darnell (2007: 561) offers another version of the duality of policy by arguing that much sport-for-development

> operates within two overlapping, yet distinct discursive frameworks: that of sport and play as universal and integrative social practices, and that of international development as the benevolent deliverance of aid, goods and expertise from the northern, 'First World' to the southern, 'Third World'.

Myths, evangelism, conceptual entrepreneurs and incestuous amplification

However, the ambiguity of the use of the terms 'sport' and 'development' is clearly politically and ideologically advantageous, permitting a number of interpretations and seeming to offer an economy of remedies to a range of problems for a variety of funders (we will explore this in Chapter 3). However, the ambiguity and relative lack of concern with robust and objective evidence among many sport-for-development proponents can partly be explained by sport's mythopoeic status (Coalter, 2007).

Mythopoeic concepts are those whose demarcation criteria are not specific, but are based on popular and idealistic ideas that are produced largely outside sociological analysis, and which 'isolate a particular relationship between variables to the exclusion of others and without a sound basis for doing so' (Glasner, 1977: 2–3). Such myths contain certain elements of truth, but elements that become reified and distorted and 'represent' rather than reflect reality, standing for supposed, but largely unexamined, impacts and processes. The strength of such myths lies in their 'ability to evoke vague and generalised images' (Glasner, 1977: 1). For example, the mythopoeic nature of sport is illustrated by the fact that it is a rich source for a wide variety of frequently positive metaphors – playing the game, fair play, level playing fields, it's not cricket, first past the post, getting to first base, throwing in the towel, being on a winning team. It is as if sport is life.

It is this mythopoeic status of sport that underpins the 'sports evangelism' that characterises much of the rhetoric of sport-for-development (Guilanotti, 2004; Coalter, 2007). This is reinforced by the fact that many of the spokespeople, or 'celebrity diplomats' (Black, 2010: 126), have been successful elite athletes and, as Kidd (2008: 374) argues, have 'imbibed the developmental rhetoric of sport throughout their lives and saw themselves as living testimonials'. In the context of their commonsense repertoires and 'tacit knowledge' (Rossi *et al.*, 2004), personal testimonies and *ad hominem* examples are presented as proof of the contribution that sport can make to 'development' – or that highly focused, obsessive and sometimes dysfunctional personal commitment to elite sport, often among already privileged individuals, can lead to personal success, celebrity and affluence. Robust research evidence illustrates that these are wholly unrealistic role models for the vast majority of participants in sport-for-development programmes (Payne *et al.*, 2003; Lyle, 2006; Kidd, 2008). As Black (2010: 123) notes, quoting Kidd's (2008: 377) comment that 'the singleminded purpose and confidence that sport instils in champions, a commendable attribute when transferred to many other settings', may be ill-suited to the uncertain landscape of development. We will return to the issue of role models in Chapters 4 and 7.

Such processes produce a number of 'conceptual entrepreneurs' (Hewitt, 1998), who offer solutions to problems via focusing on a single concept. For Hewitt (1998) this relates to the promotion of self-esteem as a social vaccine for a wide variety of personal and social problems (we will look at self-esteem in the context of sport-for-development in Chapter 5). Conceptual entrepreneurs engage in claim-making activities to persuade others of the importance of their proposed solution. They use what they claim to be scientific ideas to argue the legitimacy of their claims and they promote specific programmes based on the central concept or idea and stand to gain financially, or in terms of social and political status. Such processes are usually accompanied by 'incestuous amplification', which is defined by Jane's Defence Weekly as 'a condition in warfare where one only listens to those who are already in lock-step agreement, reinforcing set beliefs and creating a situation ripe for miscalculation' (www.cybercollege.com/ia.htm, accessed 11 December 2012). The amplification is supported and reinforced by three mechanisms: selective exposure via which individuals and organisations minimise exposure to ideas that run contrary to their own beliefs; selective perception of data and information (e.g. ignoring less than supportive research findings) and selective recall in support of their arguments.

In the sport-for-development arena such perspectives and incestuous amplification are reinforced by the promotional and self-promotional strategies of sport-for-development organisations. Such organisations proclaim their belief in the transformatory power of sport and its contribution to 'development'. Kidd (2008) refers to the increasingly vociferous and well-connected policy entrepreneurs (should this be conceptual entrepreneurs?) of the sport-for-development lobby, which has sought to convince the United Nations and other agencies about the contribution that sport could make to their aid agendas. Such organisations constantly refer to the supposed 'power' of sport, and via websites and conferences (perhaps 'congregation' would be a more appropriate term) promote the ability of sport 'to create positive social change across the world' (Beyond Sport, nd). In line with the myth making, wholly commercial sports brands such as MLB, NBA, NFL and NHL are accorded 'heroic' status and viewed as having 'the profound ability to become hubs of positive influence and resource'. It is surely a mere coincidence that Tony Blair – who has been accused of incestuous amplification regarding the war in Iraq and of being a war criminal by Archbishop Desmond Tutu – is Chairman of the Beyond Sport Ambassadors, an organisation that promotes sport for peace. It is a pity that Saddam Hussein did not play ball.

Much of this rhetoric is based on mythical tales of individual conversion, the conquering of adversity, heroic feats, personal redemption via hard work and individuals possessing the power to shape their fate through sheer self-affirmation. Such rhetoric fits well with the broader international neo-liberal policy context (Kidd, 2008) and the ignoring of broader social and economic structures – a perspective criticised by many (Giulianotti, 2004, 2011; Darnell, 2007). The quasi-religiosity combines with the hyperbole inherent in discussions of sport – where all are 'heroes', even the organisations. Although not typical, the Youth Sport Uganda website provides a rather literal example of sports evangelism, which is not wholly unconnected with sport-for-development rhetoric. It states that its 'Sports Evangelism program operates under two basic principles: One is that sports provide a platform or avenue to share the Gospel that might not exist otherwise'. The second principle is derived from Romans 12:6: 'We each have different gifts according to the grace given us ... let him use them in proportion to his faith'.

Approaches to sport-for-development

In the context of such essentialist approaches it is useful to note the range of approaches and initiatives that can be included under the designation of sport-for-development. For example, Kidd (2008) suggests that there are three broad, overlapping, approaches:

- Traditional sports development in which the provision of basic sports coaching, equipment and infrastructure are the central concern. For example, the Norwegian Olympic Committee and Confederation of Sports (NIF) started supporting sport-for-all projects in Tanzania in 1984; Olympic Solidarity distributes resources from the television rights of the Olympic Games to national Olympic Committees; the Dutch FA (KNVB) supports the development of football in countries with which it has historic links; Commonwealth Games Canada supported the Canadian Caribbean Coaching Certification Program; UK Sport, the British Council and UNICEF deliver the International Inspiration programme as part of the legacy promises for the London 2012 Olympics. However, while all contain an element of altruism, such initiatives are often undertaken for diplomatic purposes (see Kidd, 2008).

- Humanitarian assistance in which fundraising in sport is used to provide forms of aid assistance, frequently for refugees. This is exemplified by the early work of Olympic Aid, some of the subsequent work of Right to Play, the work of the British charity Sport Relief and the partnership between UNICEF and Barcelona FC to highlight issues and raise funds.
- The rather grandiosely named 'sport-for-development-and-peace', which covers a variety of organisations and loose coalitions (Kidd, 2008). It is probably the case that most organisations and projects tend to be more concerned with individual and community development, rather than the rather amorphous and ill-defined 'peace'.

Giulianotti (2011) concentrates on sport-for-development-and-peace (SDP) initiatives and offers three ideal types. These overlap Kidd's (2008) categories, but place emphasis on the institutional features of projects, the properties of the work and the types of social relations within the projects.

- The technical model is a hierarchical and directive one in which external agencies provide supposedly impartial analysis and implement problem-solving strategies. This is mostly via clinics using established sports and defined outcomes are quantified and measured. Such initiatives are often supported by celebrity-driven organisations and transnational corporations seeking to associate their products with good causes.
- The dialogical model is rooted in 'an interpretative, communicative philosophy' in which external agencies work to facilitate meaningful, sustainable contact between divided peoples, and act as independent mediators via 'dialogical pedagogy' (Giulianotti, 2011: 218). The model tends to be based on a 'training the trainers' approach and is willing to modify existing sports to achieve inclusiveness.
- Critical SDP model. This 'features a highly reflexive and critical approach towards SDP work' (Giulianotti, 2011: 220). It adopts a facilitating, bottom-up, local ownership, community-wide approach that seeks inter-communal transformation via self-directed experiential learning and uses new games that lack the cultural baggage of established sports. It also recognises that such work is complementary to wider social processes.

Burnett (2010) describes three different approaches to sport-for-development in South Africa.

- A government-initiated mass participation programme, which seems more 'top-down' and non-consultative than many of the so-called neo-colonialist programmes.
- A community-club development programme funded by AusAid and the Australian Sports Commission that was based on an 'inclusive community consultation and the needs-based, community-driven structuring of a club' (Burnett, 2010: 35, 39), which promoted 'local ownership and buy-in'. This raises questions about the one-dimensional nature of the neo-colonialist critique of such programmes (Lindsey and Grattan, 2012; Darnell and Hayhurst, 2012).
- An 'outside-in' approach promoted by GTZ and the European Union via the development of local partnerships to build capacity and spread 'development philosophy' (Burnett, 2010: 36).

Coalter (2007) suggests a broad approach to classification based on the relative emphasis given to sport to achieve certain objectives:

- Traditional forms of provision for *sport,* with an implicit assumption or explicit affirmation that sport has inherent developmental properties for participants and communities.
- *Sport plus,* in which sports are adapted and often augmented with parallel programmes in order to maximise their potential to achieve developmental objectives. This approach might be regarded as the standard sport-for-development model and the research reported in the later chapters was undertaken with organisations in this category.
- *Plus sport* in which sport's popularity is used as a type of 'fly paper' to attract young people to programmes of education and training (a widespread approach for HIV/AIDS prevention programmes), with the systematic development of sport rarely a strategic aim.

Of course such categories are ideal types and there is a continuum of *sport plus* and *plus sport* programmes, with differences not always clear-cut, with outcomes pursued via varying mixtures of organisational values, ethics and practices, symbolic games and more formal didactic approaches. As will be argued throughout the book, while participation in sport is mostly an important *necessary* condition, it is rarely a *sufficient* condition for the achievement of many outcomes (Coalter, 2007; Coakley, 1998). As we will see, this presents significant methodological difficulties in attributing any measured individual impacts or behavioural outcomes solely to 'sport'.

In addition to such variety it is essential to note that many of the radical critiques of sport-for-development tend to be aimed at top-down forms of directive intervention by external agencies, often with little local accountability – Giulianotti's (2011) technical and dialogical models. These are taken to symbolise a broader pattern of neo-colonialist and exploitative relationships and are part of a more general concern about the consequences of external aid for civil society organisations (Giulianotti, 2011; Lindsey and Grattan, 2012; Darnell and Hayhurst, 2012). As the debt-ridden crises of many African societies have led to a weakening of the state and institutions of civil society, there has been a proliferation of external non-governmental organisations (NGOs) giving them effective control of areas such as health, education and welfare provision and this has been reinforced by the HIV/AIDS pandemic (Armstrong and Giulianotti, 2004; Pisani, 2008). In such circumstances some argue that the rapid growth in influence of locally non-accountable NGOs represents new forces of neo-colonialism. With their main leadership and strategies being formulated in the West, they are viewed as having the potential to promote new forms of dependency. In an analysis of the testimonies of Right to Play volunteers, Darnell (2007: 560) has characterised such approaches as ones in which 'whiteness as a subject position of benevolence, rationality and expertise, [is] confirmed in opposition to marginalised, unsophisticated and appreciative bodies of colour' and Giulianotti (2011) criticises the technical model's reliance on externally imposed solutions.

Levermore (2008) proposes a classification based on desired outcomes, which provides a basis for the disaggregation of the summative term 'development' and a partial framework for the identification of measures of effectiveness: conflict resolution and inter-cultural understanding; building physical, social and community infrastructure; raising awareness, particularly through education; empowerment; direct impact on physical and psychological health and general welfare; economic development and poverty alleviation.

Rights or externalities?

The rapid growth of the sport-for-development movement occurred in the late 1990s with the establishment of organisations such as Edusport Foundation, Zambia (1999), Magic Bus, Mumbai (1999) and EMIMA, Tanzania (2001) and the Kicking Aids Out Network in 2001 – although organisations such as Mathare Youth Sport Association (MYSA) (1987) and Sports Coaches Outreach (1991) had existed for much longer. These initiatives were consolidated via the first International Conference on Sport and Development in Magglingen, Switzerland in 2003. The scale of this recently emerged 'movement' is indicated by the fact that 295 organisations are listed in the International Platform on Sport and Development, which Kidd (2008: 370) refers to as an admittedly loose and unorganised 'international movement for Sport-for-Development and Peace'. Kidd (2008: 371) argues this 'movement' is qualitatively and quantitatively different from previous rather fragmented and *ad hoc* interventions:

> The current manifestation is different in the rapid explosion of agencies and organisations that are involved, the tremendous appeal that it has for youth volunteering, the financial support it enjoys from the powerful international sports federations and the extent to which it has been championed by the United Nations, its agencies and significant partners.

So the question is, where did this 'movement' come from and why?

Some commentaries suggest that the current sport-for-development movement emerged from an evolutionary history of the extension of human rights. For example, the Sport-for-Development International Working Group (2008) adopts a broadly human rights framework by highlighting the inclusion of play and recreation in the 1959 UN Declaration the Rights of the Child, the 1978 UNESCO adoption of the International Charter of Physical Education and Sport, the 1979 recognition of women's right to sport and physical education in the Convention on the Elimination of All Forms of Discrimination against Women and the 1989 adoption by the UN of the Convention of the Rights of the Child, which reinforced every child's right to play.

This human rights approach is exemplified in the Norwegian Ministry of Foreign Affairs' (2006) *Strategy for Norway's culture and sports co-operation with countries in the South*. This document locates the consideration of sport within a broader context of cultural rights. Quoting the UN Declaration of Human Rights, the International Covenant on Civil and Political Rights and the International Covenant on Economic, Social and Cultural Rights as a framework, it asserts that 'the opportunity to take part in sport is a right in itself which must be promoted and safeguarded' (Norwegian Ministry of Foreign Affairs, 2006: 37). This approach was in part reflected by the earlier work of the Norwegian Olympic Committee and Confederation of Sports (NIF), which has been promoting sport in Africa since 1984, starting with a traditional sport-for-all pilot project providing facilities and equipment in Dar-es-Salaam in Tanzania. This work was subsequently extended to Zimbabwe and Zambia, where the emphasis shifted to capacity building, organisational development and sustainability. However, for a variety of reasons relating to a lack of local capacity and political commitment, this strategy proved to be difficult to achieve (NIF, nd) – an experience still common with some of the initial pioneers recently facing difficulties.

A different approach, but one still closely related to the concepts of rights of the child, is illustrated by the 'humanitarian sports assistance' (Kidd, 2008) of Olympic Aid, which is similar to Giulianotti's (2011) technical model. This was established by the Lillehammer Olympic Organising Committee in 1992 as part of the preparations for the 1994 Olympic Winter Games. In a partnership with the Red Cross, Save the Children, Norwegian Refugee Council, Norwegian People's Council and the Norwegian Church Fund, Olympic Aid used sporting personalities and sports networks to raise funds to contribute to a range of humanitarian, but largely non-sporting, projects in war zones such as Sarajevo, Guatemala, Afghanistan and Lebanon. This type of sports-related fundraising continued until 2001 when it was established as an NGO committed to a more direct delivery model, using mostly North American volunteers to deliver an initiative entitled SportWorks, working in refugee communities in Angola and Côte d'Ivoire (Darnell, 2007). In 2003 Olympic Aid rebranded itself as Right to Play and extended its direct delivery remit (Darnell, 2007; Kidd, 2008), becoming more specifically a 'sport-for-development-and-peace' organisation and a major player in the new burgeoning 'movement'.

Such a broad framework of human rights' declarations and humanitarian actions provided a legitimating framework for sporting organisations to lobby for investment to widen sporting opportunities. However, the limitations of this position, especially as a basis for practical policy and investment, and the perennial duality of policies for sport are illustrated by the Norwegian Ministry of Foreign Affairs' (2006: 11) statement that 'in practice it is neither possible nor appropriate to differentiate between culture and sports activities with a predominantly intrinsic value and those with a predominantly utilitarian value'. The essential duality continues in the statement that 'sport is a human right, has an inherent value and can be used as a tool for achieving peace and development and thus also the MDGs [Millennium Development Goals]' (Norwegian Ministry of Foreign Affairs, 2006: 37).

Consequently, although this document places itself firmly within 'a rights-based perspective' (Norwegian Ministry of Foreign Affairs, 2006: 70), it feels the necessity to outline an impressively long list illustrating the supposed 'utilitarian value' of sport, clearly based on longstanding ideologies: health improvement, reduction of the probability of contracting disease, the reduction of HIV/AIDS, job creation and stimulating local economic development, environmental awareness, an alternative to drug use and crime, improvement in academic results, peace and reconciliation, dialogue and tolerance, decreased welfare expenditure and the development of human capital. However, despite the listing of such extraordinarily wide-ranging contributions, and the assertion that it is not possible to separate sport's intrinsic and utilitarian values, the document then illustrates the fundamental ambiguity in such policies by arguing that 'it is important to have realistic expectations about what can be achieved through sport. Sport is no guarantee of peace and development, nor is it a blueprint for solving major social problems' (Norwegian Ministry of Foreign Affairs, 2006: 41).

This mixture of a bold assertion of the utilitarian benefits of ensuring human rights combined with the management of expectations is related to the essential dependency of sport-for-development organisations on funding from non-sporting sources, such as aid-agencies with very specific development agendas. Kidd (2008) comments that, despite the rhetorical and symbolic legitimation provided by the rights discourse and UN support, sport-for-development-and-peace initiatives are heavily dependent on others for funding. Although some governments were willing to fund straightforward sports development projects (e.g. Norway; Canada; UK; Holland), albeit within a broader diplomatic agenda, the increasing dominance of forms of neo-Liberalism in many Western industrialised nations led to a growing scepticism about simple rights-based arguments, especially in what might be regarded as a lower priority 'right' of sport. Consequently, sports funding would need to be sought from organisations and agencies with non-sporting agendas, with the attendant necessity to persuade them that sport could contribute to their core agendas – everything from the development of human capital and educational achievement, via the reduction of HIV and AIDS infections to economic development and regional reconciliation and peace.

Therefore, the evolutionary framework of human rights declarations may have provided some rhetorical legitimation for those lobbying for a sport-as-human-right position, especially with regard to women. However, it is undeniable that the great step, if not leap, forward for sport-for-development is to be explained not by a gradual acceptance of sport as a human right, but by broader policy changes that enabled sport to draw on long-standing ideologies to argue for its contributions to aspects of a new aid paradigm (Renard, 2006). This shifted emphasis from economic capital to human and social capital, from government agencies to civil society.

The United Nations embraces sport, with the exhortation of the evangelists

From the late 1990s an increasingly vociferous loose coalition of sport-for-development organisations sought to convince the United Nations and other agencies about the contribution that sport could make to their aid agendas. The influence of sport-for-development lobbying can be seen in the statement of Louise Fréchette, the UN Deputy Secretary General, at the World Sports Forum in 2000 that:

> The power of sports is far more than symbolic. You are engines of economic growth. You are a force for gender equality. You can bring youth and others in from the margins, strengthening the social fabric. You can promote communication and help heal the divisions between peoples, communities and entire nations. You can set an example of fair play.

The duality of the motives and probably the strength of the influence of the lobbyists can be seen in the next sentence – 'Last but not least, you can advocate a strong and effective United Nations'. The lobbying efforts were greatly assisted by the publication in 2000 of the United Nations' eight Millennium Development Goals (MDGs). These represented an attempt to achieve a comprehensive and coordinated strategic approach to tackling certain development-related issues, based on more precise definitions of priority areas for investment. Significantly, many of these were focused on personal and 'social inclusion' issues that, in the late 1990s had become associated with sports policy in the more economically developed societies (Coalter, 2007) – strengthening education, improving community safety and social cohesion, helping girls and women and youth at risk and addressing issues of public health (Kidd, 2008). The latter included HIV and AIDS, which was to provide the sport-for-development movement with a major opportunity, becoming a central component of many programmes and resulting in the establishment of the Kicking-Aids-Out! network of sport-for-development organisations (www.kickingaidsout.net, accessed 12 December 2012). The defining of such people-centred objectives clearly resonated with many of sport's traditional claims about its contribution to personal and social development, again illustrating continuity rather than 'newness'. This situation seems closely analogous to that outlined in Pisani's (2008: 31) sceptical analysis of the 'AIDS industry' and the bandwagon effect. She notes that 'as the AIDS funding honeypot began to swell', 10 UN agencies discovered that HIV was part of their core mandate.

Potential influence was increased via the appointment in 2001 of Adolf Ogi, a former Swiss politician, as special advisor on sport to Kofi Annan, the United Nations Secretary General (albeit only one of 60 such unpaid advisors). In 2002, at the Olympic Aid Roundtable Forum in Salt Lake City, Kofi Annan argued for the integration of sport into mainstream development policies in terms that are clearly rooted in the mythopoeic qualities of sport and sports evangelism:

> Sport can play a role in improving the lives of individuals, not only individuals, I might add, but whole communities. I am convinced that the time is right to build on that understanding, to encourage governments, development agencies and communities to think how sport can be included more systematically in the plans to help children, particularly those living in the midst of poverty, disease and conflict.

As Kidd (2008) records, at the instigation of Johann Koss, Chief Executive of Right to Play and several developing countries and with the support of Kofi Annan, the UN commissioned and gave approval to *Sport for Development and Peace; Towards Achieving the Millennium Development Goals* (United Nations, 2003). Subsequently, in November 2003 the General Assembly of the United Nations adopted a resolution affirming its commitment to sport as a means to promote education, health, development and peace and to include sport and physical education as a tool to contribute towards achieving the MDGs.

This dramatically increased interest and the growing sport-for-development 'movement' was given expression in 2003 via the first International Conference on Sport and Development in Magglingen, Switzerland, and was supported by the Swiss Agency for Development and Co-operation. This was accompanied by the publication of the *Magglingen Declaration*, which was mostly an old testament restatement of many of the widespread, but largely unsubstantiated, claims for sporting externalities – physical and mental health, improved educational performance, sociability, overcoming social barriers, teaching mutual respect and providing the basis for partnerships (a central mechanism in the new aid paradigm). This was followed by the establishment of an internet platform (www.sportanddev.org, accessed 12 December 2012) to contribute to a common working framework for the promotion of sport and development. In the same year, the first of a biennial series of more African-focused *Next Step* conferences was held in Amsterdam, hosted by, among others, the Dutch National Committee for International Co-operation. The effectiveness of the sport-for-development lobby is illustrated by the United Nations' declaration of 2005 as the Year of Sport and Physical Education, building on UNESCO's definition of sport and physical education as a fundamental right for all, and the Convention on the Rights of the Child's designation of the right of the child to play. However, once again the duality of motives is clear – despite the rights-based assertions, the rhetorical commitment to sport was based on its supposed ability to offer an economy of remedies as, 'the United Nations is turning to the world of sport for help in the work for peace and the effort to achieve the Millennium Development Goals' (United Nations, 2005b: v). Sport was regarded as a 'natural partner' for the United Nations and was viewed as 'a powerful vehicle through which the United Nations can work towards achieving its goals' (United Nations, 2005a: v).

The 'world of sport' responded, often in evangelical language talking about the 'power' of sport to 'transform lives'. For example, in a 2005 FIFA document entitled *Football for Hope: Football's Commitment to Social Development*, the president Sepp Blatter announced a change from FIFA's traditional charity giving to 'meaningful, responsible, involved and committed development co-operation' (FIFA, 2005: Preface). This document stated that 'our game is an ideal tool for achieving social and human development targets and tackling many of the problems faced by society today' (FIFA, 2005: 5). As part of the London bid for the 2012 Olympics, Sebastian Coe articulated the 'Singapore Vision' that led to the establishment of the International Inspiration programme, with aims to:

> use the power of sport to transform the lives of millions of children and young people of all abilities, in schools and communities across the world, particularly in developing countries. This will ... deliver the ambitions promised in Singapore – and contribute to the achievement of the Millennium Development Goals. (UK Sport, nd: 1)

From economic capital to social capital

The emphasis on personal and collective values in the UN statements could be regarded as reflecting wider and more fundamental changes in the aid paradigm (Renard, 2006), which greatly strengthened the ability of the sport-for-development-and-peace lobby to argue for a slice of the development funding cake. We have already noted the emphasis on culture in the *Strategy for Norway's Culture and Sports Co-operation with Countries in the South* (Norwegian Ministry of Foreign Affairs, 2006). Hognestad (2005) relates this to the report from the World Commission on Culture and Development (1995) – *Our Creative Diversity* – which defined development as an expansion of people's possibilities of choosing, while stressing the significance of bringing issues of culture to the mainstream of development thinking and practice – 'not to substitute more traditional priorities that will remain our bread and butter – but to complement and strengthen them' (quoted in Hognestad, 2005: 3). Consequently, this new 'paradigm for development', with its concern with the relationship between poverty and cultural conditions, placed increased emphasis on social relationships and networks, on the development of human capital as well as the investment of economic capital, on bottom-up community development rather than apparently wasteful top-down investment in often corrupt governmental agencies. As Black (2010: 124) argues, it 'stressed locality, context and responsiveness to community priorities and dynamics'.

More fundamentally, this also reflected a broad shift in approaches to the economics of development and the alleviation of poverty. In launching *Sport for Development and Peace*, the United Nations (2005b: 1) stated that, although it had collaborated with a range of organisations in the commercial, public and voluntary sectors, 'what was missing ... was a systematic approach to an important sector in civil society: sport'. In an earlier document, the United Nations (2003: 14) had stressed the centrality of *volunteering* in sport, arguing that it contributes to 'social welfare, community participation, generation of trust and reciprocity, and the broadening of social interaction through new networks. Consequently, volunteerism creates social capital, helping to build and consolidate social cohesion and stability' as a basis for development. Further, while the concept of *social capital* is not explicitly stated, it is clearly implied by the statement that there was a need to promote partnerships that enable resource mobilisation 'both for and through sport' as 'effectively designed sports programmes ... are a valuable tool to initiate social development and improve social cohesion' (United Nations, 2003: 20, 12).

Kidd (2008: 374) suggests that this new emphasis was enabled by the collapse of the Soviet Union and the triumph of Western liberalism – or neo-liberalism – which led to 'a new focus on entrepreneurship as a strategy of social development, creating new openings for the creation of non-governmental organisations and private foundations'. The linking of sport to the politics of civil society and the development of social capital certainly reflects wider shifts in the aid paradigm. Woolcock and Narayan (2000) argue that a new emphasis on civil society, social capital and culture reflected a recognition that the concentration of development policy on the economic dimension was too narrow, often dismissing various aspects of traditional social relations and networks as obstacles to development, rather than potential resources. It is suggested that where the state is weak, or not interested in particular policy areas, organisations in civil society and the trust and reciprocity they may engender can increase community participation and strengthen democracy, as well as facilitate various types of social development. In fact, Portes and Landolt (2000: 530) suggest that the new emphasis represented an attempt to repair the damage done by previous policies in which:

> the removal of state protection giving way to unrestrained market forces has produced growing income disparities and an atomised social fabric marked by the erosion of normative controls ... the trend is visible enough for policy-makers to seek ways to sensitise or create anew community bonds and social institutions.

While there is a clear theoretical logic to such analyses, there is also a more pragmatic advantage to such a policy shift and one that is a characteristic attraction of most sport-for-development organisations. Portes and Landolt (2000) conclude that the development of forms of social capital is a very attractive proposition for aid agencies because they can increase the yield of aid and investment via volunteer labour and an openness and accountability not characteristic of governments and their agencies. Within this context, the widespread and highly ambitious claims made by the sport-for-development-and-peace lobby appear to offer an economy of remedies to otherwise seemingly intractable problems. Investment in sport is relatively cheap and its high dependence on both foreign and indigenous volunteers provides a substantial value added for relatively small sums of aid.

The extent to which sport-for-development can contribute to the social capital agenda will be explored in detail in Chapter 8. Here it is sufficient to suggest that the largely untheorised assertions about sport and social capital once again illustrate the issue of displacement of scope (Wagner, 1964), in which micro-level effects are, wrongly, generalised to the macro. For example, Portes and Landolt (2000: 542), drawing on mainstream aid perspectives, argue that 'it must be recognised that local-level cooperation alone cannot overcome macro-structural obstacles to economic stability, autonomous growth, and accumulation … social capital is not a substitute for the provision of credit, material infrastructure and education'.

Unequal partners, inflated promises and mission drift

The above has attempted to provide a general framework for understanding the emergence and growth of the sport-for-development movement. However even Kidd (2008: 376), who refers to the sport-for-development-and-peace 'movement', admits that it is a movement only in the loosest of senses – it is 'still in its infancy, woefully underfunded, completely unregulated, poorly planned and coordinated and largely isolated from mainstream development efforts' (see also Levermore, 2008; Black, 2010). It is of course highly debatable whether such a disparate set of organisations, initiatives and interest groups competing with each other for political influence and limited financial resources could be regulated or coordinated in any meaningful way (see Pisani's [2008] analysis of the difficulties in achieving either international or national integration and coherence in the allied field of HIV and AIDS prevention). Banda et al.'s (2008) research in Zambia illustrates clearly the problems of integration and coordination between a limited number of sport-for-development NGOs in one relatively small country.

While the mythopoeic qualities of 'sport' might provide a symbolically unifying concept, sport-for-development will inevitably remain a subsidiary actor in areas such as HIV and AIDS, health promotion, economic development and social cohesion, especially where funding comes from core development agencies. Further, the type of coordination, cohesion and leadership implied by Kidd (2008) and Levermore (2008) entail dangers of forced and selective consolidation and a 'top-down' approach to control of which Kidd (2008) and others (Giulianotti, 2004; Armstrong and Giulianotti, 2004; Darnell, 2007; Darnell and Hayhurst, 2012) are highly critical. Critics see the growth in influence of locally non-accountable NGOs as a form of neo-colonialism and question the nature and extent of the dialogue between donors and recipients, the extent to which 'empowerment' is a clear goal and the precise nature and meaning of cross-cultural 'cooperation' between donor and recipients (Darnell, 2007). However there is a range of potential and actual relationships between a variety of types of sport-for-development organisations and funding agencies with differing, often non-sporting, agendas (Giulianotti, 2011). Consequently, these are matters for empirical investigation, rather than abstract critical assertion, or deduction from theoretical principles.

For example, Bob Munro, the founder of MYSA (often regarded as a template for such organisations) has stated that 'the best thing that happened to MYSA was that nobody was interested for the first five years' (Munro, personal communication). The implication of this was that the lack of interest and external aid permitted the establishment of locally based aims, objectives and principles and MYSA was eventually strong enough to negotiate funding on the basis of its own definition of its needs and approach. However, this option was not open to all in the late 1990s' rush to benefit from the rapid increase in international interest in, and funding for, sport-for-development. Stephan Howells (2007), the Executive Director of SCORE, comments that although the processes of aid are often formally based on values of participative processes, partnership, local involvement and responsiveness to local needs, aid is given within the predefined, often political, parameters or objectives of the developer, which are in turn influenced by the funders' own national constituency (see Kidd, 2008 for an analysis of the difficulties in persuading Canadian sports organisations of the value of sport-for-development). Further, the necessity to compete for increasingly limited resources leads to projects being developed to fit the funding criteria, with the potential to compromise beneficiaries' needs, promote organisational mission drift and there is often an acceptance of donor targets with insufficient implementation capacity (Howells, 2007). For example, although many sport-for-development organisations viewed the people-centred MDGs as a major opportunity to apply for funding, Renard (2006) suggests that donors' insistence on addressing the MDGs may lead to the development of programmes that do not reflect local issues and needs.

However, it is necessary to adopt a rather more realistic approach to funding and recognise that funding relationships based at least in part on the power and the requirements of funders are not the sole property of 'neo-colonialism'. It is understandable that funder-dependent, often marginally viable and volunteer-based local NGOs make inflated promises in order to obtain funding (in the UK as well as elsewhere) − an apparent economy of remedies is always an attractive proposition. Further, it must also be acknowledged that over-ambitious and theoretically weak grant submissions are often encouraged, or at least condoned, by many funding agencies − it is surprising how many funders and sport-for-development organisations work in a shared mythopoeic universe, or at least travel in hope. Finally, if the mission is simply to survive then there is little drift − exploitation is not always a one-way street.

The inflated promises made in the area of sport-for-development can be viewed as an area-specific example of a more general phenomenon in which the formulation of ambitious, wide-ranging, vague and ill-defined claims are a function of the processes of lobbying, persuasion, negotiation, alliance building, pragmatic opportunism and the confusion between movement and progress that are part of all policy processes (see Chapter 3). Weiss (1993: 96) emphasises the essentially political nature of much policy formulation, resource bidding and programme development, arguing that:

> Because of the political processes of persuasion and negotiation that are required to get a program enacted, inflated promises are made in the guise of program goals. Furthermore, the goals often lack the clarity and intellectual coherence that evaluation criteria should have … . Holders of diverse values and different interests have to be won over, and in the process a host of realistic and unrealistic goal commitments are made.

Weiss (1993) contends that inflated promises are most likely to occur in marginal policy areas that suffer from status anxiety and are seeking to gain legitimacy and funding from mainstream agencies. We have already noted sport-for-development's marginal status in international aid policy (Levermore, 2008; Black, 2010). Kidd (2008) comments that, despite the rhetorical and symbolic legitimation provided by a human rights discourse and UN support, sport-for-development-and-peace initiatives are heavily dependent on aid agencies who have specific, non-sporting, development agendas – with the necessity for sport to persuade them that it could contribute to their core agendas. In such circumstances the studied vagueness of sports evangelism and the use of the populist, mythopoeic view of sport with its 'ability to evoke vague and generalised images' (Glasner, 1977: 1) could be viewed as an advantage. It is not wholly clear whether this is the function of a belief system or a conscious and pragmatic strategy – some funders clearly wanted to believe. However, even within this context, some might be slightly bemused by the claim that sport can contribute to the Millenium Development Goal (MDG) of a global partnership for development by *acting as a catalyst* for 'global partnerships and increased networking among governments, donors, NGOs and sports organisations worldwide' (Right to Play, nd).

Limited focus programmes and broad gauge problems

Perhaps it is these factors – over-inflated and imprecise claims, lack of systematic monitoring and evaluation, lack of robust evidence of poorly defined (but always ambitious) outcomes – that partially explain the relative isolation from mainstream development efforts. Levermore (2008: 188) refers to the 'long-established and well documented unease with which sport has been viewed (as being exclusive, male dominated and a diversion from what is really important in development)'. However, it is probable that this unease is sometimes a reflection of a naiveté or lack of understanding by sport-for-development organisations of the policies and approaches of aid organisations (Black, 2010). For example, Banda et al. (2008) conclude that Zambian sport-for-development NGOs had a limited understanding of national HIV/AIDS policy frameworks and this led to difficulties in aligning their efforts with core policies.

At the Next Step Conference held in Nambia in 2007, I was approached by two funders from aid agencies – one government agency and one major charitable organisation – who complained that the almost evangelical presentations that they had attended provided no basis on which to make judgements about the extent to which sport could contribute to their strategic goals. One of them was moved to 'feel insulted'. In this context it is worth quoting from one of the first systematic evaluations within sport-for-development, undertaken by someone outside the sport-for-development fraternity, which concluded:

> We have not come across any systematic analysis of how to understand the relationships between sport and development or an assessment of to what

extent such a relationship exists – or in other words a discussion of the causal links between an increased emphasis on sport and a positive impact on HIV/AIDS ... . The strong beliefs seem to be based on an intuitive certainty and experience that there is a positive link between sport and development.

(Kruse, 2006: 8)

Coakley (2011: 307) refers to 'unquestioned beliefs grounded in wishful thinking' and Hartmann and Kwauk (2011: 285–286) refer to 'anecdotal evidence, beliefs about the impact of sport in sound bites of individual and community transformation, packaged and delivered more often than not by those running the programs'.

Such lack of systematic evidence, or even coherent theory-based explanations, tend to be ignored in the mythopoeic world of the sports evangelists, in which many conferences, or congregations, seem to fuel a form of incestuous amplification supported by personal testimonies and project descriptions. They are often reminiscent of Pisani's (2008: 288) ironic comment that those in receipt of HIV and AIDS funding

almost never have to show you've prevented any infections. You can be judged a success for just doing what you said you were going to do, like build a clinic, or train some nurses or give leaflets to 400 out of the nation's 160,000 drug injectors.

At such gatherings there is little space for sceptics, less for agnostics and atheists are beyond the pale. Further, it is striking how even some critics tend to retain a belief in the potential power of sport, while criticising certain types of relationships and forms of delivery. Perhaps it is pragmatism, perhaps it is a shared belief, but sport-for-development seems to be a broad church united by a fundamental belief in sport. At another conference I was approached by two young academics who wished to develop a critical perspective on sport-for-development – i.e. to undertake legitimate academic work. However, they said that they could not do so as they were afraid that this would negatively impact on their career prospects. On another occasion a senior academic pointedly referred to a lack of 'critical voices' at certain sport-for-development congregations – at many points politics trumps evidence or critical reflection.

However, when sport-for-development seeks to contribute to the broader world of 'development' – making claims about community cohesion, social capital, peace, economic growth, gender equity and healing communal divisions – such claims are inevitably treated with scepticism by agencies who have been addressing the complexities of such issues for some time. This brings to mind Weiss' (1993: 105) more general comment about social policy interventions:

We mount limited-focus programs to cope with broad-gauge problems. We devote limited resources to long-standing and stubborn problems. Above all we concentrate attention on changing the attitudes and behaviour of target groups without concomitant attention to the institutional structures and social arrangements that tend to keep them "target groups".

In this regard Hartmann and Kwauk (2011: 292) refer to underpinning assumptions via which 'the whole concept of development is depoliticized and serves to reinforce and reproduce the social status quo'.

It is possible that in communities dominated by extreme poverty, lacking a range of welfare services, lacking educational and employment opportunities, having weak civic organisations and where daily life is not yet dominated by consumerism, sport, or more importantly, sporting organisations, can make a much greater impact than in more economically advanced, market-based and organisationally complex societies (see Chapter 8). However, again we are faced with issues of displacement of scope (Wagner, 1964) and the precise nature of the claims being made for sport-for-development. It is clear that participation in certain types of sporting environments *may* have an impact on *some* participants' self-efficacy, self-esteem or broader social skills (Coalter, 2007). Nevertheless, even at the level of the individual, the extent to which this will, or can, lead to changed behaviour (e.g. safer sex, improved educational performance) or, more ambitiously, improved real life chances is very difficult to assess and the limited evidence that exists is not wholly optimistic (Botcheva and Huffman, 2004; Kruse, 2006).

Consequently, it is suggested that there is a need to recognise that actions and choices take place within the material, economic and cultural realities within which the 'empowered' live (Mwaanga, 2003; Morris *et al.*, 2003). Mwaanga (2003) argues that raising expectations and aspirations of young women without changing their economic circumstances may have limited impact on their more instrumental sexual behaviour. Or, the literature that emphasises the deep-rooted cultural nature of sexual behaviour and associated risks of HIV and AIDS (Pisani, 2008; McNeill, 2009). Such analyses illustrate the complexity of the issues, which is often ignored in policy rhetoric, and too often reduces complex social issues to individual behaviours, ambitions and actions. In fact, an over-concentration on traditional individual impacts is, in many cases, misguided, with a clear need to develop a more informed, grounded and contextual understanding (Burnett, 2001). One might also argue that there are moral and political dangers in de-contextualised, romanticised generalisations about the 'power' of sport to 'transform' lives.

Conclusion: hope is not a plan

Levermore (2008: 189) argues that 'the use of sport for developmental purposes should be considered in a more nuanced manner' and, much more challengingly, that it should be 'evaluated relative to other engines of development'. In relation to HIV and AIDS, Banda *et al.* (2008: 7) suggest that the relative marginalisation of Zambian sport-for-development NGOs from national HIV and AIDS policy was because of their 'potentially narrow conception of the contribution of sport-for-development NGOs'. However, as Kruse (2006) concludes, the precise nature of this contribution – either theoretically or practically – is often poorly articulated.

The frequent failure to address such issues reflects Weiss' (1993: 103) concern that many social interventions fail because they are 'fragmented, one-service-at-a-time programs, dissociated from people's total patterns of living'. In this regard Pawson's (2006: 5) comment that all social interventions are 'complex systems thrust amidst complex systems' seems appropriate to an approach to understanding the role and operation of sport-for-development organisations – rather than simple one-off or short-term projects. Rather than seeking simply to assert sport's almost magical properties (Papacharisis *et al.*, 2005), or commission 'research' that proves 'success' (Koss in van Kampen, 2003: 15), what is required is a developmental approach based on the 'de-centring' (Crabbe, 2000) or de-reification of 'sport' and a concentration on understanding the social processes and mechanisms that *might* lead to desired impacts for *some* participants or some organisations in *certain circumstances* (Pawson, 2006). Of course, proving that such possible impacts lead to developmental *outcomes* – changed behaviour, changed prospects, social cohesion – presents substantial difficulties, as is indicated by the research that is systematically ignored.

From this perspective, monitoring and evaluation need to pursue *understanding* via participatory, process-centred and formative evaluation (Coalter, 2006, 2007; Shah *et al.*, 2004). Such an approach can: contribute to organisational capacity building; develop greater ownership and understanding of the often complex relationships between aims and objectives; provide the basis for an integrated and coherent organisational culture and associated programmes; assist in the development of a self-critical and self-improving organisational culture (Department for International Development, 2005). In addition to improving the design and implementation of sport-for-development programmes and defining more realistic and contextually relevant impacts and outcomes (Burnett, 2001), such an approach could have a more strategic political function. Hopefully it would provide the basis for a constructive dialogue, or 'conversation' (Weiss, 1993; Pawson, 2006), between a variety of funders and sport-for-development organisations and the development of real partnerships (Banda *et al.*, 2008). (These issues will be explored in more detail in Chapter 3.)

However, as will be argued in Chapter 3, it is not wholly clear that such an approach – the intellectual development of sport-for-development – would be welcomed in the world of evangelical testimonies, mythopoeic perspectives, political lobbying, incestuous amplification, the seeking of organisational advantage and intense competition for funding by vulnerable organisations. In the related area of HIV and AIDS programmes Pisani (2008: 300) suggests that 'doing honest analysis that would lead to programme improvement is a glorious way to be hated by just about everyone'.

We now turn to issues of research and evaluation.

3

CONCEPTUAL ENTREPRENEURS, LIBERATION METHODOLOGISTS AND RESEARCH AS A DIRTY WORD

Politics, ideology and faith: who needs evidence?

In Chapter 2 it was argued that a combination of sports evangelism, underpinned by the mythopoeic character of sport, promoted by conceptual entrepreneurs and supported by forms of incestuous amplification tends to generate a particular attitude towards knowledge and evidence. In fact belief and faith by definition do not depend on, or need, proof or evidence. In this regard commentators have pointed to the tendency towards 'unquestioned beliefs grounded in wishful thinking' (Coakley, 2011: 307). Where evidence is offered it is often in testimonial form with 'heartfelt narratives, evocative images, and quotable sound bites' (Hartmann and Kwauk, 2011: 286). Others simply point to the general lack of systematic analysis and assessment (Kruse, 2006). It is an interesting question as to whether this situation reflects the political desire to view it as an emerging 'new field' in its 'formative stage' (Kay, 2009: 1177), or whether the very ideological and political construction of the policy area mitigates against objective analysis, or an acknowledgement of the not wholly positive implications of a substantial body of existing research on the use of sport for personal and social change (Coalter, 2007; Coakley, 2011).

However, although this seems to have taken a rather extreme form in sport-for-development – where even critics of supposed 'neo-colonialist' funders seem to retain a basic *belief* in the developmental potential of 'sport' (Lindsey and Grattan, 2012), it also reflects the more general problem that 'evaluation is a rational exercise that takes place in a political context' (Weiss, 1993: 94). Others have suggested that it is naive to confuse research findings with *evidence* and therefore fail to understand that even robust research competes for attention with a range of other, often more influential, factors (Solesbury 2001). Davis (2004) argues that policy making involves a range of factors that act to filter and interpret the value of evidence – values/ideologies/political beliefs, habit and traditions, lobbyists, pressure groups and resources available for policy implementation all work in various ways to determine the perceived need for information and, more especially, its relevance. Pisani (2008), in the closely related field of HIV and AIDS prevention, argues that many programmes are based on false assumptions because of the systematic ignoring of morally or politically uncomfortable evidence. For example, despite clear evidence that the use of condoms and needle exchanges substantially reduces infection rates, such policies are opposed by those who reject birth control, or argue that needle exchanges simply encourage drug use – a position adopted by USAID until the election of Barack Obama as president of the USA.

In Chapter 2 we noted Weiss' (1993) argument that policies and programmes are the products of processes of lobbying, persuasion, negotiation and alliance building and holders of diverse values and different interests have to be won over. This frequently produces inflated promises and unrealistic goals and that this is most likely to occur in marginal policy areas – such as sport-for-development (Levermore, 2008; Kidd, 2008). These result in the formulation of desired impacts and outcomes that lack the clarity and intellectual coherence that evaluation criteria should have. Consequently, the programmes that researchers seek to evaluate are not neutral experiments, but are the product of political decisions and strategic partnerships. In fact, in sport-for-development such partnerships often seem as important as the programmes that they deliver – especially partnerships with influential UN agencies or international governing bodies of sport. In this context Weiss (1993: 96) reminds us of realpolitik by arguing that 'a considerable amount of ineffectiveness may be tolerated if a program fits well with prevailing values, if it satisfies voters, or if it pays off political debts'. Consequently, a lack of clarity, precision and intellectual coherence regarding evaluation criteria might simply reflect political necessities and be inherent in such processes.

Such a position has clear, but not particularly positive, implications for the role and function of monitoring and evaluation. Such processes and a desire to offer an economy of remedies often result in situations where 'intermediate objectives are missing, providing targets for how much and when results were expected', and 'indicators are used in the application for funds, but not for actual monitoring and reporting', with the absence of clear targets 'making it difficult to assess performance' (Kruse, 2006: 27; see also Coalter, 2006; 2007). For example, the research reported in later chapters was undertaken as part of an attempt to build a strategic alliance between a generic aid organisation and a quasi-governmental sports promotion agency. Perhaps this explains the somewhat imprecise aims 'to test the hypothesis that sport contributes to the personal development and well-being of disadvantaged children and young people and brings wider benefits to the community'. One might regard this statement as indicating politically necessary studied vagueness. The precise meaning of such terms, the nature of relevant indicators and the problems involved in definition and measurement will be discussed in later chapters.

A useful illustration of the relationship between ideology, politics and research evidence is provided by the allied area of self-esteem (which we will look at in-depth in Chapter 5). In 1986 the Californian State Legislature funded the Task Force to

Promote Self-esteem and Personal and Social Responsibility. This explored the potential of self-esteem to help to solve problems of crime, teen pregnancy, drug abuse, school under-achievement and pollution (Baumeister *et al.*, 2003; Hewitt, 1998). The final report's conclusion was unequivocal: 'People who esteem themselves are less likely to engage in ... crime'. However, the Task Force's own academic consultants, Scheff *et al.* (1989), found the opposite message in the same evidence: 'the conclusion we draw from the reviews, [is that] the relationships reported between self-esteem and deviance have been weak or null' (Emler, 2001b: 18). In the Introduction to the report it is stated that:

> Diminished self-esteem stands as a powerful independent variable (condition, cause, factor) in the genesis of major social problems. We all know this to be true ... The real problem is ... how we can determine that it is scientifically true.
>
> *(quoted in Emler, 2001b: 17)*

As Emler (2001b) concludes, this is to reduce the role of science to confirming what we already think that we know to be the case. Not surprisingly we can offer two examples of this perspective from sport-for-development, which indicate at best an ambivalent attitude to the purpose of monitoring and evaluation. The first is from a key strategic lobbyist and provider – Johan Koss, President of Right to Play. At a Next Step Conference in 2003 he stated: 'We do not evaluate enough and so we invite people to do research into things like sport and development, sport and peace. We need to prove what we say that we do' (van Kampen, 2003: 15). Second, a UNICEF (2006: 1) workshop report on monitoring and evaluation concluded that there was 'a shared belief in the power of sport-for-development [and] a shared determination to find ways to document and objectively verify the positive impact of sport'.

The view that research simply functions to affirm belief is an odd perspective on both faith, which does not require proof, and scientific endeavour. However, it fits well with the ideological and belief structures that characterise sport-for-development. Kruse (2006: 8) refers to the intriguingly vague definitions of sport-for-development and that practice was not based on evidence, but 'on an intuitive certainty and experience that there is a positive link between sport and development'. As argued in Chapter 2, this reflects a mythopoeic conception of sport (Coalter, 2007), which contains some elements of truth – most forms of social intervention will have *some* positive outcomes for *some* people – but these elements also become reified and distorted and 'represent' rather than reflect reality, in which particular relationships are emphasised to the exclusion of others, without a sound basis for doing so (Glasner, 1977). The lobbying processes produce extremely wide-ranging claims, with sport contributing variously to inclusion, citizenship, community cohesion, tolerance and respect, reduction of cultural and ethnic divides, peace, discipline, confidence, leadership, learning the value of effort and how to manage victory and defeat (United Nations, 2005). In the context of such wide-ranging, amorphous and often contested definitions, it is not wholly clear what would constitute proof of 'success'.

Admitting the difficulties

From a social science perspective many of the rather commonsense terms used in such rhetoric present complex problems of definition and measurement. The failure to address systematically such issues greatly reduces the ability to fully understand the nature of any impacts and outcomes, and our ability to compare the *relative effectiveness* of various programmes. As we will see in subsequent chapters, many of the commonsense terms used in policy rhetoric are the subject of substantial theoretical debate and there is often a lack of consensus as to how such terms should be defined, measured and what their significance for 'development' is. For example, the widespread claim that participation in sport leads to increased 'confidence' (Kay, 2009) is faced with Bandura's (1997: 382) comment that 'confidence is a catchword, rather than a construct embedded in a theoretical system'. In such circumstances the meaning of confidence may vary substantially between participants in a programme and between programmes and cultures (we will deal with this in detail in Chapter 4).

In addition to such conceptual issues, it has to be acknowledged that in multi-faceted social interventions – *plus sport* or *sport plus* – it is difficult to attribute any measured change to a single component – sport. As with the term 'development', 'sport' is a collective noun that encompasses a wide variety of mechanisms – contexts, relationships, rules, experiences and a wide variety of types of participants. For example, there are individual, partner and team sports; there are sports that are based on the development of cognitive and spatial skills and those based on motor skills; there are non-contact, contact and collision sports and there are sports based on self-assessed criteria and objective norm evaluations. In this regard the President's Council on Physical Fitness and Sports (2006: 4) refers to

> the importance of not lumping all sports or sport participants together. For several reasons, broad generalizations about "sports" are unlikely to be helpful. For one, the rule structures of the various sports promote different types of social interaction. The developmental stimuli provided by a boxing match are likely to differ from those of a golf tournament. In addition, each sport tends to have its own subculture and implicit moral norms. The culture of rugby is quite different from that of competitive swimming. There are also differences based on age and competitive level. Major league baseball and Little League provide quite different social experiences. Even within a single sport area and developmental level, individual sport teams are different because each team develops its own unique moral microculture through the influence of particular coaches, athletes, fans, parents, and programs. Moreover, even within a single team, participants' own appraisals of the experience may vary substantially.

Consequently, although an essentialist view of sport combines with ill-defined notions of 'development' to underpin a potent ideology, as with all forms of mythopoeic thought, this is based on popular ideas produced largely outside sociological analysis. In fact existing sociological analysis and research raise significant questions about many of the assertions (Coalter, 2007; Coakley, 2011). As with the use of the term 'development', it seems that there is political advantage in employing the summative concept of sport in vague, amorphous and theoretically inclusive ways.

As argued in Chapter 2, discussions of sport-for-development are constructed as if it is a new field and a new area of study (Kay, 2009) – an industry of conceptual entrepreneurs seeking to establish opportunities and influence with new journals, academic courses, departments, websites, organisations, conferences and congregations. However, all of the assertions in United Nations' policy documents and manifestos such as the *Magglingen Declaration* are restatements of social policy rationales dating from at least the nineteenth century. Much of the rhetoric of sport-for-development is based on long-standing policy rationales and it is not clear why it is claimed that it is an area in its formative phase. Is there no relationship with the huge volume of research on sport and its supposed individual and group developmental impacts (e.g. Coalter, 2007; Collins *et al.*, 1999; West and Crompton, 2001; President's Council on Physical Fitness and Sports, 2006; Coakley, 2011; Value of Sport Monitor, www.sportengland.org/research/value_of_sport_monitor.aspx, accessed 18 December 2012)? In this regard it is worth quoting from the World Health Organisation's (2006: 333) review of HIV and AIDS programmes for young people, which states: 'the evidence for the effectiveness of interventions in developing countries needs to be viewed within the wider evidence base from developed countries'.

Existing research indicates that issues relating to the definition and measurement of the individual and social developmental potential of sport are many:

(i)   Participation in sport is just one of many things that people do. Therefore its impact will depend on the relative salience of the experience compared to other factors e.g., criminal sub-cultures, peer groups, family, wider social, cultural and religious norms, school, economic imperatives and so on.

(ii) Effects will be determined by the frequency and intensity of participation and the degree of participants' adherence over time. Although these factors are especially important for fitness and health benefits, they also have clear implications for the development of values and attitudes that underpin behaviour.

(iii) Rarely do sport-for-development programmes rely solely on sport to address issues of personal development. Most are sport-plus programmes or even plus sport, in which sport might be reduced to the role of 'fly paper' to attract young people to a range of education and training programmes. In such circumstances isolating the 'sport effect' is nearly impossible (Coakley, 2011; Hartmann and Kwauk, 2011). Of course, this might not be deemed important if the required impacts are achieved, although this would seem to raise questions about the specificity of a field called 'sport-for-development'.

(iv) The nature and extent of any impact on individual participants will depend on the nature both of the experience and of the participants – a fact frequently ignored. Many programmes seem to be based on a form of environmental determinism and a deficit model in which it is assumed that deprived communities produce deficient people who can be 'developed' through sport.

However, as will be illustrated in Chapters 4 and 5, this assumption might be wrong.

(v) In addition to the heterogeneous nature of participants, sports are not a homogenous, standardised product or experience. Clearly participation in sport, however defined, is a necessary condition to obtain any of the hypothesised benefits. However, as impacts and outcomes are only a possibility (Svoboda, 1994) there is a need to consider *sufficient conditions* – the conditions under which the potential outcomes are achieved. It cannot be assumed that any, or all, participants will automatically obtain the presumed benefits in all circumstances and we have relatively limited understanding about which sports and processes produce what *impacts,* for which *participants* and in what *circumstances.* As Patriksson (1995: 128) argues:

> Sport, like most activities, is not a priori good or bad, but has the potential of producing both positive and negative outcomes. Questions like 'what conditions are necessary for sport to have beneficial outcomes?' must be asked more often.

In a similar vein, Coakley (1998: 2) argues that we need to regard 'sports as *sites* for socialisation experiences, not *causes* of socialisation outcomes'. Hartmann and Kwauk (2011: 290) argue that 'the educational experience within the sporting experience is the most critical space'. These issues will be explored in Chapter 7.

(vi) Even if sports participation does assist in the development of certain types of *individual* competence, efficacy, self-esteem, values, attitudes or even expressed intention to change behaviour, this cannot simply be taken to imply that these will be transferred to behavioural change, or wider social or community benefits. For example, the transtheoretical theory of behaviour change (Prochaska and Velicer, 1997) illustrates that the relationship between changed attitudes, intentions and subsequent behaviour is not unilinear and may often be reversed. Consequently, even if we can illustrate changes in values, attitudes and self-perceptions we are still left with the generic methodological problem of relating this to subsequent behaviour change – which surely must be part of any definition of development? For example, Taylor (1999) argues that the major problem in identifying and measuring the effects of sports participation on crime is that this influence (even if it is effective) is essentially indirect, working through a number of intermediate processes, such as improved fitness, self-efficacy, self-esteem and locus of control and the development of social and personal skills. Consequently, in most cases it is misleading to argue that 'sport' reduces crime, or leads to improved educational performance. Such issues are compounded by the difficulties in controlling for intervening and confounding variables that will also influence attitudes and behaviour (Hartmann and Kwauk, 2011). Grissom (2005: 13), discussing research on the contribution of sport to educational achievement – a central component of many sport-for-development projects – points to the widespread failure of experimental designs to find statistically significant differences between experimental and control subjects and argues that this

> is due in part to the difficulty in raising academic achievement. It is very difficult to raise student achievement, beyond what might be expected, even when that is the specific focus. A study intended to affect achievement indirectly [i.e. via participation in PE and sport] would encounter even more difficulty.

(vii) The above relates to the essentially individualistic nature of the sport-for-development paradigm and this again leads to the issue of 'displacement of scope' (Wagner, 1964) with a failure to relate individual values, attitudes and expressed intentions to social contexts. We have already noted Weiss' (1993) generic comment about policy interventions seeking to change the attitudes and behaviour of target groups without addressing structures that define them as target groups. In a comprehensive study of self-efficacy Ungar (2006: 3–4) pithily summarises the general conclusion that 'changing the odds' is preferable to resourcing individuals to 'beat the odds' (see Chapter 4). In the area of sport-for-development Jeanes (2011) argues that even where programmes are successful in educating young people about the dangers of HIV and AIDS, they are unlikely to be able to challenge damaging adult attitudes, beliefs and behaviour. Mwaanga (2003) argues that raising expectations and aspirations of young women without changing their economic circumstances may have limited impact on their more instrumental sexual behaviour. Even political power and influence can be important. In an interview with a peer leader in South Africa he emphasised that his training had added to his employability via an increased sense of self-efficacy, improved time management, problem-solving skills, programme-related administrative skills and report writing. However, when asked if this would lead to employment he said that this was unlikely, as he was not a member of the ANC! (Coalter and Taylor, 2010.)

The above are generic issues relating to all forms of social intervention and are not intended to suggest that sport-for-development programmes have no value or impact on participants. However, the domination of the area by evangelical rhetoric and forms of incestuous amplification means that relatively standard issues of social science methodology are simply ignored. Sceptics and agnostics are marginalised and atheists ignored, placing substantial pressure on academics seeking to develop a career in this area. Without addressing such issues the intellectual development of sport-for-development will be very limited. More prosaically there is a strong probability that research results will not be comparable – the idea that evidence for the success of 'sport-for-development' is simply a matter of accumulating a series of impact and outcome measurements grossly over simplifies the issues involved. Clearly most forms of social intervention are likely to have some positive impacts on some participants and it is relatively easy to produce ad hominem evidence – 'sport saved me from a life of crime'. But two questions remain – *why* did a programme work for some and not others – we are rarely presented with evidence of failed programmes or unchanged participants – and what have positive individual self-assessments to do with 'development'?

Wagner (1964) argues that the issue of displacement of scope is inherent in the tremendous range of sociological subject matter and this clearly applies to sport-for-development. Perhaps, following Levermore (2008), it might be better to talk of a number of sports for developments: sport for individual development in which participation is presumed to change values, attitudes, knowledge and aptitudes for some; sport-for-development for behaviour change, in which the concern with the individual is complemented by a concern with the context of behaviour and enabling structures; sport for community development, which deals with issues at a meso level of collective organisation and forms of social capital (Burnett, 2001). Although it could be argued that all are in some way related, the intellectual development of these various aspects of sport-for-development would benefit greatly by drawing on a range of different academic disciplines and perspectives (Crabbe, 2000; Coalter, 2007; Coakley, 2011; Hartmann and Kwauk, 2011).

However, even here we need to take into account the implication of Pawson *et al.*'s (2004: 7) argument that 'rarely if ever is the "same" programme equally effective in all circumstances because of the influence of contextual factors' (which includes the frequently ignored issue of the nature of participants). Consequently, attempts to illustrate 'success' may need to adopt rather different approaches and we will examine one such approach later in the chapter.

As a limited contribution to addressing some of these issues, most of the rest of this book will draw on original research (Coalter and Taylor, 2010; Coalter, 2011) that has sought to address one of these areas – sport for individual development – to explore if and how such programmes work (Chapters 4 and 5). It will also draw on other theory and research to make some speculative comments on the second – sport-for-development for behaviour change – especially related to HIV and AIDS education (Chapters 6 and 7). Finally, in Chapter 8, it will draw on theory and research to explore sport for community development and issues of social capital.

Liberation methodology and research as a dirty word

So far we have referred to three obstacles to undertaking research in sport-for-development. First, the policy-lobbying processes that produce 'ill-defined interventions and hard to follow outcomes' (Pawson, 2006). Second, evangelical policy makers and many providers have a relative indifference to research and evaluation, viewing this simply in terms of producing proof for their beliefs or legitimating their funding. Both of these make objective research in this area extremely difficult and, in some quarters, unwelcome. Third, there are generic methodological difficulties in defining and measuring impacts and outcomes and also attributing them solely to sport in any simple and straightforward way. These issues are illustrated by the wide variety of relevant research on sport often ignored within sport-for-development.

However, in addition to these issues, a form of 'liberation methodology' among some sport-for-development academics seems to argue that the attempt to define and especially measure and quantify impacts and outcomes – the purpose of much of this book – is illegitimate. Traditional social science debates are used to raise questions about the very nature and purpose of research and, especially, evaluation. Issues of ontology, epistemology, methodology and methods are combined in abstract ways and mixed with diffuse notions of politics, power and liberation. This results in the designation of the type of quantitative research reported in this book as being unavoidably part of neo-colonialist hegemonic repression and contributing to the reproduction of unequal power relations (Lindsey and Grattan, 2012; Darnell and Hayhurst, 2012; Nicholls, Giles and Sethna, 2011). For example, Kay (2009), who is one of the more reasonable and informed of the critics, nevertheless uncritically quotes Tuhiwai Smith (1999: 1) to the effect that 'the term "research" is inextricably linked to European imperialism and colonialism. The word itself, "research", is probably one of the dirtiest words in the indigenous world's vocabulary'.

Various aspects of methodology and methods are labelled in a flurry of quotation marks, as if to signal the toxic and corrupting nature of such perspectives as positivism, rationality, objectivity, academic, scientific, truth, linear causality and management-oriented research (Lindsey and Grattan, 2012; Nicholls, Giles and Sethna, 2011) – a form of naming and shaming, although guilt seems to be by association. It is asserted that the majority of empirical sport-for-development research has been conducted by researchers from the so-called Global North and that the findings of many of these studies are 'internationally-oriented' (Lindsey and Grattan, 2012) – although no worked examples are provided. In a neat paradox, academics from the Global North (often funded by Global North agencies) reject the validity of research by those from the Global North – although *their* commentary and analysis is to be taken as correct! In part, this is because it is asserted that as this research is undertaken for policy makers it is 'primarily an instrumental means of improving the effectiveness of sport-for-development programmes and organisations' (Lindsey and Grattan, 2012: 94; Kay, 2011). It is not clear what is wrong with improving programmes – unless the sport-for-development programmes are deemed to be rigidly imposed, inherently wrong and improving them simply contributes to the interests of funders and continues the neo-Liberal, neo-colonialist oppression (Darnell and Hayhurst, 2012).

The arguments are framed in terms of homogenising polarities – Western and non-Western societies; Global North and Global South; high-income and low-income countries (Woodcock et al, 2012); Cartesian and non-Cartesian epistemologies (Kay, 2009) and positivism and its supposed alternative – 'decolonising, feminist-oriented, participatory action research' (Lindsey and Grattan, 2012). Non-indigenous researchers are all from the Global North and the oppressed are from the Global South – the relationships and the epistemologies are homogenised and derived from structure and ideology. Such terms may serve the interests of political activism and political correctness but, paradoxically, do little to further the call for greater specificity and understanding of both policies and context. It is not always clear precisely what is being argued. Is it that anyone from outside a participant community – or even worse, from the Global

North – has no legitimate right to research sport-for-development; has no understanding of the Global South, a term that denies specificity, especially for empirical research; is inevitably part of hegemonic, neo-colonialist oppression and, if associated with funders, is irredeemably epistemologically and ideologically contaminated? However, even if some of these issues are addressed via developmental and collaborative research of the type reported in this book, it seems that there is an even more fundamental objection.

'It is too scientific'

The above quote relates to a comment made when I presented the finding of the research contained in later chapters to a workshop of practitioners and policy makers in Cape Town. I had presented the various graphs, which indicated that some common deficit assumptions about participants needed to be reconsidered, that the impact of programmes was varied and was often not as assumed. When the audience was asked to comment, one participant informed me that my work was 'too scientific' – a rather odd comment. Perhaps it was too technical for an audience with little formal research training. Perhaps it departed too far from the simple and always positive testimonial approach beloved of practitioners and used as evidence for funders and at the various sport-for-development congregations. However, it is possible that a more fundamental objection informed this reaction and this is one that informs liberation methodology. This is that any form of *quantitative* research – stereotyped and reduced to the dreaded, crude positivism – seems to be condemned as inherently flawed. Of course this raises the unanswered question as to whether *indigenous* researchers who work in the positivist tradition are also agents of neo-colonialism. For example, as we will see in Chapter 6, Cyprian Maro, the founder of EMIMA (Dar-es-Salaam), used both survey data and statistical analysis to explore issues relating to the effectiveness of his programme, as has Sarah Forde, the founder of Moving the Goal Posts (Kenya) (Woodcock et al., 2012) – do we regard them as having gone over to the other side?

The basic premise seems to be that quantitative knowledge is inevitably 'oppressive' and that qualitative knowledge is liberating. While there are many legitimate criticisms of the so-called positivist tradition, they are not articulated and italicised polarities do not represent an informed debate about the strengths, weaknesses and limitations of *all* social science methodology. Positivism is attacked (although not coherently defined) not because of epistemological and methodological issues – if methodology and method were serious considerations there would be a recognition of long-standing, wider and sophisticated debates within social science and also about differing types of policy-oriented research and different relationships between researchers and policy makers (Bulmer, 1982; Cantley, 1992; Hammersley, 1995; Hammersley and Gomm, 1996; Nutley et al., 2007).

Rather, positivism seems only to be a hook on which to hang a rejection of Western (or is it Northern?) rationality and Cartesian dualism and all forms of 'managerialism' aimed at programme improvement. That this is as much a political as a methodological argument is indicated by calls to '"de-colonise" methodologies and postcolonial, hegemonic approaches to researching SDP' (Darnell and Hayhurst, 2012: 120) and 'the need to subvert enduring "colonial" power relationships' (Kay, 2009: 1188; see also Lindsey and Grattan, 2012; Nicholl, Giles and Sethna, 2011). In a slightly more moderate vein, Kay (2009: 1118) warns against 'an uncritical assumption about the universality of methodology and its epistemological and ontological underpinnings'.

We are informed of the evils of rationality and objective analysis and that the 'instrumental use of rationalistic models' undervalues practical knowledge … among field-level practitioners (Nicholls, 2009; Nicholls et al., 2011). It is hoped that 'decolonising, feminist-oriented, participatory action research may provide a means through which to reinvigorate the SDP research agenda in a more positive, socially charged and meaningful way' (Darnell and Hayhurst, 2012: 120).

Nicholls et al. (2011) draw on Foucault's generic analysis of the relationship between power and definitions of legitimate knowledge to criticise policy makers in the Global North for 'subjugating' the sport-for-development practitioners' knowledge. However, there seem to be a number of possible paradoxes in the analysis. First, they are speaking about those implementing Kicking AIDS Out – a programme developed and designed to reflect local conditions by practitioners in the Global South. Second, because Foucault's analysis is generic it says little about 'neo-colonialism', which is simply a specific case of a general argument. Such relationships between strategic policy makers and practitioners are commonplace, even *within* the Global North, and references to a 'colonial legacy' and 'colonial power relations' (Nicholls et al., 2011: 261) seem like ideological over-reach. Third, their work was funded by a major Global North funder – Commonwealth Games Canada – an exception to the neo-colonialist rule? Fourth, despite criticising the privileging of academic knowledge it is only this that has enabled them to identify the supposed relevance of Foucault's analysis, propose a liberating perspective and to suggest that academics are 'critical to the growth and "legitimization" of sport-for-development as contributing to development issues' (Nicholls et al., 2011: 259).

In part the supposed liberationist nature of these epistemological and methodological proposals is related to the importance, or at least symbolic significance, attributed to sport-for-development – either as a source of liberation (Lindsey and Grattan, 2012; Kay, 2009) or an example of neo-liberal oppression (Darnell and Hayhurst, 2012). For example, reference is made to a case study of a local football programme in Zambia (Lindsey and Grattan, 2012), as illustrating 'place-based struggle' in SDP (Darnell and Hayhurst, 2012: 121) and that this can also be used to illustrate

> struggles as they are produced and constrained within the global politics of unequal development. That is, in addition to making sense of local actions, scholars should also now connect and communicate such understandings of sport-for-development in ways that challenge or contribute to broader structures of knowledge and power on a global scale.
>
> *(Darnell and Hayhurst, 2012: 121)*

We are warned that if such issues are not recognised, sport-for-development may 'fail to address, and thus implicitly contribute to the continuation of, the structured nature of poverty and global inequalities' (Lindsey and Grattan, 2012: 95).

Such claims for the real, or even symbolic, importance of a peripheral and locally focused programme indicate a failure to address issues of displacement of scope. Perhaps I am naive, but can we really define a football programme in Zambia in terms of 'development efforts initiated in the Global North as being aligned with the hegemonic maintenance of power relations which continue to subjugate those in the Global South' (Lindsey and Grattan, 2012: 94)? Is this not attributing a symbolic and political importance to such initiatives out of all proportion to even their local significance? Is this not another example of ideological over-reach? Perhaps it is not surprising that some of the liberationist methodologists seem to share the sports evangelists' grand designs for sport-for-development, if not their approach to evaluation and improvement.

Liberation, standard research practice or good manners?

However, despite such heated abstract rhetoric and attempts to conflate positivism and neo-colonialism, much of this seems to amount to little more than an age-old debate about the relative merits of quantitative and qualitative research. Reflecting the rhetoric of sport-for-development evangelism, this is presented not as a standard evaluation of the relative merits of two approaches that are often regarded as complementary, but as a form of contestation and liberation. Kay (2009: 1189) informs us that 'basing research inquiry on an implicit model of western scientific rationality carries the danger of dismissing ... authentic local voices'. Quantitative research – or 'positivism' – is viewed as inherently oppressive and a tool of neo-colonialism rationality and linear thinking. In this context a 'decentred and actor-centred approach' (Lindsey and Grattan, 2012: 107) is viewed as inherently liberating.

However, the examples offered from the application of such a liberating methodology seem less than revolutionary. For example, Lindsey and Grattan (2012), via a series of so-called decentred and actor-centred in-depth interviews with those delivering a Zambian football programme, inform us that sport is viewed as having value for its popularity, its 'associative value' and its ability to bring young people together, especially in the context of the breakdown of traditional family structures. In addition, it has an ability to act as a diversionary activity and reduce crime and to enable young people to develop physically and to improve their health and a compensatory mechanism for those who are less academically gifted. Further, it is viewed as a vehicle for various 'educational messages' and the 'malleability' of sport permits it to address a number of interconnected issues. It is not clear how this differs from the views of the neo-colonialist funders from the Global North – or are we to view these not as legitimate voices, but simply reflecting neo-liberal ideology? Such views seem relatively standard expressions of populist ideologies of sport and are very similar to those found by Burnett (2001: 51) in South Africa, where she states that many respondents 'approached and interpreted change very much from a functionalist perspective, because "educational" and "functional" outcomes were held in high regard by all'.

Kay (2009) uses in-depth interviews with female participants and providers in a Delhi-based sport-for-development programme to illustrate a similar, but not unusual, analysis of the perceived positive impacts of participation – increased self-confidence and aspirations. This is presented as illustrating

> some of the contributions qualitative study can offer to our understanding of the social impact of sport in development contexts ... the young women's narratives describe in detail how the programme impacted positively on their own behaviour and self-perceptions and also affected how others viewed and treated them.
>
> *(Kay, 2009: 1187–88)*

Kay (2009: 1188) argues that this work illustrates the value of qualitative investigation and its ability 'to capture the complex and multi-faceted process through which individuals experience beneficial social outcomes from sport' – something with which I agree and seek to illustrate in Chapter 7, although I suggest that much more than 'sport' is involved. However, following this relatively standard research approach and findings of the type desired by the neo-colonial Western Cartesian rationalists who fund such programmes, we are informed that there is 'a radical contrast ... between Indic epistemology and ontology and the modern Western one'. Further, it is asserted that there is a need for Western researchers to be alert to 'the cultural specificity of the Western ontological cleft between the human mind and the rest of the world' (Kay, 2009: 1189). Despite this apparently radical statement we are not then informed as to the implication of this for the previously offered insights and defence of the value of qualitative approaches implemented by a Western academic. Are the presented analysis and insights legitimate or not? Do they take account of Indic ontology and epistemology? If not, what is their value?

Although the liberation methodologists issue a wide variety of ontological and epistemological health warnings they rarely offer examples of the implications of this for research and interpretation. It seems that the radical politics of liberation require, or are reinforced by, the acknowledgement of the existence of alternative epistemologies but we are offered limited practical illustration of the implications for research and programme improvement.

It is not wholly clear why a standard approach to research, even in Western rationalist environments – in-depth interviews – is deemed to be 'liberating', especially how this can be linked, however loosely, to structured poverty and neo-colonialist hegemonic power relations. It is relatively standard research practice to use in-depth interviews, either as a basis for questionnaire design for a more representative survey, or as a basis for the exploration of meaning following the collection of survey data. The polarised epistemological and methodological choice simply ignores actual research practice, in pursuit of what seem to be political ends.

However, perhaps it is not the relatively unsurprising information that is the key, but the *processes* of asking, consulting and involvement in 'feminist-oriented, participatory action research' that is 'decolonising'. This seems analogous to the Marxist, or Christian, view that the oppressed contain the seeds of their own liberation, or Freire's (1970) famous pedagogy of the oppressed. While helping to design a research project in India I was informed that some of the females would have difficulties in answering the survey questions, which were designed in close collaboration with the indigenous female programme providers. At first I thought that this related to language, or the complexity of the Likert scales. However, it referred to the fact that women in the slum communities were not used to being consulted, or asked their opinion and they might suffer from a form of cognitive disequilibrium – a disorientation relating to being asked about their attitudes and opinions and subsequent confusion about if, or how, to answer. In such circumstances one might view involvement in the research process as some-how 'liberating', although it could be argued that this experience would be a very minor element within their broader socio-cultural and economic lives. To view this as 'de-colonising' and relate it to matters of structured poverty, neo-colonialism and broader structures of knowledge and power on a global scale seems to be several steps too far. The desire to confront perceived oppression, forms of neo-colonialism, to be on the side of the oppressed seems to lead to epistemological and methodological over-reach.

In this respect it is worth again noting Kay's (2009: 1180) more sober recognition of the limitations of such work. Although arguing that the 'insights … have value in themselves' and 'are important for their reflexive representation of local knowledge' it is acknowledged 'from the outset that small-scale, qualitative, exploratory studies of this type have limited application'. It might even just indicate good manners. For example, Nicholls et al. (2011: 260) agree with Kay (2009) stating that 'it is problematic to accept uncritically subjugated knowledges, these contributions should not be ignored' but argue that there is a 'need for respectful consideration of cultural repre-sentations' – even if they might have limited value. Hardly the liberationist claims of Lindsey and Grattan (2012).

Are researchers simply agents of neo-colonialism?

My response to much of this debate is that of Hammersley (1995: 19), who argues that 'philosophy must be not be seen as superordinate to empirical research … research is a practical activity and cannot be governed in any strict way by metho-dological theory'. Allied to this is Sugden's (2010: 267) advocacy of a form of critical pragmatism that 'places emphasis on theoretical development and refinement through critical, practical, empirical engagement, rather than fixating upon abstract debate and unmoveable theoretical principles'. Second, following Cantley (1992), questions about the nature of funders' influence on the validity and reliability of research are not dealt with by crude assertions and polarities and the absence of worked illustrations – it is an empirical question. In my experience such research needs to be viewed as a *process of negotiation* around such things as issues for investigation, the strength and limitations of research methods, the utility of research findings and assumptions about the role of the researcher. It is interesting to note that the meanings and intentions of Global North policy makers and researchers are simply ascribed – no participatory action search for meaning here! The crude and essentialist idea that all research funded in the Global North is tainted and purely instrumental ignores the variety of relationships between research, researchers and types of funders. It also conveniently ignores the fact that many of the critics are funded by Global North funders.

Reflecting this, there are several typologies illustrating possible outcomes of such negotiations and the potential variety of policy-oriented research (e.g. Weiss, 1997; Silverman, 1985; Bulmer, 1980). Bulmer (1980) suggests that there are three broad types of policy-oriented research: analytic description entailing the gathering of primary data to 'map out the terrain'; testing of a theoretical model to address issues of concern to funding agencies; generalised understanding or enlightenment that provides policy makers with facts, analytic descriptions or technical solutions to put problems into a broader context in relation to general theoretical concepts. More comprehensively, Weiss (1986) identifies seven possible relationships between research and policy that are based on empirical work rather than politically oriented epistemological affirmation:

- The knowledge-driven model: research is driven by curiosity and moves from basic to applied and programme development. This approach would apply to one of the funders of the research reported in the book (Coalter and Taylor, 2010).
- The problem-solving model: research is driven by finding solutions to social problems.
- The interactive model: policy makers acquire input from various sources, including researchers.
- The political model: policy-makers draw on research to justify decisions already taken. This approach could be taken to apply to one of the funders of the research reported in this book (Coalter and Taylor, 2010).
- The tactical model: research is a delaying tactic to avoid making decisions.
- The enlightenment model: research might not have a direct impact on policy but may permeate the policy process with the general intellectual conditions for problem solving – to put problems into a broader context in relation to general theoretical concepts. In a very limited way this is the approach adopted by the researchers on the project reported in later chapters (Coalter and Taylor, 2010).
- The intellectual enterprise of society model: research and policy influence each other and in turn are influenced by social and political processes.

As indicated above, the relationships between funders and researchers for the research reported in this book and their various perspectives were more complex and nuanced than implied by the liberation methodologists. I am *not* arguing that there are no abuses of power nor that research can be constructed to suit the purposes of funders – legal constraints prevent me from offering such examples from my own experience. However, such typologies at least suggest that there is a need for greater care in evaluating the motives and actions of policy-oriented researchers, their relationships with policy makers/funders, the motives of funders and the validity and value of their data. The empirical investigation of such relationships might be more useful than simply dismissing them on the basis of geopolitics, geography and crude stereotypes of methodology. As Black (2010: 124) argues 'emancipatory possibilities arise in and through what are widely perceived as top-down policies and institutional structures associated with official development agencies'.

Logic, what logic?

Finally, Lindsey and Grattan (2012: 94) congratulate me on capturing

> a common belief in the functional and managerial purpose of evaluation in suggesting that development interventions utilizing sport 'require a clear, articulated understanding and evaluation of the conceptualisation, design and delivery of a programme'. This quote, and Coalter's (2009) explanation of the use of logic models in sport-for-development evaluation, also suggests the need to conceptualize sport-for-development interventions as linear processes which progress through a series of stages towards outcomes that can then be evaluated.

This is either a misunderstanding or a strawman construction on which to hang an essentialist argument. Logic models form the basis for theory-based evaluation, but are less a method and more of a framework for understanding and analysis. A programme theory does seek to identify the components, mechanisms, relationships and sequences of cause and effect that are *presumed* to lead to desired impacts and outcomes, of the type articulated, but not explained by Lindsey and Grattan's (2012) respondents. However, such programme theories must be developed in close cooperation with those designing and running a programme, as they represent an articulation of *their* assumptions. Consequently such an approach actually addresses a fundamental issue for the liberationists – the inclusion of local practitioners, local knowledge and local understanding. The key idea of theory-based evaluation is that we can express both policy makers' and programme providers' beliefs and assumptions in terms of their programme theory, or theory of change (Granger, 1998) – and articulate a *presumed* sequence of causes and effects (Weiss, 1997).

However, as will be emphasised throughout this book, the logical exposition of the assumptions underpinning a programme certainly does *not* imply simple linear causality (World Bank, 2004; Pawson, 2006) – this is the province of sports evangelists. This will be explored in detail in Chapter 7, where a programme theory is offered that is based on in-depth interviews with participants, although I certainly would not claim that the interview process liberated them. The interviews indicate that impacts are contingent, that programmes affect different people in different ways and that the road to liberation, being better informed, prevention or rehabilitation is certainly not a straight and linear one. Some participants inevitably will continue to struggle with issues of values, attitudes and behaviour and live in environments where there are constant pressures, temptations and obstacles.

Rather than articulating a set of linear processes the collaborative exercise in developing programme theory-based logic models has a number of important advantages:

- It serves to de-reify sport by emphasising the essential distinction between *necessary conditions* and *sufficient conditions* – the processes and experiences necessary to maximise the potential to achieve desired impacts and reduce potentially negative ones.
- This relates to the need to move away from the universalism of the sports evangelists and the liberation methodologists and to explore middle-range mechanisms

(Pawson, 2006) and to develop middle-range theory (Merton, 1968). For example, in programme design and daily practice across a range of seemingly different programmes, certain mechanisms or processes will result in the development of (say) self-efficacy by certain participants and not by others (Chapter 4). The identification of the potential communalities of such mechanisms across a range of interventions can lead to the development of, or linking with, broader analytical frameworks. This can provide a much more robust and potentially generalisable version of 'what works', in what circumstances, for whom and why, rather than a simple accumulation of impact studies or 'heartfelt narratives' (Hartmann and Kwauk, 2011: 286).

- It assists in the formulation of theoretically coherent, realistic, precise and relevant impacts related to programme context, processes and the nature of participants – i.e. the definitions of impacts, or their measurement, is not imposed by neo-colonialist positivists from the Global North. In the developmental work for the project underpinning this book substantial renegotiations took place in order to revise wholly unrealistic impacts and outcomes agreed between projects and funders that, if insisted on, would have led to inevitable failure. Once again, it is essential to understand the role of a researcher – often as mediator – in the various relationships between the 'oppressed' and the 'oppressors', both of whom are often trapped within the incestuous amplification that characterises some policy worlds.
- It enables the identification and awareness of critical success factors, enabling a much more informed approach to programme management, evaluation and, dare I say it, improvement.
- It provides the basis for formative, rather than simply summative (i.e. impact/outcome), evaluation and contributes to the improvement of interventions. Monitoring and evaluation become developmental, as formative evaluations are concerned with examining ways of improving and enhancing the implementation and management of interventions. It is not clear why such improvement should not be a legitimate aim.

However, more importantly from the liberationist perspective:

- It identifies and seeks to resolve different programme theories held variously by providers, policy makers and funders. They are all required to think harder and deeper about their assumptions and the programmes. In this regard many of the programme personnel and the funders of the research reported here would agree that this process proved to be significant in developing a mutual understanding, more realistic expectations and overcoming the rather mythopoeic approaches to sport that informed several perspectives. Again the image of researcher as always the agent of neo-colonialism seems misplaced.
- It contributes to capacity building, to developing a greater sense of ownership, understanding, integration and an organisational ability to reflect on and analyse attitudes, beliefs and behaviour. Much of this could be contained under a definition of 'development'.

A major attraction of theory-based approaches to evaluation is that they provide an opportunity to close the distance between academic research, policy makers and practitioners – surely a legitimate goal for liberation methodologists? Weiss (1980) argues that a theory-based approach entails a 'conversation' between researchers, policy makers and practitioners, Pawson (2006: 169) refers to 'sense-making' and Pawson and Tilley (2000: 201) refer to mutual 'teaching and learning interactions'. Bailey *et al.* (2009: 31) suggest that:

> One of the key tasks for researchers is to work with programme developers and sponsors to analyse the outcomes for which they are hoping. More importantly, the analysis reveals assumptions (and micro-assumptions) that have been made about the ways in which programme activities will lead to intended outcomes. A theory of change approach to evaluation argues that this clarification process is valuable for all parties, particularly in making explicit powerful assumptions that may or may not be widely shared, understood or agreed.

Why do you think it works?

Everyone involved in the research reported in this book (Coalter and Taylor, 2010) initially had difficulty in formulating project impacts with the conceptual precision required for evaluation. Further, they simply took the developmental potential of sport for granted and made homogenising assumptions about participants' needs. Such difficulties also reflected the very ambitious and poorly defined outcomes that had been proposed and accepted as a basis for funding by both the funders, with its references to 'personal development', 'well-being' and 'wider benefits to the community'. It is worth noting that many of the programmes initially were concerned about questioning the agreed impacts and outcomes and were fearful that the research would reveal failure – they were not delivering what they had promised in the funding application. However, in discussions with the funders it was agreed that if we could explain 'failure' – something that is inherent in a programme theory approach, but less appreciated by sport-for-development rhetoricians and liberation methodologists – and this could be used to improve the effectiveness of programmes, then all would benefit. Again, we see much more fluid and pragmatic relationships than implied by the universalising pespective of the liberationist methodologists.

All found it difficult to outline a basic programme theory, i.e. to define precisely how they thought that sport, or their programme, would achieve the desired impacts and outcomes. However, via an ongoing, fieldwork-based, collaborative process all developed a better understanding of *their assumptions* as to how such programmes might and might not work. They developed more realistic assessments of what could and could not be expected and a much greater degree of ownership of their programmes. One story might illustrate this. While driving to the airport having worked with an organisation developing a programme-based logic model, a young man placed his hand on my shoulder and said, 'I want to thank you Fred … I now understand much better why I do what I do'. Some may view this as an indication of neo-liberal neo-colonialist indoctrination, while others might see it as contribution to an increased sense of ownership, perceived self-efficacy and maybe even 'empowerment'. Who knows?

Finally, and fundamentally, such an approach shifts the focus from families of programmes (sport-for-development) to *families of mechanisms*, with the key issue being the assumed and often unexamined programme *mechanisms* that underpin policy makers' investment decisions and providers' design and delivery of the programmes. While relevant quantitative impact and, the more difficult, outcome measurements are not precluded, the emphasis is on *process evaluation* and *how* it was achieved: is the basic plan theoretically sound and plausible, what are the key variables to be studied and key stages at which to collect information, is the programme being delivered as theoretically intended and consequently can it legitimately be subjected to impact measurement?

Despite policy rhetoric and evangelical testimonies, the perspective underpinning much of this book is that 'sport', in an essentialist sense, does not really exist and does not have causal powers; impacts on individuals, however defined, are contingent, i.e. not guaranteed and variable between programmes and participants; outcomes (e.g. changed behaviour) are even more contingent, as they are mediated by a wide range of non-sporting factors. Even the most robust impact- and outcome-based evaluations are often unable to *explain* either success or failure – the 'how and why?' questions. Given the variety of sport-for-development programmes, the huge diversity of socio-cultural contexts in the so-called Global South and the, often ignored, variety of participants, it is unlikely that sport-for-development can develop via an accumulation of testimonies and measured impacts and outcomes. However, if we shift our focus from families of *programmes* to families of *mechanisms* (or programme theories), we might discover that apparently diverse interventions share common components. For example, Pawson (2006: 174) suggests:

> There are probably some common processes (e.g. how people react to change) and thus generic theories (about human volition) that feed their way into all interventions. If synthesis were to concentrate on these middle-range mechanisms, then the opportunities for the utilisation of reviews [of research] would be much expanded.

Therefore Pawson (2001a) argues for a configurational approach to causality, in which impacts can only be understood as being *produced* by the interaction of a particular and often complex combination of circumstances. This perspective, which emphasises the need to understand mechanisms and processes, is closely allied to theory-based evaluation, which Weiss (1997: 520) argues is most appropriate 'when prior evaluations show inconsistent results' – which is quite clearly the case for sport and sport-for-development (Coalter, 2007; Coakley, 2011; Hartmann and Kwauk, 2011).

Leaving aside the more complex issues about the precise relationship between certain impacts (e.g. increased self-efficacy; physical self-worth; self-confidence; self-esteem; acceptance of certain values and attitudes) and subsequent behavioural outcomes, it is clear that many sport-for-development programmes are seeking to achieve many of the same basic impacts on participants. Further, other non-sporting programmes are also seeking to address the same issues, via broadly similar mechanisms (Hartmann and Kwauk, 2011). For example, Tacon (2007) argues that football-based social inclusion projects have much in common with social work and health work practice, as they seek to promote tolerance, reduce youth offending and drug use. Biddle (2006) stresses social climates, intrinsic motivational approaches, task and mastery orientation and Witt and Crompton (1997) highlight 'protective factors' referring to *generic* mechanisms, with 'sport' being a site for, but not cause of, socialisation experiences (Coakley, 1998; Hartmann and Kwauk, 2011). (These issues will be explored and illustrated in Chapter 7.)

The implication of such an approach is that there is a need to understand the nature of such middle-range mechanisms, which programme providers either assume or try to build into their programmes. For example, in programme design and daily practice across a range of seemingly different programmes, certain mechanisms or processes will result in the strengthening of (say) self-efficacy by certain participants and not others. The identification of the potential communalities of such mechanisms across a range of interventions can lead to the development of, or linking with, broader analytical frameworks, providing a much more robust and potentially generalisable version of what works, in what circumstances, for whom and why. For example, Weiss (1997: 154) suggests that theory-based evaluation, by shifting focus from categories of activities to the categories of mechanisms by which change is achieved, 'can track the unfolding of events, step-by-step, and thus make causal attributions on the basis of demonstrated links. If this were so, evaluation would not need randomized control groups to justify its claims about causality.'

The approach potentially provides *explanations* for particular impacts and a basis for informed generalisation, or as Pawson (2001b: 4) suggests 'a tailored, transferable theory' – this programme theory works in these respects, for these subjects, in these kinds of situations. Clearly such a concentration on middle-range mechanisms would enable programme designers to adopt a broader view of the world of evidence and draw on a wide range of generic research and practice (this is done in Chapter 7). It should also lead to conceptual clarification and improved programme design and, probably, increased ability to achieve the desired impacts. Perhaps most importantly it points to the question raised at the start of Chapter 2 – the extent to which sport-for-development is a new and developing academic field in its formative stage, or is one that simply ignores a vast array of research on the nature of the efficacy of sport and related forms of intervention that seek to promote individual and social change. From the perspective of potentially common processes, generic theories, middle-range mechanisms and programme theories it is odd to define sport-for-development as a new field with little connection with previous research – unless the implication is that such programmes and contexts in the 'Global South' are so specific that previous research on sport and personal and social change has no relevance. This would seem to be an odd conclusion as the historic rhetoric surrounding such policies and interventions provides the contemporary rationale and legitimation for sport-for-development.

Conclusion: beyond incestuous amplification

Rather than seeking simply to assert sport's magical properties, or commission 'research' that proves 'success' and contributes to incestuous amplification, or collect local knowledge and cultural representations, what is required is a developmental approach based on the de-reification of 'sport' and a concentration on understanding the social processes and mechanisms that *might* lead to desired impacts and outcomes for *some* participants, or some organisations, in *certain circumstances* (Pawson, 2006). From this perspective, monitoring and evaluation need to pursue *understanding* via participatory, process-centred and formative evaluation (Coalter, 2006, 2007; Shah *et al.*, 2004). In addition to improving the design and implementation of sport-for-development programmes and defining more realistic and contextually relevant impacts and outcomes, such an approach could have a more strategic political function. It requires a conversation (Weiss, 1993) – a collaborative approach by policy-makers, funders, providers and managers to articulate much more clearly and precisely the nature of their programme theories, tacit knowledge and professional repertoires and to seek to reconcile different perspectives. This requires a consideration as to how participation in specific *sport, plus sport* or *sport plus* programmes is presumed to lead to certain impacts, which then supposedly lead to broader outcomes. The evidence from Lindsey and Grattan (2012), Kay (2009) and Burnett (2001) seems to suggest that there will be little disagreement about desired impacts and presumed outcomes. From certain perspectives this could be interpreted as 'de-colonising' and surely if sport-for-development programmes are concerned with 'development', however defined, to abjure programme improvement is self-defeating?

4

SELF-EFFICACY BELIEFS

Not so deficient after all?

Touching virtually every aspect of people's lives

Much of the policy rhetoric about 'development' and 'empowerment' tends to be vague and imprecise. While such studied vagueness might be advantageous for partnership and alliance building it does not provide a basis for robust definition and evaluation of the impact of participation on individuals, or an understanding of the presumed processes and mechanisms involved. As already noted, the hypothesis underpinning the project reported in this book was that sport contributes to 'the personal development and well-being of disadvantaged children and young people'. Attempts to operationalise 'personal development' led us to the concept of *perceived self-efficacy* as there are strong arguments for regarding this as a core component of any definition of personal development. For example, Pajares (2002: 1) argues that

> self-efficacy beliefs touch virtually every aspect of people's lives – whether they think productively, self-debilitatingly, pessimistically or optimistically; how well they motivate themselves and persevere in the face of adversities; their vulnerability to stress and depression, and the life choices they make.

Graham and Weiner (1996) argue that, especially in psychology and education, self-efficacy beliefs have proven to be a more consistent predictor of behavioural outcomes than other motivational constructs. Further, while acknowledging the possibility of cultural differences in the relevance or meaning of this construct, it is interesting to note Luszczynska, Scholz and Schwarzer's (2005: 439) conclusion that 'general self-efficacy appears to be a universal construct that yields meaningful relations with other psychological constructs' such as self-regulation, goal intentions and outcome expectancies. Further, as we will see, Bandura (1994) places notions of self-efficacy at the centre of social learning theory, which seems to inform the practice of many sport-for-development projects and is a central component of the transtheoretical theory of behaviour change (Prochaska and Velicer, 1997). Consequently, the issue of perceived self-efficacy can be regarded as lying at the centre of concerns with personal development and is a desired impact that is implicit, although rarely systematically articulated, in many sport-for-development programmes.

What is perceived self-efficacy?

Perceived self-efficacy refers to an individual's belief in her/his ability to plan and perform a task, to achieve a particular outcome, to address difficult issues – 'individuals with high levels of self-efficacy approach difficult tasks as challenges to master rather than as threats to be avoided' (Williams and Williams, 2010: 455). This is one aspect of *resilience* – the ability to deal with difficult situations, to cope with stress, to overcome setbacks, to learn from defeat, and can be regarded as a fundamental component of personal development and achievement motivation. It is worth noting Bandura's (1997: 382) distinction between self-efficacy beliefs and a more general commonsense notion of 'confidence' – a notion widely used in sport-for-development, especially the testimonies of participants (Kay *et al.*, 2007; Kay, 2009).

> Confidence is a non-specific term that refers to strength of belief but does not necessarily specify what the certainty is about. I can be supremely confident that I will fail at an endeavour. Perceived self-efficacy refers to belief in one's agentive capabilities that one can produce given levels of attainment. A self-efficacy belief, therefore, includes both an affirmation of a capability level and the strength of that belief. Confidence is a catchword, rather than a construct embedded in a theoretical system.

Bandura (1994: 2) defines *perceived self-efficacy* as 'people's beliefs about their capabilities to produce designated levels of performance that exercise influence over events that affect their lives. Self-efficacy beliefs determine how people feel, think, motivate themselves and behave'. Bandura (1994) suggests that those with high perceived self-efficacy attribute failure to insufficient effort or deficient knowledge and skills, which they can acquire. However, those with low self-efficacy tend to view poor performance as reflecting their deficient aptitude and personal inadequacy (see also Dweck, 1999). From this perspective an individual's belief that he/she has the capability to perform a task is closely associated with their level of motivation, perseverance and eventual performance. This raises important questions about the rather homogeneous view of participants 'in need of development', which underpins the rhetoric of sport-for-development.

How is perceived self-efficacy developed?

Bandura (1994: 2) states that 'the most effective way of creating a strong sense of self-efficacy is through mastery experiences'. In this regard the nature and practice of sport would seem to provide a potentially effective medium for the development of certain self-efficacy beliefs. The emphasis on practice, skill development, mastery and dealing with, and learning from, defeat all seem to be important potential contributors to the development of perceived self-efficacy – the sense that particular competencies can be developed and particular tasks achieved. However, such a perspective places strong emphasis on the need to understand the *context* in which this occurs and the processes and experiences involved. For example, via negative experiences it is also possible to reduce a sense of self-efficacy. This requires us to abandon simple de-contextualised and untheorised notions of 'sport' – such outcomes are only a possibility and a linear relationship between the complex processes of participation and positive impacts cannot be assumed (Svoboda, 1994; Patriksson, 1995). For example, Biddle (2006) emphasises the importance of the 'social climate' of sport-for-development programmmes. He argues that the enhancement of perceived self-efficacy is most likely to be achieved in programmes that seek to develop intrinsic motivational approaches based on a task-oriented, mastery orientation. In such a context participants' skills are matched with the challenges they face, cooperative learning is encouraged, clear experiences of personal success are provided and effort is supported with positive encouragement and affirmation. Conversely, for many young people a social climate based on performance and competition, in which there is constant comparison with others, punishment for mistakes and unequal recognition ('good' and 'bad' players), is unlikely to be inclusive or to support the development of perceived self-efficacy among certain participants.

As Bandura (1994: 2) argues, 'successful efficacy-builders structure situations … in ways that bring success and avoid placing people in situations prematurely where they are likely to fail often'. In this regard Pajares (2002: 7) argues that

> just as positive persuasions may work to encourage and empower, negative persuasion can work to defeat and weaken self-efficacy beliefs. In fact, it is usually easier to weaken self-efficacy beliefs through negative appraisals than to strengthen such beliefs through positive encouragement.

In addition to issues relating to the social climate of programmes, social cognitive theory proposes that learning occurs via observation and imitation. This is most likely to occur when:

- there is a lack of social distance and a perceived similarity between the teacher and the learner. This may be especially important for females in cultures with few public female role models (Brady and Kahn, 2002; Saavedra, 2007);
- there is a *self-efficacy expectation* on the part of the learner, i.e. she/he is capable of developing the skill/completing the task. This is strengthened by perceived similarities with the teacher – 'if she can do it then so can I' – what Bandura (1994) refers to as 'vicarious experience';
- and there is an *outcome expectancy* that the performance of the activity will have desirable outcomes, which can be affirmed and reinforced by the social climate of the programme.

Many of these elements – lack of social distance, self-efficacy expectation, outcome expectancy – are inherent in the community-based, local peer-leader approach adopted by many sport-for-development programmes. However, such a perspective raises significant questions about the relative effectiveness of programmes based on short-term volunteers from other cultures – an approach widely used in financially weak sport-for-development programmes. As Bandura (1994: 2) states, 'if people see the models as different from themselves their perceived self-efficacy is not much influenced by the models' behaviour and the results it produces' (we will deal with issues relating to peer leaders in more detail in Chapter 6).

The significance of the social cognitive approach to learning and personal development is that it emphasises the importance of active cognition and agency in people's capability to construct reality, self-regulate, encode information and perform behaviours. In such circumstances impacts are not inevitable and pre-given, as seems to be assumed by the concepetual entrepreneurs of sport-for-development. Pajares (2002: 2) argues that this perspective is

> in contrast to theories of human functioning that over-emphasise the role that environmental factors play in the development of human behavior and learning. Behaviorist theories, for example, show scant interest in self-processes because theorists assume that human functioning is caused by external stimuli. Because inner processes are viewed as transmitting rather than causing behavior, they are dismissed as a redundant factor in the cause and effect process of behavior and unworthy of psychological inquiry.

With this emphasis on context, social and learning relationships and active cognition, the social cognitive approach has similarities with the realist evaluation approach of Pawson and Tilley (2000). This emphasises that social intervention programmes 'work' by enabling participants to make different choices, although choice making is always constrained by participants' previous experiences, beliefs and attitudes, opportunities and access to resources. The making and sustaining of different choices requires a change in participants' reasoning (e.g. values, beliefs and attitudes, or the logic they apply to a particular situation) and/or the resources they have available to them (e.g. information, skills, material resources, support, experiences). This combination of 'reasoning and resources' – the programme 'mechanism' – is what enables a programme to 'work'. In this regard Pajares (2002: 7) states that sources of self-efficacy information (e.g. various programme experiences) are not necessarily translated directly into judgements about personal competence. He suggests that individuals' sense of self-efficacy is based on active selection, integration and interpretation of information. Bandura (1986: 25) emphasises human agency and the view that individuals proactively engage in their own development and that they possess self-beliefs that enable them to exercise some control over their feeling and actions – 'what people think, believe and feel affects how they behave'. In such circumstances the mere participation in a sport-for-development programme is unlikely to be sufficient to ensure the development of perceived self-efficacy for all participants – especially if the improved skills and expertise are not regarded as important for self-definition (Fox, 1992). This is also an issue of direct relevance to self-esteem and will be dealt with in more detail in Chapter 5.

Of course perceived self-efficacy is subjective – it is not an 'objective' measure and does not necessarily reflect people's actual capacity to achieve certain tasks. However, this does not undermine its relevance and importance to the understanding of people's behaviour. As Bandura (1997: 2) contends, 'people's level of motivation, affective states, and actions are based more on what they believe than on what is objectively true'. Further, Pajares (2002: 4) states that 'self-efficacy beliefs are themselves critical determinants of how well knowledge and skill are acquired in the first place'. We have noted Bandura's (1994) comment that those with high perceived self-efficacy will attribute failure to insufficient effort and that those with low self-efficacy tend to view poor performance as reflecting personal inadequacy. In this regard Dweck (1999) suggests that there are two types of views on ability and intelligence. The *entity view* regards intelligence as fixed and stable and success is related to this, rather than effort. Such individuals have a high desire to prove themselves to others and to be seen as smart and to avoid looking unintelligent. However, it is also possible that they are susceptible to learned helplessness and avoidance of challenging situations, feeling that circumstances are outside their control. The *incremental view* regards ability and intelligence as malleable, fluid, and changeable and personal satisfaction is gained from processes of participation, challenge, learning and mastery.

Such analyses raise two major issues that are rarely addressed systematically by sport-for-development programmes and almost wholly ignored in the homogenising rhetoric of conceptual entrepreneurs – the nature and variety of participants and how this might mediate the impacts of the programme. Much of the rhetoric of sport-for-development is based on what seems to be a necessary assumption that participation in programmes leads to 'development'. Consequently, much policy and many programmes seem to be based on a crude environmental determinism that assumes that deprived environments produce 'deficient' people and that they are in need of 'development'. However, it is highly improbable that the self-selecting participants in a wide variety of contexts will have uniform self-evaluations of their self-efficacy (or self-esteem, or knowledge of HIV and AIDS, or aspirations). However, as we will see below (and in Chapter 5) many of the unexamined assumptions about participants and their 'needs' might be ill-conceived. Second, such variations mean that 'participation' will be perceived and experienced differently by different individuals and this may lead to a variety of results.

Is perceived self-efficacy enough?

Before we turn to the research data, we again need to remind ourselves of the dangers of displacement of scope. This relates to the dangers of an overly individualised analysis and the fact that the ability to perform certain tasks and to achieve particular outcomes is dependent on the resources available to an individual and the context in which they operate. For example, referring to the closely allied area of resilience, Gilligan (2001: 94), in a manual for child and youth care workers, states:

> While resilience may previously have been seen as residing in the person as a fixed trait, it is now more usefully considered as a variable quality that derives from a process of repeated *interactions* between a person and favourable features of the surrounding context in a person's life. The degree of resilience displayed by a person in a certain context may be said to be related to the extent to which that context has elements that nurture this resilience.

Ungar (2006), in a major cross-cultural review of resilience, makes a distinction between 'navigation' and 'negotiation'. Navigation refers to an individual's capacity to move towards resources that are available and easily accessed, whereas negotiation is the provision of resources in ways that are meaningful to individuals and 'health enhancing'. Ungar (2006: 8) offers an example relevant to sport-for-development when he suggests that even education can be problematic when it is 'devalued within the discourse of success particular to a child's community'. He continues:

> In such cases the child may be able to navigate his or her way to school and access appropriate educational experiences tailored to his or her level of study. However, if that education is provided in ways that are culturally less meaningful to that student, with outcomes that are likely not realizable such as a good job or advancement to university (due to the child's poverty or experience of racial discrimination) then we might say that the child's resilience remains contingent upon his or her negotiation for education and a place in society that is more responsive to his or her context and cultural realities. As hardy as the individual child may be, it is the child's environment that lacks the resilience to negotiate with the child and provide what is needed. In this case, it is the child's environment that lacks resilience, not the child per se.
>
> *(Ungar, 2006: 8)*

Ungar (2006: 3–4) more pithily summarises the conclusion of general literature as being that 'changing the odds' is preferable to resourcing individuals to 'beat the odds'. In many ways this seems to express the dilemmas and limitations of sport-for-development and needs to be borne in mind in our analysis of the strengths and limitations of an approach based on the strengthening of perceived self-efficacy. Jeanes (2011) makes a similar point in relation to HIV and AIDS education and subsequent behaviour; we will return to this in Chapter 6.

Measuring perceived self-efficacy

Perceived self-efficacy is often context- and/or activity-specific, and Bandura (1986: 396) states that 'measures of self-precept must be tailored to the domain of psychological functioning being explored'. Consequently, the development of *sporting self-efficacy,* or a sense of efficacy within the supportive environment of a sport-for-development programme, may not go 'beyond the touchline' i.e. be transferred to a wider sense of self-efficacy when the individual confronts other tasks or difficulties. This is an empirical question and is rarely considered by sport-for-development organisations, which have tended to offer individual testimonials about how participation has increased 'self-confidence' while often ignoring significant issues of social desirability bias. This refers to the tendency of respondents to reply in a manner that will be viewed favourably by others, or which will affirm themselves and is present when issues involve self-evaluations of personal abilities and qualities. This may be a particular concern in sport-for-development programmes, in which relatively vulnerable young people are dependent on programme providers for access to free programmes that they value highly. The social climate of such programmes constantly emphasises notions of self-improvement, achievement and 'development'. In such circumstances there will be pressures to provide the expected responses and to affirm the value of the programme.

An interesting take on this in relation to perceived self-efficacy was provided by a local programme leader in Gulu (Northern Uganda), who was providing a soccer programme in camps for internally displaced people. Following my explanation of the nature and meaning of perceived self-efficacy and a discussion of the relevant scale he suggested that the respondents would deliberately underestimate their self-efficacy and provided an interesting insight on the potential negative impact of aid. Many of the displaced people had been subsistence farmers and since they had been in Gulu they had been provided with free food by the World Food Programme via huge brown tents in the town. There was a fear that they were losing their agricultural skills, which would have made resettlement difficult. The programme leader's suggestion was that they would feel that they would risk losing the food programme and have to return to farming if they indicated that they had high perceived self-efficacy and they would adjust their responses accordingly! However, as we will see, this was an example of local knowledge, cultural representation and interpretation that the quantitative data proved to be wrong.

Partly to address the issue of context and/or activity-specific perceived self-efficacy we used a generic measure that sought to explore issues of more general self-efficacy beliefs (Coalter and Taylor, 2010). In light of Bandura's (1986) comments about the need for domain, or activity-specific, measures we have to acknowledge the possible imprecision of such a measure – it is unlikely that respondents will encounter all tasks and situations with the same degree of perceived self-efficacy. However, the use of a sports-specific measure would have raised substantial concerns about its generalisability to wider contexts and would have been a very limited measure of 'development' – unless the key issue was sports development. Further, because people's motivations and actions are based largely on what they believe, such general self-evaluations can be regarded as being broadly indicative of how they assess their ability to address general issues in their lives, taking into consideration the concerns about navigation and negotiation outlined above. Despite its limitations, we think that this approach has theoretical value because little research in sport-for-development has sought to address such key issues systematically – this is at least a first step, providing a basis for a more theoretically and methodologically informed debate.

	Strongly disagree	Disagree	Agree	Strongly disagree
If something looks too complicated, I will not even bother to try it.	☐	☐	☐	☐
I avoid trying to learn new things when they look too difficult.	☐	☐	☐	☐
When trying something new, I soon give up if I am not initially successful.	☐	☐	☐	☐
When I make plans, I am certain I can make them work.	☐	☐	☐	☐
If I can't do a job the first time, I keep trying until I can.	☐	☐	☐	☐
When I have something unpleasant to do, I stick to it until I finish it.	☐	☐	☐	☐
When I decide to do something, I go right to work on it.	☐	☐	☐	☐
Failure just makes me try harder.	☐	☐	☐	☐
When I set important goals for myself, I rarely achieve them.	☐	☐	☐	☐
I do not seem to be capable of dealing with most problems that come up in my life.	☐	☐	☐	☐
When unexpected problems occur, I don't handle them very well.	☐	☐	☐	☐
I feel insecure about my ability to do things.	☐	☐	☐	☐

FIGURE 4.1 Perceived self-efficacy scale

In the research drawn on here (Coalter and Taylor, 2010) self-efficacy was measured using a scale developed by Sherer *et al.* (1982) and modified by Bosscher and Smit (1998). This is a 12 item Likert scale based on a series of positive and negative statements, with respondents asked to strongly agree/strongly disagree. The statements illustrated in Figure 4.1 were each allocated a score of 0–3 for negative statements and 3–0 for positive statements, with an overall score produced for each respondent.

Implementation ... nearly

Not all programmes involved in the study used the full scale or the standard response system. The reasons for this illustrate some of the difficulties encountered in under-taking collaborative work, in a wide variety of contexts, with relatively inexperienced people working at arm's length. First, despite prior agreement, some simply did not use all the statements. Second, some argued that the scale was too complicated for many of their participants and chose to use simple yes/no responses. While this did provide some useful information for the programme personnel in terms of developing their thinking about the meaning of 'development' and the nature of possible programme impacts, it undermined the validity of the scale and reduced inter-programme comparability. That this is not unusual in such circumstances is illustrated by the work of Woodcock *et al.* (2012) in which local volunteers regarded questionnaires as too long and complex, even with simplified response formats. Burnett's (2001: 47) experience in her extensive and systematic work in South Africa was that questionnaires were continually changed and shortened to accommodate all levels of literacy and time constraints ... this resulted in the simplification of questions, scaling (a reduction from a five- to a three-point Likert scale ... . The need to adapt methodology to be flexible and context-sensitive may have impacted negatively on the sophistication of results but was envisaged to be an important result in itself.

Despite this, we can use data from three of the programmes to explore issues relating to (i) the assumptions made about participants and their developmental 'needs' and (ii) the apparent impact of participation on perceived self-efficacy.

The programmes are (see Chapter 1 for more details): the Kids' League providing sports programmes for young people in camps for internally displaced people in Gulu in northern Uganda; an all-female football programme provided by EMIMA in Dar-es-Salaam, Tanzania; Magic Bus, working with young people from Mumbai slums. Only the Kids' League can be regarded as a true 'before' survey, as respondents in the other surveys had been taking part in this or associated organisational programmes before the initial survey. However, although this might strictly be regarded as a limitation, it probably reflects the situation in most sport-for-development organisations and illustrates the need for a pragmatic approach to research. Ongoing programmes embedded in a wider set of organisational activities are relatively widespread. Waiting for a substantial number of new recruits and identifying precise sports-specific effects is very difficult – especially given the project timescales. In such circumstances the data are offered as indicative and a basis for exploring issues that are frequently left unexamined.

'You would not survive three days here'

Although few programme personnel could provide precise definitions of what was meant by 'development', most had some vague idea that the programmes would develop the young participants' self-confidence and associated aspirations. Consequently, the largely unexamined assumption was that participants would come to the programme with relatively low self-confidence, or, more precisely, low perceived self-efficacy – if this was *not* an assumption, what are sport-for-development programmes trying to achieve?

The first important finding is that the groups were not homogeneous – contrary to an implicit assumption in universalising sport-for-development rhetoric. In all three samples the distribution of 'before' data on self-evaluations conformed broadly to a bell-shaped curve (Figures 4.2–4.4). Although respondents recorded both low and high self-evaluations, the majority fell within the mid range – they were certainly not uniformly deficient. Such data raise questions about overly generalised deficit models, which assume that poor communities automatically produce deficient people, or that there is a standard, universal, need for 'development'.

Given the diversity of populations, cultures and contexts it is not surprising that there were slight variations in average scores between the three samples. The Kids'

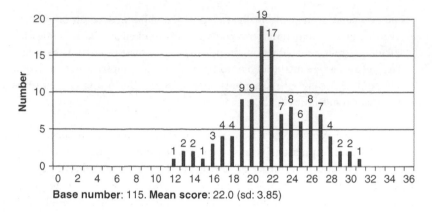

FIGURE 4.2 The Kids' League: Perceived self-efficacy: before

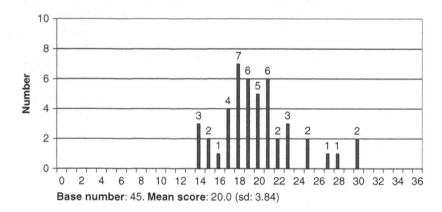

FIGURE 4.3 Magic Bus Voyagers: Perceived self-efficacy: before

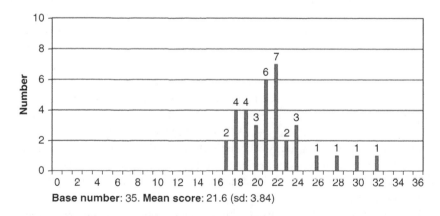

FIGURE 4.4 EMIMA: Perceived self-efficacy: before

League (the largest sample and the true 'before' sample) had the highest average score (22), followed by the all-female EMIMA (21.6) and then Magic Bus (20). It is worth noting that, on average, the Magic Bus sample recorded lower average scores on both perceived self-efficacy and self-esteem (Chapter 5) than the Tanzanian and Ugandan samples. It is not possible to be definitive about the reasons for these differences. They might indicate the distinct population from which Magic Bus recruited and that targeting had identified relatively vulnerable young people – Magic Bus used social workers to gain access to the communities, whereas the other programmes were relatively open access. Alternatively, this might reflect cultural differences and a modesty and humility that produce rather self-effacing assessments. For example, Oettingen and Zosuls (2006: 259) refer to the research finding that 'a comparatively lower sense of efficacy is often observed in Asian adolescents compared to Western adolescents', although this does not lead to lower academic achievement.

However, although the Kids' League and Magic Bus contained a number of individuals with lower self-efficacy scores than the more homogeneous, all-female EMIMA sample, there was little overall difference in the *distribution* of values, with each group containing the same degree of individual diversity. It could be argued that such data indicate that, in terms of their self-perceptions, these were relatively ordinary groups of young people who happened to live in exceptionally deprived circumstances.

When I expressed some surprise about such data it provoked three reactions:

- 'Fred, you would not survive three days here'. A long-standing programme provider in a very large African slum asked me how I thought that young people were able to deal with the day-to-day struggle for survival and the economic and familial responsibilities they often assumed without a relatively high level of perceived self-efficacy and resilience.
- 'Yes, they tend to be very assertive'. This was a reaction from another African programme provider who stated that the young women were especially demanding and assertive about what they wanted from the programme.
- 'Perhaps we are not targeting the right people'. Participation in such programmes is voluntary and most that choose to take part are likely to have a reasonable level of perceived self-efficacy – the confidence to participate. For example, Feltz and Magyar (2006: 168) illustrate that research indicates that 'when young people feel confident in their ability to participate in a given activity in the face of barriers, they are more likely to engage in that activity'. The trans-theoretical theory of behaviour change (Sonstroem, 1988) posits that there are several stages involved in behaviour change – precontemplation of the behaviour; contemplation of the behaviour; preparation to adopt the behaviour; action in which the behaviour is adopted; and maintenance of the new behaviour. It suggests that shifts from pre-contemplation to contemplation to action (e.g. joining a sport-for-development programme) depend on a certain level of perceived self-efficacy. Consequently, it is not unreasonable to assume that most participants already had a reasonable degree of perceived self-efficacy – a belief that they are capable of performing the

desired tasks, acquiring a certain level of skill without being socially embarrassed. Further, some element of self-efficacy belief is necessary to acquire knowledge and skill (Pajares, 2002). Consequently, it is not immediately obvious that the proposal that the programmes were not targetting the 'right people' is accurate. Further, it is not clear how or if this could be done, as we will see below in the data relating to non-participants.

An additional issue that needs to be borne in mind is that the nature and meaning of perceived self-efficacy cannot be taken for granted. Researchers have found that in certain circumstances there are self-protective and survival forms of resilience that include such behaviours as denial, suppression, resistance and aggression (Jenkins, 1997; Hunter, 2001). This has similarities to narcissistic and protective expressions of self-esteem that will be explored in Chapter 5. This can even lead to forms of dysfunctional and damaging behaviour. This may be an underlying factor explaining some of the highest individual scores, although we have no information as to the extent of such self-protectiveness.

Whatever the reasons, the data indicate that although these respondents come from very economically deprived communities, they can be viewed as a relatively normal selection of young people and certainly not uniformly 'deficient'.

Programme impacts and beyond averages

In the absence of control groups (and the limited nature of the 'before' data), it is very difficult to attribute changes in self-evaluations simply to participation in the programmes – and certainly not to 'sport'. Respondents were not simply 'sports participants' – many were involved in other non-sporting activities run by the organisations and all were involved in a wide variety of experiences in schools, communities, peer groups, families and churches. However, the data do enable us to begin to ask better informed questions about the impact of participation.

The two African programmes – the all-female EMIMA and the Kids' League – recorded statistically significant increases in their average perceived self-efficacy scores. The EMIMA average increased from 21.6 to 23.9 and Kids' League from 22 to 24 (Table 4.1). However, indicating that programme impacts are contingent and probably culturally specific, Magic Bus experienced a marginal and non-statistically significant *decrease* – from 20 to 19.8. The contingent nature of such impacts was also illustrated

TABLE 4.1 Perceived self-efficacy data: before and after

Programme	Before average score	After average score	Statistical significance p
EMIMA	21.6 (sd:3.84)	23.9 (sd:3.18	0.000
Kids' League	22.0 (sd:3.85)	24.0 (sd:3.68)	0.000
Magic Bus	20.0 (sd:3.84)	19.8 (sd:3.18)	0.846

in the two projects that used the more limited scales, with the mixed-sex KCCC (Kampala, Uganda) recording a statistically significant *decrease* and the all-male Praajak (Kolkata, India) a non-statistically significant *increase*.

However, one change was common to the three samples – a reduction in diversity. For example, the all-female EMIMA group, which recorded the greatest increase in perceived self-efficacy, became a less diverse group (sd: 3.84–3.18); the Kids' League also increased the average score and became a slightly less diverse group (sd: 3.85–3.68); Magic Bus Voyagers experienced a *decrease* in average scores and also became a less diverse group. Such shifts could be regarded as desired impacts of such programmes. One might hypothesise that a social climate that emphasises inclusion and team building should lead to less diverse groups. However, the processes via which these changes occur are not straightforward. We will illustrate this in the next section.

Beyond averages

In certain approaches to monitoring and evaluation the increased average scores in two out of three projects might be presented as an indication of the success of the programme and affirmation of the simple rhetoric of sports evangelism – sport works. This could even be supported by selective individual testimony to illustrate how participation had increased selected participants' 'confidence'. However, the use of averages disguises a more complex and important set of effects, which illustrate the importance of understanding mechanisms, processes and participant experiences and reactions. Just as the young people could not be regarded as uniformly deficient, the impact of participation in the programme was varied and not uni-directional. Adjustments included both increases and *decreases* in self-evaluations – a more complex set of impacts than is assumed in much sport-for-development rhetoric.

The all-female EMIMA sample exhibited the clearest positive changes, with only 17 per cent decreasing their self-evaluation, while three-quarters (76 per cent) increased. However, these data contain the possibility of a social desirability bias, as some of the second phase data were collected by personnel involved directly in delivering the programme, despite strong and consistent advice that this should not happen. Nevertheless, although the strength of the impact might have been over-estimated in this sample, the overall direction of change was similar in the other two programmes. In the Kids' League two-thirds (67 per cent) improved their self-evaluation, with a quarter (26 per cent) recording a decline. Among Magic Bus participants the impact of the programme was spread more evenly, with half (49 per cent) increasing their perceived self-efficacy and 44 per cent decreasing. This process of re-evaluation also occurred in the two programmes that used the limited scales – half of mixed-sex KCCC participants recorded a *reduction* in perceived self-efficacy, with about one-quarter increasing their evaluation. Among the all-male Praajak participants, 57 per cent increased their self-evaluation, with 43 per cent recording a *decrease*. In other words different programmes, with different social climates, different participants in different contexts had different effects on different individuals – whence sport-for-development?

Before score *below* average and then increased	Before score *above* average and then increased
Before score *below* average and then decreased	Before score *above* average and then decreased

FIGURE 4.5 Key to reading scattergrams (Figures 4.6–4.8)

Figure 4.5 provides a guide to reading Figures 4.6–4.9, which illustrate the nature and degree of changes – each point on the graphs represents an individual respondent and the *degree to which their self-evaluation changed* between the two survey points. Where scores are exactly the same the points will represent more than one person. The data in all figures are all statistically significant, with only one chance in a 1,000 that this could have happened by chance.

While all changes are worth noting, the top-left and bottom-right quadrants could be regarded as the most interesting. The top-left quadrant represents a key claim of sport-for-development – that participation in such programmes increases participants' initially weak perceived self-efficacy. It is clear that in Figures 4.6–4.8 substantial proportions of participants in the three programmes increased their scores from below

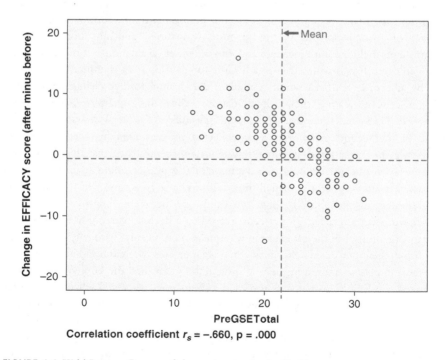

Correlation coefficient $r_s = -.660$, p = .000

FIGURE 4.6 Kids' League: Degree of change in perceived self-efficacy

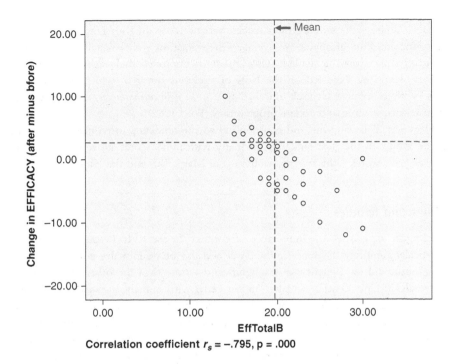

Correlation coefficient $r_s = -.795$, p = .000

FIGURE 4.7 Magic Bus Voyagers: Degree of change in perceived self-efficacy

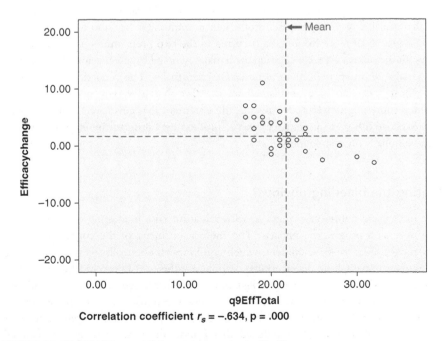

Correlation coefficient $r_s = -.634$, p = .000

FIGURE 4.8 EMIMA Degree of change in perceived self-efficacy

average. Although there were project-specific variations – in the Kids' League (Figure 4.6) more increased an already above average self-evaluation – the overall picture is that many of those with the weakest self-evaluations improved their score. This general impact would be expected on the basis of previous research, which indicates that those with lower perceived self-efficacy have, *in the right circumstances*, the most to gain from participation in appropriate programmes (Fox, 1992).

However, balancing this and contributing to the tendency to reduce the diversity of the groups, is the clear tendency for many with initial scores above the average to *decrease* their scores – this was most obvious in Magic Bus and the Kids' League.

Males and females

Here again we can see the importance of context. In the Kids' League there was no statistically significant difference in the *degree of change* between males and females – the programme did not benefit one sex significantly more than the other. The majority of females (51 per cent) and males (55 per cent) with initially *lower-than-average* self-efficacy scores increased their scores – with a quarter of females and one-fifth of males with above average scores reducing them. However, females in Magic Bus increased their average score to exceed that of boys, whose average score decreased. However, because the female sample was very small (n: 9) such data can only be regarded as indicative, if thought provoking. For example, it is not clear if such effects related to the nature of the programme and its ethos, or reflected the processes involved in a small, coherent and mutually supportive group of females taking part in activities not usually available to young women from their communiites (see also Kay, 2009).

This process of re-evaluation also occurred in the two programmes using the limited scales. In the mixed-sex KCCC group the females, who had a lower prior self-evaluation than males, also experienced a greater *decline* than males. This reduction in perceived self-efficacy may be partly explained by the fact that in survey questions females adopted more negative attitudes towards the statement that girls *have less talent for sport than boys* and this view might have been reinforced by a programme ethos that placed some emphasis on competition.

Stating the bleeding obvious?

The extent and nature of changes in self-evaluation raise interesting questions about how we assess programme impacts. The rhetoric of many of the conceptual entrepreneurs of sport-for-development, which combines an essentialist view of sport with an implicit universalistic deficit model, implies a rather uni-linear and homogeneous process, in which all participants will *increase* their perceived self-efficacy – all will 'develop'. For whatever reason, this is clearly not the impact recorded in our data – while the overall picture is that many of those with the weakest self-evaluations improved their scores, others reduced theirs and, for some, participation had no impact. There are several possible explanations for this.

First, there may be a methodological testing re-testing effect in which respondents were more familiar with the scale on the second occasion and gave a more considered, or more self-affirming response. Second, it is possible that some who recorded a high initial perceived self-efficacy might have overestimated their abilities and that a failure to develop certain skills and competence, or recognition that they overestimated their abilities *in comparison to others*, caused them to readjust. A third possibility is that the social climate and approach to teaching and learning was more appropriate for some participants than others. This seems most obviously the case in KCCC, where female perceived self-efficacy declined and in Magic Bus where female perceived self-efficacy increased. However, it is clear that we need more information about the variety of mechanisms – context, relationships, rules, experiences and participants' 'reasoning and resources' (Pawson and Tilley, 2000) – which led to such differences and generalisations about 'sport-for-development' are of little assistance.

It seems to be 'stating the bleeding obvious' to say that participation in different programmes in different contexts will affect different people in different ways and it would be very surprising if decreases in self-evaluation did *not* occur (Patriksson, 1995; Coakley, 1998; Pawson, 2006; Biddle and Mutrie, 2001). Even in the exceptionally positive results produced by the all-female EMIMA, about one-fifth of participants reduced their self-evaluations and a number of individuals who started with below average scores *decreased* their evaluations. Clearly perceptions of self-efficacy are tested constantly and more so when participating in new activities, or in mixed-ability groups – you discover that you are better or worse than you thought, especially in comparison to others. However, how this is interpreted depends partly on the social climate of the programme, or if individuals have an entity or incremental view of abilities (Dweck, 1999), or if the activity and experiences are deemed to be important to self-definition. Further, it is possible that a reduction in perceived self-efficacy is merely a realistic adjustment based on practical experience. This is not necessarily a negative outcome and is a possibililtiy that programme providers should be aware of, although it is an impact that is rarely, if ever, recorded in personal testimonies – congregations like simple and positive messages.

Further, the various shifts in self-evaluation are reflected in reductions in the relative diversity of the groups. Such outcomes should not be a surprise if the aim of most sport-for-development organisations is to emphasise inclusivity – if the programmes achieve their inclusive aims then groups are likely to become less diverse over time. However, it is important not to over-emphasise this trend because the groups remained diverse and there were real differences between the three programmes. Such effects are mediated by the nature of participants, programme practice, ethos and cultural context.

Participants and non-participants: spot the difference

Although we were unable to use control groups to identify the comparative impact of participating in the programmes, we undertook two sets of participant/non-participant surveys related to EMIMA and KCCC (Coalter and Taylor, 2010). The EMIMA programme was not the all-female one reported on above and respondents had been taking part in sport and sport-related activities for at least 18 months; the KCCC respondents for between six months and two years. It seems reasonable to presume that the sport-for-development assumption would be that participants who had been taking part for a minimum of six months would score higher on many of the personal development factors than non-participants, irrespective of their pre-participation scores – unless it is assumed that those recruited to the programmes would have systematically lower levels of perceived self-efficacy. However, as we have argued, this seems unlikely.

In the case of EMIMA there were no consistent or statistically significant differences on issues of perceived self-efficacy, with differences being largely random. In both samples males had slightly higher perceived self-efficacy than females. There was little difference between both sets of females, with non-EMIMA females scoring marginally higher (Coalter and Taylor, 2010).

In the case of KCCC they chose to use a yes/no option, preventing the calculation of an overall score. However, we were able to compare various elements of the scale, which provided some indicative comparisons. We were able to do this because it is possible to subdivide the scale to explore issues of *initiative* (the extent respondents are willing to deal with difficult issues), *effort* (the extent to which respondents are willing to stick at a task) and *persistence* (respondents' general assessment of their ability to deal with unexpected issues and stick at a task) (Coalter and Taylor, 2010). With KCCC the picture was slightly more complex, with some statistically significant differences for partial measures in favour of both groups, which are difficult to interpret. In terms of measures of *effort,* non-KCCC respondents had statistically significant higher scores, but in relation to *initiative* and *persistence* KCCC participants recorded higher scores than non-participants. Perhaps reflecting the before-and-after data above, non-KCCC females recorded higher scores than the KCCC females, although most of the differences were not statistically significant – i.e. they could simply reflect chance, or the type of people attracted to KCCC.

Overall, there were no consistent statistically significant differences between participants and non-participants. On the basis of self-evaluation, the participants in the sport-for-development programme remained broadly representative of the communities from which they were drawn. It would seem that some factors influencing perceived self-efficacy lie beyond the touchline.

Training peer leaders

So far we have explored the impact of participation in sport-for-development programmes on general participants. However, we also collected data relating to a more focused attempt to address the issue of perceived self-efficacy – peer leader training (Coalter and Taylor, 2010). In Chapter 6 we will deal in more depth with issues relating to peer leaders and it is worth noting that many commentators suggest that peer leaders are the main beneficiaries of sport-for-development programmes, but that insufficient attention is paid to their training. Here we will examine the impact of a training programme on those who many regard as practically, ideologically and symbolically central to sport-for-development programmes (Nicholls, 2009; Jeanes, 2011).

We undertook a before-and-after survey of 17 participants in the Magic Bus peer-leader training programme – in my experience this is one of the most systematic programmes of its type. Trainee peer leaders were selected from the Magic Bus Voyager programme (aged 15 plus) because they had shown most interest, commitment and were regular attendees over a three-year period. The training programme was designed to build on the competencies that it was presumed the young people had developed via participation in Magic Bus programmes. In 35 sessions over one year the training combined workshops and practical training sessions, in which the trainees assisted in the delivery of activity sessions and eventually delivered sessions under supervision. Issues dealt with included awareness of self, community and personal and social change, personal and social development, gender and HIV and AIDS, leadership, facilitation and sports skills.

The data on self-efficacy (and self-esteem) indicate that Magic Bus chose a distinctive group of people for peer-leader training. As they were selected for exhibiting commitment to, and initiative in, the programme it is not surprising that their average self-efficacy score (21.4) was higher than the Voyager sample (20). Of course, it is possible that simply being chosen for the training boosted their self-evaluations. With an initial score already higher than the group from which they were selected it was not surprising that training produced only a marginal and non-significant increase in the average score – 21.4 to 21.6.

Again this marginal shift in the average score of a relatively small sample disguises differential impacts. As with the broader, less focused, participation programmes, the experience of training and being closely monitored led some to readjust self-evaluations – it would be surprising if a training programme in which participants are required to take increasing responsibility and are monitored closely by programme staff did not have such an effect. As with the general participation programmes, the majority with initial *below average* scores increased their evaluations (Figure 4.9), some made no adjustments and several reduced their perceived self-efficacy.

Reduction in perceived self-efficacy might not be unusual. Seeking to develop peer-leaders involves a different and more objectively assessed set of skills and competencies from those derived from being a relatively anonymous programme participant. In fact, in some cases a reduction in perceived self-efficacy might represent a more realistic level and might be viewed as a positive outcome. However, a few were left with relatively low self-evaluations that must raise questions about their suitability for the peer-leader role. It seems clear that some of those who exhibit commitment and enthusiasm as participants might not always be suitable candidates for peer leadership. These data raise issues about peer-leader training that are rarely dealt with systematically and we will return to this in Chapter 6.

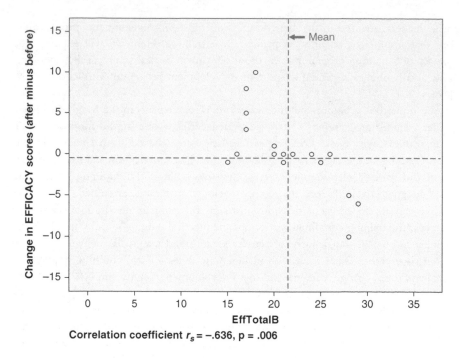

Correlation coefficient $r_s = -.636$, p = .006

FIGURE 4.9 Magic Bus Peer Leaders: Changes in self-efficacy

Conclusions

The deficit model

The data raise significant questions about simple deficit models of young people and easy generalisations about 'development needs'. Although all of the respondents lived in extremely deprived social and economic circumstances they cannot be regarded as uniformly 'deficient'– at least not in terms of their self-perceptions of their self-efficacy. In fact it might be conjectured that living in such deprivation means that many have to develop relatively high levels of *perceived* self-efficacy in order to survive and to remain positive. Of course it is possible that some of these evaluations reflect a certain self-protective element, with a degree of denial and suppression (Jenkins, 1997; Hunter, 2001) – we have no way of knowing from our data, although this cannot explain the relatively normal distribution of self-perceptions across a variety of contexts.

Nevertheless, the young people in these programmes were not homogeneous groups and there was a range of self-evaluations, with many expressing quite strong self-beliefs. To ignore this as a result of an unquestioned deficit model contains obvious ideological and pedagogic dangers. Such diversity raises interesting questions about the definition of 'target groups' and their presumed 'needs', programme design, social climate, content and delivery and the definition of appropriate performance indicators. For example, one organisation over-reacted to such data by questioning the very rationale for the programme – rather than adopting a more realistic, participant-focused approach and seeking to adapt the programme and to build on the participants' self-beliefs, which seem often to be ignored.

Changes in self-evaluation

The extent and diversity of changes in self-evaluation raise interesting questions about how we assess programme impacts, especially as the uni-linear deficit model would imply that all, or most, will *increase* their perceived self-efficacy – often reflected via selective testimonies. First, it is inevitable that participation in different programmes, in different contexts will affect different people in different ways and it would be very surprising if decreases in self-evaluation did not occur. Clearly perceptions of self-efficacy are tested constantly and more so when participating in new activities, or in mixed-ability or mixed-sex groups, or in peer leadership training – you discover that you are better or worse than you thought, often in comparison to others. It is possible that a reduction in perceived self-efficacy is merely a realistic adjustment based on practical experience, which is not necessarily a negative impact.

The directions of change

Although there were project-specific variations, the overall picture is that many of those with weaker self-evaluations improved their score. This reflects previous research which indicates that those with low perceived self-efficacy have, in the right circumstances, the most to gain (Fox, 1992). Also there was an associated pattern of those with initially higher than average self-evaluations lowering these as a result of participation. This pattern was most obvious in Magic Bus and the Kids' League. In the only robust mixed-sex data set – the Kids' League – there was no significant difference in the *degree of change* between males and females – this programme did not benefit significantly one sex more than the other. On the other hand, on the more limited data from KCCC, the programme had a negative impact on several female participants.

Group diversity

These various changes in self-evaluation are reflected in the shifts in the relative diversity of the groups, with all becoming slightly less diverse goups (sometimes explained by the reduction of some initially relatively high self-evaluations). Perhaps such outcomes are not surprising. If the aim of sport-for-development organisations is to emphasise inclusivity, then groups are likely to become less diverse over time. However, it is important not to over-emphasise this trend, as the groups remained diverse and, most importantly, there were real differences between the three programmes.

Although much of this may seem self-evident, it is often ignored in the universalising rhetoric of many in the sport-for-development 'movement'. Although the data indicate general *tendencies,* the variations between the programmes indicate that, not surprisingly, there is no simple and predictable 'sport-for-development effect' – would we expect a universal 'education effect', or a 'crime prevention effect'? As with all forms of social intervention, causation is contingent, reflects the nature of participants, circumstances, relationships and interactions and no impacts are guaranteed. In this regard Pawson *et al.* (2004: 7) state that: 'It is through the workings of entire systems of social relationships that any changes in behaviours … are effected … . Rarely if ever is the "same" programme equally effective in all circumstances because of the influence of contextual factors'.

Was it sport?

In the absence of a control group – i.e. an equivalent sample of young people who had not participated in the programmes – it is difficult to attribute any changes in self-evaluations simply to participation in the programmes. Further, the data *cannot* be viewed as providing an indication of the impact of 'sport' in the essentialist sense it is often used in sport-for-development. All programmes contained a number of non-sporting elements and a wide variety of social relationships and experiences. Perhaps most importantly, and remembering the absence of consistent significant differences between participants and non-participants, many young people may live in reasonably homogeneous cultural and/or religious communities that serve to sustain relatively normal levels of self-efficacy beliefs – albeit with individual differences. For example, Hunter (2001: 175) in a comparative qualitative study of resilience among adolescents from New England and Ghana, found that responses had little to do with culture, socio-economic group, age or gender but rather 'with the participants' perceptions of and the activities of the support systems in their lives; those adolescents with loving, involved and caring support systems and those without' – in her sample this was predominantly among the Ghanaian respondents, who were members of a Christian youth group. Earlier we noted Gilligan's (2001) argument that, rather than adopting an individual perspective on resilience, it is more useful to view it as being related to the extent to which the context has elements that nurture this resilience. Likewise, Ungar (2006), in a review of international research on resilience, argues that

> while self-efficacy was initially hypothesized to be an individual characteristic, response patterns … show that children linked questions that appear logically to relate to aspects of self-efficacy at the individual level with self-efficacy in relationships and in community and cultural contexts (political efficacy, influence on parents, etc.). Youth in different research sites attribute different aspects of resilience to different factors when tests of validity are performed. It is worth noting that factor analysis of the entire sample did not produce a coherent factor structure … majority world boys sorted themselves into two groups, those in communities with high social cohesion such as Israel, Palestine, India, Tanzania, the Gambia and Russia, where there is a sense of common purpose, and those from communities with low social cohesion where a common purpose is

not evident. These communities included Cape Town, Medellin and the northern Canadian aboriginal community of Sheshatshiu.

Ungar (2006) admits that the distinction between high and low social cohesion is based mostly on qualitative data and that more objective data are required. Nevertheless, Ungar (2006: 2) argues that 'aspects of children's lives that contribute to resilience are related to one another in patterns that reflect a child's culture and context'. This of course raises significant questions about the precise contribution of sport-for-development programmes in such complex socio-cultural landscapes. It also raises questions about the analytical utility of over-generalised references to the components of 'development' and the homogenising use of the term 'Global South' when discussing sport-for-development work.

5

SELF-ESTEEM

Best taken in moderation

Why self-esteem, why sport?

In the previous chapter we explored issues relating to perceived self-efficacy and the varying impacts that participation in the various programmes appeared to have. Perceived self-efficacy relates to an individual's perception of her or his ability to achieve a task or to solve a problem and is usually based in practical experiences. However, self-esteem relates to an individual's assessment of her or his own self-worth, which may or may not relate to actual capabilities. In fact, research indicates that there may be little relationship between self-esteem and objectively measured abilities (Baumeister *et al.*, 2003) – an issue to which we will return.

Self-esteem is regarded as consisting of a *relatively* stable and enduring personality characteristic (trait self-esteem) and subject to short-term variations (state self-esteem). The strength of one's self-evaluation can change with circumstances and is also dependent on how one is treated by significant others – this is especially so if trait self-esteem is weak. A sense of self-esteem may relate to performance in a variety of roles and the *relative importance* attributed to each – son/daughter, friend, student, father/mother, partner, footballer, coach or peer leader. In other words, aspects of self-esteem are dependent on a range of often changeable factors and are, to some degree, dependent on how individuals are treated by others – recognition, acceptance, status and appreciation are important to a sense of self-worth. As Emler (2001a) summarises – we discover who we are and what we are through our interactions with others.

The United Nations includes self-esteem as a desired impact of sport-for-development in many of its publications. For example, *Sport-for-development and Peace: Towards Achieving the Millennium Development Goals* (United Nations, 2003) includes self-esteem as one of the skills and values learnt through sport and one of the life skills that 'empowers' individuals, especially young women. The *Final Report on the International Year of Sport and Physical Education* (United Nations, 2005: 16) lists a number of sport-for-development organisations that 'use street football as an educational tool in projects that promote self-esteem'.

More generally, self-esteem has been viewed as a central aspect of psychological health and personal and social development. For example, in the classic Maslow (1987) hierarchy of human needs, following the fulfilment of basic needs for physiological survival, safety and social belonging, esteem needs, the respect of others and self-respect, are regarded as the necessary basis for the next stage of 'self-actualisation' and the reaching of individual potential. In passing, it is worth noting issues that this raises for sport-for-development, when basic physiological needs and safety and security – i.e. basic aspects of 'development' – have to be achieved before issues of perceived self-efficacy, self-esteem and self-actualisation can be addressed.

In the research reported in this chapter (Coalter and Taylor, 2010) self-esteem was included as a measure of personal development because of the propositions of the hierarchical competence-based model of self-esteem (Sonstroem and Morgan, 1989; Harter, 1999). For example Shephard (1997) suggests that it is possible that an increased sense of self-efficacy might be developed via increased motor skills and a sense of achievement in physical activity or sport. This, in turn, might lead to increased self-esteem, if the achievement is valued in terms of self-definition – an important *sufficient condition* usually ignored in generalised rhetoric. Further, in terms of notions of 'development', the presumption is that this combination of strengthened perceived self-efficacy and improved self-esteem might encourage and enable improved learning – some approaches to HIV and AIDS' education view this combination as central to behaviour change (Chapter 6). This appears to lend support to the traditional belief that participation in, and achievement through, sport can contribute to the development and strengthening of self-esteem by proposing that the lower levels of the hierarchy are related to the development of perceived self-efficacy.

Such an approach is based on the view that the concepts of self and self-esteem consist of multiple components, each of which is not of equal importance to all individuals. For example, Harter (1988) suggests that some of the components of self-esteem are perceived intelligence, scholastic competence, social acceptance, *athletic competence, physical self-concept* and *physical appearance*. From this perspective, the hypothesis is that the lower-level development of a sense of *physical self-efficacy* may lead to a sense of *physical competence* (a general evaluation of the self as possessing overall physical fitness based on feelings of self-efficacy via specific exercise activities) and *physical (self) acceptance*, which is a more general satisfaction with various aspects of the body. In turn this is regarded as one possible component of global self-esteem. Sonstroem and Morgan (1989) also speculate that *perceived physical appearance* may be an important aspect of self-acceptance. In this regard Leith (1994) argues that the close link between body image and self-image may help to explain the apparently strong theoretical link between exercise and self-esteem, especially for many young women, although increasingly so for some young men (see also Fox, 1999). Ferron (1997) suggests that this reflects the experience of bodily changes and growing interest in the opposite sex and Harter (1990) argues that for adolescents, especially girls, physical self-esteem is consistently an important predictor of global self-esteem

(McDermott, 2000) – although the extent to which this is culturally variable is an important empirical issue.

In terms of the relative role of sport and exercise, Fox (1992) agrees that participation in sport may lead to a sense of competence or physical strength. However, he emphasises that the effect of these on physical self-worth and *then* self-esteem is filtered by the relative importance attached to them, compared to other sources of self-esteem. Sport *may* contribute to the strengthening of self-esteem, but, being good or bad at something about which one cares little will have limited impact on how one values oneself. In this regard James (1890) defined self-esteem as success divided by pretensions (or aspirations) and what matters is whether successes are relevant to pretensions (Emler, 2001a). For example, Zaharopoulos and Hodge (1991) found that although US high school athletes had higher levels of physical ability self-acceptance than non-athletes, they did not have higher global self-esteem. Bowker, Gadbois and Cornock (2003) report no significant relationship between sports participation and global self-esteem for senior US high school students. Also the effects may vary by sex. For example, a large-scale survey of English school pupils (Mason, 1995) found that boys placed a much higher emphasis than girls on sport and physical education in terms of their self-definition, preferred areas of achievement, sources of social acceptance and friendship networks. Related to this Saga, Boardley and Kavussanu (2011) found male and female differences in how fear of sporting failure affected self-esteem. For young males the fear was that under-performance would negatively affect the opinion of significant others and threaten their social standing. Females were more likely to be concerned with a fear of devaluing their own self-estimate, perhaps leading to a lowering of the significance that they attributed to sport in terms of self-perceptions.

Fox's (2000) research review indicates that from late adolescence onwards taking part in regular sport or exercise is moderately associated with more positive physical self-perceptions, including body image. Although for some people appropriate provision and experiences of participation in sport can serve to enhance a sense of self-efficacy and physical self-esteem, Fox (2000: 97) concluded that in general, 'participation in sport and exercise was weakly associated with global self-esteem'. The relationship is dependent on the nature of the population, environment and individual characteristics. Spence, McGannon and Poon (2005) in a systematic review of 113 studies found that exercise participation appears to lead to small, if significant, increases in global self-esteem (GSE). However, they conclude that, overall, 'the benefits of exercise for GSE are overstated' (Spence *et al.*, 2005: 322).

Sport and exercise are weakly and inconsistently associated with global self-esteem because the relationship seems to be heavily dependent on context – the nature of participants, the type of social climate and even individual characteristics. Fox (2000) summarises the general practical implications of existing knowledge as follows (see also Biddle and Mutrie, 2001):

- The greatest improvements are likely to occur in those who are initially low in self-esteem, physical self-worth and body image. Spence *et al.* (2005) also suggest that those with the lowest initial levels of physical fitness have most to gain.

- The 'attractiveness' factors that make people stay with such programmes cannot be separated from those that promote self-esteem – for example, the qualities of the leader, the exercise setting and relationships with other participants appear to be significant programme mechanisms.

This last point again raises fundamental issues about context, process and participant experience. For example, Biddle *et al.* (2004) suggest that while physical activity may enhance psychological well-being, it is likely that the prevailing psychological climate and social interactions will be more crucial than the actual physical activity. Sonstroem and Morgan (1989) also accept that the social and psychological processes involved in participation may be as important as any objective, or even subjective, improvements in fitness or physical competence. In this regard, Fox (2000) hypothesises that the relationship between exercise and any measured increases in self-esteem may be explained by perceived autonomy and personal control and/or a sense of social belonging and significance within the group. With regard to autonomy and control, Biddle (2006) argues that the enhancement of physical self-efficacy and (possibly) self-esteem is most likely to be achieved in a social climate that seeks to develop intrinsic motivational approaches based on a task-oriented, mastery orientation. Participants' skills are matched with the challenges they face, which facilitate clear experiences of personal success and positive encouragement is provided. In other words, for many of the groups likely to benefit most from improved physical self-worth, body image and self-esteem, traditional competitive, ego-centred sports might not be effective.

The relationship between sports participation and improved self-esteem is at best variable – individual characteristics, context, process, experience and relative importance are all mediating factors. Consequently, there is a danger in adopting a simple, one-dimensional, abstracted sports-centred approach – sport-for-development – which ignores the social climate in which sports participation takes place. Again we are reminded of Coakley's (2004) distinction between sport as a cause and a site of socialisation. Further, as with perceived self-efficacy, there is a danger of adopting overly individualised versions of self-esteem, which ignore the wider social, cultural and economic environments that strongly influence how individuals are able to view themselves and on which participation in a single sports programme is likely to have minimal effect. Here it is worth remembering Pawson and Tilley's (2000) emphasis on participants making choices that depend on previous experiences, beliefs and attitudes, opportunities and access to resources. However, even if participation in sport can improve self-esteem, there is a range of fundamental concerns about the validity and utility of the concept.

Cultural relevance

The Maslow (1943) hierarchy is criticised for being ethnocentric, especially for its emphasis on individualism. It is argued that it ignores the possibility that in more collectivist cultures, acceptance in the community and the respect of others may be much more important than the emphasis on individuality and ego-centred self-actualisation. For example, during the development phase of the project informing this book, a programme provider in the majority Muslim Senegal expressed some concern about the use of the concept of self-esteem, viewing it as a Western, market-driven individualistic notion. It was suggested that in many communities the sub-ordination of the self to the collective good was a way of achieving status and esteem rather than overly individualistic behaviour. A slightly different issue was raised in India where it was suggested that because many women are taught to subordinate their sense of self and where their opinions are not sought or valued, they might suffer a type of cognitive dissonance when asked for their opinions – especially about their own value and worth. Baumeister, Campbell, Krueger and Vohs (2003) also argue that even in some Judeo-Christian traditions modesty and humility are regarded as virtues, with high self-esteem being associated with pride and vainglory. While such possibilities cannot be ignored, there is a considerable consistency in our data (Coalter and Taylor, 2010) across programmes and cultures and samples in which Muslims are the majority. Also, it is possible to offer some reasonable explanations for the measured differences between the various samples, where the main divide seems to be between the East African and Indian data – we will return to this below. Finally, although there is evidence that the *average strength* of self-esteem is mediated by certain aspects of cultures, research evidence suggests that self-esteem functions in similar ways in different cultures and that, in terms of correlates of self-esteem as a psychological construct, there is a good deal of cross-cultural generality (Brown, Cai, Oakes and Deng, 2009). Within the debate about cultural relativism, which seems to underpin much of the concerns of the liberation methodologists, it is worth at least noting the comment by Brown *et al.* (2009: 154) that 'cultural differences in the magnitude of some phenomena may not necessarily translate into functional differences between cultures' and that 'a complete understanding of culture requires understanding cultural similarities as well as cultural differences'.

A social vaccine?

A more fundamental critique of the individualism underpinning the concept of self-esteem is provided by Hewitt (1998). Reflecting Weiss's (1993) concern about limited-focus programmes seeking to deal with broad-gauge problems, Hewitt (1998: 22) states that:

> Psychological myths explain and justify social reality by attributing problems to individuals rather than to the social world. The belief that individuals can improve their chances in life by improving their self-esteem seems to be a doctrine that celebrates the power of the individual … the individual possesses considerable power to shape his or her fate through sheer self-affirmation … but this myth of self-esteem also assigns great responsibility to the individual … it is the individual who must recover self-esteem and thereby overcome adversity and if the individual fails to do this, he or she is to blame. The possible influence of the social world is simply left out of the picture

Like the mythopoeic nature of sport that underpins sports evangelism (Coalter, 2007) Hewitt (1998: xii–xiii) argues:

> [S]elf-esteem, has all the earmarks of a reigning cultural myth, a tale that informs us what we should strive for, explains how to reach it and warns about the pitfalls that lie in wait for us … And just as heroic myths embellish the lives of historic figures, and even invent them when necessary, the myth of self-esteem decorates the bare facts of human psychology with ideas that are grounded in the needs of American culture and coated with the legitimacy of science.

In an analysis that has strong similarities to the politics and rhetoric of sport-for-development, Hewitt (1998) argues that 'conceptual entrepreneurs' have promoted the idea that 'low self-esteem lies at the root of individual and thus societal problems and dysfunction' (Baumeister *et al.*, 2003: 3). In other words self-esteem can be both a *cause* of, and a cure for, a variety of social problems – a type of social vaccine (Emler, 2001a), providing an all-purpose solution to a range of social problems such as crime, low educational achievement, drug taking and may contribute to the ill-defined 'development' and 'empowerment'. In Chapter 3 we noted the strength of this belief that underpinned the rejection of the negative conclusions of its researchers by the Californian Task Force to Promote Self-esteem and Personal and Social Responsibility. The optimism of the will, or in this case wishful thinking, drowned out the voice of the pessimistic, or realistic, intellect.

However, Emler's (2001a) comprehensive review of research evidence suggests that young people with low self-esteem are *not* more likely to commit crimes, including violent crimes; use or abuse illegal drugs; drink alcohol to excess or smoke; or fail academically. Commenting on his review, Emler (2001b: 1) states:

> Many of the claims made about self-esteem are not securely rooted in hard evidence. Indeed where many of the biggest and most expensive social problems are concerned – crime, violence, alcohol abuse and racism – there is no warrant for the view that low self-esteem plays a significant role.

In terms of personal development and learning it is worth noting Emler's (2001a: 19) conclusion that high self-esteem can be a source of problems, as 'young people with very high self-esteem are more likely than others … to reject social pressures from adults and peers and engage in physically risky pursuits'. Also, in relation to attempts to use sport-for-development to increase self-esteem as part of a strategy to reduce HIV and AIDS, it is useful to note Baumeister *et al.*'s (2003) warning that high self-esteem can foster experimentation and may increase drinking and early sexual activity (see Chapter 6).

These potentially negative outcomes are in part related to the heterogeneity of high self-esteem (Baumeister *et al.*, 2003). Similar to the issues of potential denial, suppression, resistance and aggression in terms of high perceived self-efficacy (Chapter 4), measures of self-esteem can indicate genuine, defensive or narcissistic self-esteem – the latter referring to favourable, even grandiose views of self and personal capabilities and a belief in entitlement to privileges. Such heterogeneity can result in individuals with seemingly similar scores acting is very different ways – e.g. high self-esteem is related to both high and low levels of hostility and violence (Emler, 2001a). Because of this Emler (2001a: 26) suggests that 'the optimal level of self-esteem is not high. If self-esteem is a favourable opinion of oneself, then people with very high self-esteem will also sometimes be described in less positive terms – overbearing, arrogant, self-centred, narcissistic, egotistic, smug, vain'. This also raises significant methodological issues about the use of self-report for evidence of behaviour – a widespread approach in sport-for-development. This is because those who think highly of themselves also have a tendency to, often wrongly, think highly of their actions. For example, 'researchers obtained more impressive evidence of the benefits of self-esteem when they relied on self-reported outcomes than when they relied on objective outcomes' (Baumeister et al., 2003: 7) – perhaps de-colonising, feminist-oriented, participatory action research (Lindsey and Grattan, 2012) has certain limits.

Doing well and well-being

Baumeister et al. (2003) raise a further issue related closely to the concept of perceived self-efficacy and of direct consequence for any definition of 'development'. They argue that if self-esteem is an outcome rather than a cause, then it is plausible that to seek systematically to raise self-esteem via affirmation (often an aim of child-centred sport-for-development programmes) could have undesirable results – people enjoying the rewards of self-esteem without making the effort and thereby developing an unwarranted sense of privilege. Reflecting this analysis Reasoner (nd) argues that:

> Attempts by pro-esteem advocates to encourage self-pride in students solely by reason of their uniqueness as human beings will fail if feelings of well-being are not accompanied by well-doing. It is only when students engage in personally meaningful endeavors for which they can be justifiably proud that self-confidence grows, and it is this growing self-assurance that in turn triggers further achievement.

Baumeister et al. (2005: 91) conclude: 'We have found little to indicate that indiscriminately promoting self-esteem in today's children or adults, just for being themselves, offers society any compensatory benefits beyond the seductive pleasure it brings to those engaged in the exercise'.

This is related to Spady's (1970) warning of the dangers involved if sporting activities stimulate participants' status perceptions and future goals without providing the skills and orientations required for occupational success – sport needs to be a *complement* to education and development, not a substitute. This is central to sport-for-development and raises issues about the relationship between improved perceived self-efficacy, changes in self-esteem and 'development'. For example, Mwaanga (2003), a pioneer of sport-for-development, warns against the dangers of raising expectations and aspirations of young women without changing their economic circumstances. We will return to this later.

We now turn to issues relating to the definition and measurement of self-esteem.

Measuring self-esteem

Unlike perceived self-efficacy there is a widely accepted 'gold standard' scale for measuring self-esteem (Emler, 2001a) – the Rosenberg (1965) self-esteem scale. Nevertheless Emler (2001a) refers to a study that identified at least 200 different measures of self-esteem, indicating that great care needs to be taken in the populist use of the term and when comparing studies. The Rosenberg scale is a ten-item Likert scale with items answered on a four-point scale – from strongly agree to strongly disagree (figure 5.1). It is based on the conception of self-esteem as an evaluative attitude towards the self, with only two questions being comparative but only about parity and not perceived superiority or inferiority. Further, because the statements are very general self-evaluations, it is usually referred to as a measure of 'global self-esteem' – rather than being related to any specific domain, similar to the perceived self-efficacy scale used in Chapter 4.

The individual's score is calculated by scoring all positive statements from 3–0 and all negative statements from 0–3. The self-esteem score is the sum of these values. The presumed 'normal' range for responses has been regarded as lying between 15 and 25. However, as noted above, there is a strong possibility of cultural variations. There is a general tendency for scores to be skewed towards higher self-esteem

Below is a list of statements dealing with your general feelings about yourself. Please state whether you strongly disagree, disagree, agree or strongly agree with each statement.

	Strongly disagree	Disagree	Agree	Strongly agree
On the whole I am satisfied with myself	☐	☐	☐	☐
At times I think I am no good at all	☐	☐	☐	☐
I feel that I have a number of good qualities	☐	☐	☐	☐
I am able to do things as well as most other people	☐	☐	☐	☐
I feel I do not have much to be proud of	☐	☐	☐	☐
I certainly feel useless at times	☐	☐	☐	☐
I feel that I am a person of worth, at least equal with others	☐	☐	☐	☐
I wish I had more respect for myself	☐	☐	☐	☐
All in all, I am inclined to think I am a failure	☐	☐	☐	☐
I take a positive attitude towards myself	☐	☐	☐	☐

FIGURE 5.1 Rosenberg self-esteem scale

(Adler and Stewart, 2004) and this is especially so in some Western cultures that emphasise individualism and rights more than collectivism and responsibilities – something that has increased in recent decades with the domination of neo-Liberal social and economic policies. Evidence indicates that this has now reached rather extreme proportions among young people in the USA, where an emphasis on self-esteem is a central part of the education system, often separated from objective academic achievement (Hewitt, 1998). Further, Emler (2001a: 45) offers the cautionary note that

> very few people have low self-esteem in an absolute sense – in that they more often describe themselves in negative than in positive terms ... Therefore, the references in research to low versus high self-esteem almost always mean a distinction between those whose self-esteem is very positive and those whose self-esteem is slightly positive.

Indeed, Blascovich and Tomaka (1991: 123) argue that 'an individual who fails to endorse self-esteem scale items at least moderately is probably clinically depressed' – suggesting that even the restricted range of self-esteem scores is useful among, and representative of, non-depressed individuals.

Social desirability bias

Krueger (1998) suggests that the standard finding that most self-esteem scores are high indicates the possibility that at least some scores are affected by deliberate or unwitting self-enhancement. This raises the possibility of social desirability bias, which refers to the tendency of respondents to reply in a manner that will be viewed favourably by others, or which will affirm themselves. This issue is present in most research where respondents are asked to provide self-evaluations of their personal abilities and qualities. However, we have already raised concerns that this may be a particular concern in sport-for-development programmes, in which vulnerable young people are dependent on programme providers for access to free programmes that they value highly. The rhetoric of such programmes systematically emphasises notions of self-improvement and self-worth and there will be obvious pressures to provide the expected responses and to affirm the value of the programme. This is most obviously seen in selective testimonies, heartfelt narratives (Hartmann and Kwauk, 2011) and case study evidence. Also, in certain circumstances some extreme responses may be indistinguishable from narcissism and adolescent bragging. This bias is most likely when personnel involved in programme delivery and propagating programme ideology collect data via face-to-face interviews. All projects in the research were strongly advised not to adopt such an approach to data collection although, as we will see, not all conformed (Coalter and Taylor, 2010).

Self-selection and self-esteem

In Chapter 4 we noted the possible implications of self-selection and the need for a reasonable degree of perceived self-efficacy in order to decide to take part in sport-for-development programmes. This may also be the case in relation to self-esteem. For example, Lindner (1999) cites longitudinal studies that found that US high school athletes were different from non athletes *before* they entered high school, with those with lower abilities and/or low self-esteem dropping out of sport. This type of dilemma is acknowledged by Biddle and Mutrie (2001: 184) who distinguish between two perspectives on the relationship between self-esteem and physical activity. The 'motivational approach' (or 'self-development hypothesis') postulates that individuals with high self-esteem (or physical self-worth) 'are more likely to exercise, as this is an area where competence and self-worth can be maintained or enhanced'. On the other hand the 'skill (personal) development hypothesis' is that self-esteem is an *outcome* of participation in physical activity, and that self-esteem can be changed through experience. However, Biddle and Mutrie (2001: 185) suggest that these two perspectives are not mutually exclusive, 'as initial involvement in physical activity, which may be externally motivated, may lead to enhanced self-perceptions of esteem and worth which in turn, become motivators of subsequent activity'. Within this context we now turn to explore the survey data (all programmes used the standard Rosenberg scale).

Participants and non-participants: beyond sport

Although we were unable to use control groups to identify more precisely the impact of programmes, we did undertake two sets of participant/non-participant surveys related to EMIMA and KCCC (Coalter and Taylor, 2010; see Chapter 1). The mixed-sex EMIMA respondents (a different sample from the all-female one used for the before-and-after study) had been taking part in sport and sports-related activities for at least 18 months before the survey and the mixed-sex KCCC respondents for between six months and two years. The sport-for-development assumption might be that participants who had been taking part for a minimum of six months would score higher on many of the 'personal development' factors than non-participants, irrespective of their pre-participation scores – unless it is assumed that those recruited to the sport-for-development programmes would have substantially lower levels of self-esteem. However, theory tells us that this is unlikely, especially as both programmes were open access and self-selecting.

Despite having been in the EMIMA programme for at least 18 months, participants appear to have remained relatively representative of the community from which they were drawn in terms of self-esteem. The non-participant sample had a marginally higher average score and was a slightly more diverse group than the participants – 22.4 (sd: 3.79) compared to 22.0 (sd: 3.2) – with the difference not statistically significant.

However, the KCCC sample presents a different picture, with the participants' average score (18.43; sd: 1.57) statistically significantly *lower* than the non-participant sample and with much less diversity (20.5; sd: 3.71). This pattern – which might be described as humble and homogeneous – in which all but one of the participants scored within the 'normal range' might in part be explained by a 'levelling' impact of participation in team sports. However, data from the other surveys suggest this is unlikely to produce such a low average and lack of diversity. Alternatively, the lack of diversity might reflect the fact that the KCCC respondents were drawn from a distinctive and tightly defined geographical area, with a strong sense of local identity created and supported by shared poverty and membership of a programme run by a strongly religious organisation that has a major presence in the slum. It has its own chapel, primary school, HIV and AIDS clinic, a small micro-bank and parents were involved closely in the running of the soccer programme. This might have produced elements of the strong and cohesive communities that Hunter (2001) and Ungar (2006) suggest underpin high levels of resilience (see Chapter 4).

Consequently, both of the sport-for-development participant samples had lower average scores for self-esteem than non-participants – one marginal and one statistically significant. However, it is not wholly clear how to interpret this. Other than assuming that those recruited to the programme were particularly distinctive groups, and this seems not to be the case for the EMIMA sample, it is possible to interpret these data as indicating that there is a variety of sources of self-esteem and participation in a sports-for-development programme will be only one, relatively minor, influence for many participants.

Before-and-after surveys

Before

As with the data on perceived self-efficacy, the first important finding is that the groups were not homogeneous – they held a variety of self-evaluations and were certainly not uniformly 'deficient'. Although each project had a slightly different profile, in all samples the distribution of self-evaluations conformed broadly to a bell-shaped curve – a relatively 'normal' distribution (this term is not used in a precise statistical sense). Although some respondents recorded both low and high self-evaluations, the majority fell within the range usually regarded as normal (15–25). Such data conform to the theoretical expectations discussed in the previous sections and once again raise questions about overly generalised deficit models, which assume that poor communities automatically produce deficient people, or that there is a standard, universal need for individual 'development'.

Given the diversity of populations, cultures and contexts it is not surprising that there were variations in average scores between the samples (Table 5.1). Two East

TABLE 5.1 Self-esteem data: before

Programme	Sample size	Average score	Standard deviation	% below 15	% above 25
EMIMA	33	20.8	3.65	3	12
Kids' League	117	20.4	4.18	7	13
Praajak	31	18.9	3.61	16	3
Magic Bus	44	18.8	4.63	14	11
KCCC	44	18.4	1.57	2	0

African samples had the highest average scores – the all-female EMIMA (20.8) and the mixed-sex Kids' League (20.4). Both also had the highest proportion above the top of the presumed normal range, with the Kids' League containing some *very* high individual self-evaluations.

As with perceived self-efficacy, excluding the Kampala-based KCCC, both Indian samples recorded lower average scores – Magic Bus (18.8) and the all-male Praajak (18.9) – with the Magic Bus sample containing the widest diversity (sd: 4.63), although there were no systematic sex-related differences. Significantly, both Indian samples had the highest proportion falling below the lower end of 15–25 'normal' range – Praajak (16 per cent) and Magic Bus (14 per cent). It is difficult to be definitive about the reasons for these differences – they might indicate the distinct populations from which Praajak (railway children) and Magic Bus recruited and that targeting had identified relatively vulnerable young people. For example, Magic Bus often used social workers to gain access to the slums and to recruit participants. Alternatively this might reflect cultural differences. Wood, Hillman and Sawilowsky (1995), using a different measure of self-esteem, found that scores for heterogeneous groups of 10–14-year-old Americans were significantly higher than those of Indian pupils.

However, as already noted, the 'humble and homogeneous' KCCC sample presents an apparent anomaly and one that might illustrate the important influence of social and cultural factors. The sample had the lowest average score of 18.4 and much less diversity than the others – its standard deviation was 1.57 compared to 4.63 in Magic Bus – and there was a distinct skew towards the lower end of the 15–25 'normal' range, with no-one above 25. We have already noted the distinctive context from which the participants were drawn. In addition, the other organisations can be regarded as largely 'secular' and certainly not as dominant as KCCC was in the area from which participants were drawn.

After

The average self-esteem scores increased for all samples, except the railway children of Praajak, which recorded a minor decline – although they also had taken part in a distinctly different type of programme. Once again, despite some adjustments, the two Indian samples had the lowest average scores and the highest proportions still

TABLE 5.2 Self-esteem data: before and after

Programme	Before average score	After average score	Statistical significance p	Standard deviation	% below 15	% above 25
EMIMA	20.8	23.0	0.017	3.88	0	33
Kids' League	20.4	20.9	0.210	3.12	3	5
Praajak	18.9	18.5	0.409	4.16	19	6
Magic Bus	18.8	18.9	0.961	3.92	14	7
KCCC	18.4	19.1	0.315	3.7	9	9

remaining under 15. However, in all but one sample, the changes were not statistically significant, meaning that they could have occurred by chance.

The exception to this was the all-female EMIMA sample, which also recorded a statistically significant increase in perceived self-efficacy. There were a number of *very* high scores, with one-third being above 25 and several near the maximum. There are several ways to view such scores. First, this might reflect the fact that this was a relatively coherent and supportive all-female group – evidence from other research indicates that young women prefer single-sex PE and sport environments. Second, it might simply reflect a methodological aberration with a small group working out how to achieve a maximum score, although this was not repeated in the other surveys. Third, such scores might be regarded as indicating a degree of narcissism, reflecting and reinforced by the programme ideology. Fourth, there is the possibility of a social desirability bias in *some* of the responses because part of the data collection was undertaken by those directly involved in programme delivery, despite being strongly advised not to in all training sessions. Once again this illustrates the type of practical difficulties faced in such collaborative and developmental research – pragmatic completion and conformity to funding agreements to 'collect data' may have been privileged over the methodological requirements of robust research and organisational learning.

Beyond averages

Unlike perceived self-efficacy, participation during the survey period had much less impact on average self-esteem scores. However, as with perceived self-efficacy, the averages disguise a complex and important set of effects, which once again illustrate the importance of understanding mechanisms, processes and differing participant experiences and reactions. Although only one of the programmes recorded a statistically significant change in the average score, all recorded statistically significant adjustments in *individual* scores, which in terms of averages largely cancelled each other out. In all cases there is only between one and four chances in 1,000 that such adjustments could have happened by chance.

As with self-efficacy, there was a general tendency in all projects for those with scores at or below the average to *increase* their scores and for those with scores above the average to *decrease*. Because of space we will present only one figure to illustrate the issues (the others can be seen in Coalter and Taylor, 2010). Figure 5.2, using data from the Kids' League, illustrates the broad general pattern seen in all projects, with the top-left quadrant representing a key claim of sport-for-development – that participation in such programmes increases the scores of those who initially were below the average, although mostly within the 'normal' range. Once again some individuals with *above average* initial scores also *increased* their scores – most clearly in KCCC and EMIMA (although here we have noted a concern about possible social desirability bias). These of course are the two quadrants from which the always positive testimonies are selected. However, as also illustrated in Chapter 4, they only tell us about one aspect of a programme's impact and little about the complexity of responses. This is

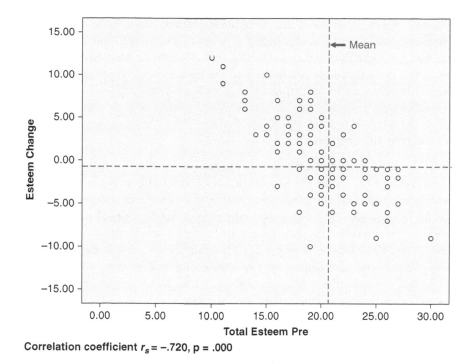

Correlation coefficient r_s = –.720, p = .000

FIGURE 5.2 Kids' League: degree of change in self-esteem

because, as with perceived self-efficacy, several individuals with before scores *above* average decreased their score – this was most obvious in Magic Bus, Praajak and the Kids' League (the bottom right quadrant in Figure 5.2).

The all-female EMIMA sample exhibited the highest proportion of positive changes, with 58 per cent increasing their evaluation. Despite this, one-third of the sample recorded a *decrease* in self-esteem scores. In the Kids' League 47 per cent increased and 40 per cent decreased their scores; changes in KCCC were evenly balanced, with just under half recording both an increase and a decrease.

However, the two Indian programmes were once again distinctively different. In Magic Bus only one-third (34 per cent) increased their scores, with 45 per cent recording a decrease. The correlation coefficients indicate that the Magic Bus programme had the strongest and most diverse impact – in part accounted for by some strongly negative adjustments. This might reflect the lack of sporting culture in the slums and poor levels of physical literacy among many of the participants, many of whom live in slums with little open space and have been economically active since an early age, with organised physical activity not a major part of their lives.

The largest proportion reducing self-esteem was recorded by the railway children of Praajak – 55 per cent. This may partly reflect the fact that elements of their social status and self-esteem were context specific, referred to as 'platform confidence' by a staff member of Praajak. Changed contexts such as camping, hiking and mountain-based adventure training and new and more intense relationships based on different expectations and forms of accountability (e.g. one was expelled from the camp for drug taking) might have led to a re-evaluation. However, it must be remembered that during the long period before the first and last camps all were involved in the ongoing Praajak activities and relationships (see Chapter 1).

Sex-related differences

Excluding the all-female EMIMA data, nearly half (46 per cent) of the female partici-pants experienced an increase in self-esteem, compared to 41 per cent of males. Males were slightly more likely to experience a reduction – 44 per cent compared to 39 per cent for females. However, each programme produced different results – once again indicating the difficulties in generalising about sport-for-development in meaningful ways. In the Kids' League, among those who started with *below average scores* more males (52 per cent) than females (37 per cent) increased their score. Conversely, in Magic Bus more females than males did so and in KCCC equal proportions of below-average males and females increased their scores.

In the two most robust mixed-sex samples – the Kids' League and KCCC – there were no significant differences in the *degree of change* between males and females. In other words these programmes did not seem to benefit significantly one sex more than the other. In the much smaller Magic Bus sample there was a significant difference between the *degrees of change* for females compared to males – similar to the situation with perceived self-efficacy. However, because of the very small sample size of females (n: 9), this can only be regarded as indicative. Further, it is not clear if such effects related to the nature of the sporting activities, affirmative aspects of the social climate or the processes involved in a small, coherent and supportive group of females undertaking unfamiliar activities.

Diversity

Unlike the shifts in perceived self-efficacy, the various adjustments to more ego-centric self-esteem did not always lead to reduced diversity within the groups. In the cases of KCCC, EMIMA and Praajak diversity increased. In EMIMA, this was caused by the emergence of some *very* high individual self-evaluations, which theory and research warn us is not necessarily a positive impact. Although the KCCC sample had been participating for some time, there was a rather dramatic increase in diversity, with the standard deviation increasing from 1.57 to 3.7, explained by an increase in respondents both below and above the normal range. It is difficult to explain such a growth in diversity of self-esteem and individuality among people who had been in the programme for some time when the initial measure was taken. It is worth noting that the male average increased much more than the female and of those who now recorded scores above 25 three were males and only one was female. However, what is more interesting is that this increase in self-esteem and increased diversity occurred in parallel with a *decline* in the average perceived self-efficacy score (we will explore these relationships below).

Self-esteem and five sport-for-development programmes: conclusions

The deficit model

As with perceived self-efficacy, the key conclusion is that all programmes contained a diversity of self-evaluations and in all cases the majority of young people had 'normal' evaluations of their own self-worth. Again this raises important questions as to the use of unexamined deficit models, how 'need' and 'development' are conceptualised and how desired impacts are defined and measured. The requirement for greater clarity is also emphasised by the apparent diversity among the so-called 'Global South' participants – both between the East African participants and, most especially, between them and the Indian participants. It is not wholly clear if such differences reflect cultural and community attitudes to self-esteem, the highly deprived nature of participants and their communities or the targeting policies of projects. But a greater specificity is required than is implied by terms such as Global South.

Changes in self-evaluation

Except for the railway children of Praajak, all samples recorded an increase in the average score, although only the all-female EMIMA was statistically significant, with the highest proportion of scores above the top of the normal range. This might be explained by it being an all-female programme, with no comparisons with male players, which seems to have produced some negative female responses in KCCC, although not in the Kids' League or Magic Bus. However, our concerns about social desirability bias must be borne in mind, especially in relation to some of the extremely high scores, which may have exaggerated an underlying but less extreme trend. Although higher proportions of females increased their scores, overall there were no significant differences in the *degree of change* between males and females. In other words, as with perceived self-efficacy, these programmes did not benefit significantly one sex more than the other, other than in the exceptional circumstances of the small sample of females in Magic Bus.

The contingent and possibly cultural nature of these outcomes is illustrated by the fact that the two Indian projects both finished with the lowest average scores and the greatest degree of variety. The all-male Praajak average score declined and the Magic Bus score increased only marginally, although the small sample of females out-performed the males. We are left with the possibility that the nature of the two programmes and associated relationships and activities are less effective than many of the East African projects. Or, the nature of the male participants was substantially different from many of the East African respondents. Or, there are cultural and contextual issues about such an ego-centric measure, which limit our ability to compare East African and

Indian projects or, more importantly, to make any meaningful generalisations about 'sport-for-development' or the Global South.

Directions of change

As with perceived self-efficacy (Chapter 4), the strong tendency was for those with initial scores at or *below average* to increase their scores – a potentially positive impact and one to be expected on the basis of existing research (Fox, 1992: 2000). However, an impact that is rarely considered in the rhetoric of sport-for-development, or presented in the various heartfelt testimonials, is that substantial proportions *reduced* their self-esteem, as also happened for perceived self-efficacy. In most cases this resulted in those with an initial *higher-than-average* self-esteem reducing their score. This may reflect a more considered approach to the completion of the questionnaire on the second occasion, or that the experience of sport and associated collective activities and comparative performance led to reconsideration, if such comparisons were deemed to be important. Such re-evaluations cannot automatically be considered to be negative impacts – appropriate levels of self-esteem might be a better policy aim than some of the rather extreme levels achieved in EMIMA. However, such impacts are rarely reflected in testimonial evidence, which almost uniformly emphasises increases rather than adjustments in self-evaluation. As noted above, very high levels of self-esteem – especially if not grounded in achievement – are not always a positive trait (Emler, 2001a; Baumeister *et al.*, 2003). In such circumstances the results produced by EMIMA can at least be viewed as requiring further examination. How one assesses such findings depends on how self-esteem is viewed, the aims and the approach of the programmes. However, the evidence suggests that such issues were not considered in any systematic manner, with these data being viewed by those involved in the programme simply as indicating success, especially when only quoting the average.

Group diversity

Unlike the shifts in perceived self-efficacy, the various adjustments to the more ego-centric self-esteem did not always lead to reduced diversity. In the cases of KCCC, the all-male Praajak and the all-female EMIMA diversity increased. The extent to which this was desired and the nature of its impact on group dynamics is something for the programme providers to consider. However, in one case the selection of an individual who exhibited high self-esteem as a peer leader was viewed as a mistake because of a negative impact on some group dynamics.

The contingent nature of impacts: stating the obvious?

However, the key issue to emerge from the above data and on perceived self-efficacy is that it is highly questionable to talk about 'sport-for-development' in essentialist and abstract ways. Although there are some identifiable general trends – e.g. for those with below average self-esteem and perceived self-efficacy to increase their evaluations – the data again indicate the contingent, context-specific, often individual and unpredictable nature of the impact on self-evaluation of such diverse programmes. Clearly participation in these programmes led to increases in the self esteem of many participants – often those who started with *below average* self-evaluations and they were frequently, but not always, female. Perhaps, reflecting Fox's (2000) analysis, these were those with most to gain, starting with initially lower self-esteem, physical self-worth and body image. Perhaps it was the social climate and the attractiveness factors (Fox, 2000) rather than the activities to which they responded. For example, Morris *et al.*'s (2003) research review, which concludes that *any* programme where there had previously been none was the most important factor, provides some food for thought.

It is likely to be many of these individuals who are chosen to offer testament to the 'success' of such programmes. However, it is clear that such testimonies do not tell the full story of how such programmes operate, or their overall impacts – however 'liberating' they may be for the testifiers. Despite the obviously positive impacts on a number of individuals, in all but one of the projects the aggregate changes were not statistically significant – they could have happened by chance. This finding parallels other researchers (Zaharopoulos and Hodge, 1991; Bowker *et al.*, 2003) who found little systematic relationship between sports participation and global self-esteem.

We have already noted the concerns about simply increasing self-esteem in isolation from achievement (Baumeister *et al.*, 2003; Reasoner, nd) and we now turn to examine the relationship between improved self-efficacy beliefs and self-esteem and the extent to which this might give some clue about how changes were effected.

Perceived self-efficacy and self-esteem: doing well and feeling good?

An implicit assumption of the ideology of sport and reproduced in sport-for-development is that participation in 'sport' will lead to an increased sense of competence and achievement and this will develop or strengthen perceived self-efficacy. In turn this combination of sense of achievement and belief in one's ability to plan and implement a course of action will lead to increased self-esteem. However, Fox (1992) emphasises the contingent and mediated nature of this process – improved performance (e.g. football skills) *may* lead to an increase in physical self-efficacy, which, if valued, *may* lead to improved perceived self-efficacy, which *may* contribute to a strengthened sense of self-esteem, *if* such achievements are deemed to be important and defining of a sense of self. The combination of strengthened perceived self-efficacy – I can do – and improved self-esteem – I am a person of value – therefore *may* lead to desired individual 'development outcomes' such as improved educational performance (Shephard, 1997) or changed sexual behaviour (see Chapter 6). The complexity of such processes and the varied approaches to definition and measurement might explain the varied nature of research findings in this area (Gruber, 1986; Harter, 1988; Ekeland *et al.*, 2005).

Clearly the measures of perceived self-efficacy and self-esteem are conceptually distinct and have no *necessary* relationship. Further, any measured relationships might simply reflect how the concepts were defined and measured. However, because they are measures of self-evaluation, it might be assumed that in certain circumstances there might be *some* relationship between them – James' (1890) comment that self-esteem is success divided by pretensions. Further, *if* sport-for-development programmes aspire to improve both perceived self-efficacy and self-esteem (the vague terminology used to describe most programmes does not assist in analytical clarity), then an exploration of possible relationships between these two measures of self-evaluation has potentially important implications for programme design and delivery. It may also contribute to progress towards greater clarity in the definition of desired impacts and behavioural outcomes and discussion of the meaning of 'development', at least at the micro level.

The approach and results: contingency again

Self-evaluations are dependent on a variety of personal, social and contextual factors and we do not have the detailed data to explore all aspects of such relationships. Also, because both measures were taken at the same point in time we cannot explore the *direction of cause* – whether perceived self-efficacy impacts on self-esteem or vice versa. However, we can look at the broad *relationships between movements* in self-efficacy beliefs and self-esteem for those projects that collected data on the full self-efficacy scale – the all-female EMIMA, and the mixed-sex Magic Bus and Kids' League. Interestingly, the project hierarchy of average scores for perceived self-efficacy is the same as that for self-esteem, with EMIMA having the highest average, followed by Kids' League and then Magic Bus – indicating some degree of consistency between the two *sets* of self-evaluations. To explore the strength of the correlations between the *degree of change* in perceived self-efficacy and self-esteem we used two statistical tests: a *correlation coefficient (r)*, which tells us the extent to which there is a relationship between both measures and the strength of this relationship; a *significance test (p)*, which took into account issues such as sample size and the probability that the measured relationship is a product of chance (see Chapter 1).

Kids' League

In the Kids' League there were statistically significant increases for both male and female perceived self-efficacy, with males having the larger increase. In the case of self-esteem there were marginal and statistically non-significant increases for both sexes. In both cases there was no statistically significant difference in the *degree of change* between males and females – the programme did not benefit significantly one sex more than the other.

The Kids' League produced the strongest correlation between changes in perceived self-efficacy and self-esteem – especially for males. For males there was a relatively strong relationship between *changes* in self-efficacy and self-esteem ($r_s = 0.505$), with a very strong level of significance ($p = 0.000$) – it is unlikely that this relationship occurred by chance. This may reflect the widespread research finding that young men place a relatively high emphasis on sport in terms of their self-definition – although as the correlation coefficient indicates, this relationship varied between individuals.

The correlation coefficient for females was weaker ($r_s = 0.357$), but nevertheless there was some relationship between changes in the two evaluations. Also, with a significance level of $p = 0.004$, it is unlikely that this relationship is a product of chance. Existing research would suggest that this effect – where there is a close relationship between the two measures for some individuals but not others – might reflect either a positive attitude to body image and physical self-worth and/or sources of social acceptance and friendship networks. However, the relationship is weaker than for males and certainly indicates a variety of relationships between the two approaches to self-evaluation.

EMIMA

The increase in the average perceived self-efficacy score in this all-female group was statistically significant. This group had the highest initial score and this increase was the strongest effect in all the projects, although we have noted some reservations about this. The increase in the average self-esteem score was also statistically significant, although this contained some extremely high individual scores. Presenting both these averages could lead to the conclusion that the programme confirmed the hierarchical competence-based model of self-esteem and conformed to the expectations of sport-for-development proponents.

However, despite these increases, the correlation coefficient for *changes* in perceived self-efficacy and self-esteem was relatively weak ($r_s = 0.229$). Further, the level of significance ($p = 0.200$) indicates that there is a 20 per cent chance that the relationship was random. In other words, although EMIMA exhibited statistically significant increases for both perceived self-efficacy and self-esteem, the relationship between the *changes* in these two self-evaluations was not particularly strong and was subject to a considerable degree of individual randomness. Change in one facet of self-evaluation did not strongly predict change in the other.

Magic Bus

Once again this Indian programme illustrates a substantially different picture from the other two, with a statistically non-significant *decline* in the average self-efficacy score. However, although the average score for males decreased slightly, the score of the very small female sample increased to exceed the boys. There was a minimal increase in the average self-esteem score. Again the nine females started with a much lower average score than males, yet finished with a higher average score. Not surprisingly, in both cases the difference in the *degrees of change* was statistically significant, with the programme having its biggest positive impact on the small group of females. The correlation coefficient for females is strong ($r_s = 0.622$) and the significance test indicates that there is only a 10 per cent possibility that the relationship is by chance. However, as this is a very small group, care needs to be taken and such data should only be regarded as indicative. The correlation coefficient for males is weak ($r_s = 0.217$), as is the significance ($p = 0.203$). This indicates that the relationship between *changes* in perceived self-efficacy and self-esteem is weak, with a large element of randomness.

Conclusions

Although such data certainly cannot be regarded as definitive, they provide food for thought. The verdict must be the Scottish legal one of 'not proven' – we do not have sufficient evidence to decide on guilt or innocence, or cause and effect. The data from the mixed-sex Kids' League and Magic Bus samples indicate the possibility that there is a relationship between changes in perceived self-efficacy and self-esteem for females, but this is not supported by the all-female EMIMA data. The data from the Kids' League illustrates a strong relationship for males between changes in perceived self-efficacy and self-esteem, but this is not confirmed by the Magic Bus data.

The explanation for some of these differences clearly lies in the programme processes, relationships, experiences and the individuals' priorities that 'produced' them. We have emphasised that we do not know the direction of cause – whether perceived self-efficacy impacts on self-esteem or vice versa. Some of the programmes may, for example, place a strong emphasis on developing perceived self-efficacy and emphasising its relationship to self-worth – 'your skill as a footballer and your performance in this programme indicate that you are a good person'. Further, this may or may not be more effective for females than males. On the other hand it is quite possible that a third factor – a set of experiences, what Fox (2000) refers to as the 'attractiveness factors' – leads to a parallel increase in both measures. Both measures are subjective evaluations and known to be influenced by a range of environmental factors and social processes. Some programmes may be successful at increasing both sets of beliefs, with no necessarily *causal* relationship between the two.

These data indicate that, in certain circumstances, for certain people there is a relatively strong relationship between *changes* in perceived self-efficacy and *changes* in self-esteem, even in programmes where the overall statistical significance of change is weak. That in itself is an important finding. However, the limitations of our ability to explain these changes and the nature of the relationship points to significant, and unexplored, questions about programme processes that lead to such differing outcomes. The answers to such questions have substantial implications for the development and delivery of sport-for-development programmes, but will probably not be reducible to the easy generalisations desired by conceptual entrepreneurs.

We now turn to consider an area that many argue is a key rationale for sport-for-development and in which perceived self-efficacy and self-esteem are regarded as central – HIV and AIDS education.

6

SPORT-FOR-DEVELOPMENT, PEER LEADERS AND HIV AND AIDS

A method in search of a theory?

Introduction

A widespread rationale for sport-for-development programmes, reinforced by the publication of the UN Millennium Development Goals (MDGs), relates to their supposed ability to contribute to the reduction of the incidence of HIV and AIDS. However, Kruse (2006: 8), in one of the first comprehensive reviews of the contribution of sport-for-development to the prevention of HIV and AIDS, stated that:

> We have not come across any systematic analysis of how to understand the relationships between sport and development ... or ... a discussion of the causal linkages between an increased emphasis on sport and a positive impact on HIV and AIDS. What is it with sport that could lead to such impact – what and where are the linkages and can they be documented? Most of the assumptions and statements about positive linkages may be true or partly true, but they are still not well understood and supported by empirical evidence ... The strong beliefs seem to be based on an intuitive certainty and experience that there is a positive link between sport and development.

We share this scepticism and in this chapter will explore some of the often unexamined assumptions and what the emerging evidence tells us.

Knowledge, informed choice and the irrationality of sex

It is argued that the widespread appeal of sports programmes (nearly always soccer) enables them to provide access to at-risk populations that traditional methods of information dissemination might not reach (e.g. young people not in school). Most programmes are based on two inter-related basic assumptions. First, that a major cause of the spread of HIV and AIDS is a lack of relevant and demystified information. Second, this results in a lack of informed choice and risk-taking sexual behaviour (Delva and Temmerman, 2006). A third more implict assumption seems to be that participation in sport-for-development programmes leads to a strengthening of perceived self-efficacy and the confidence to make positive decisions (Mwaanga, 2010; Maro, Roberts and Sorensen, 2009; Maro and Roberts, 2012). Consequently, increased knowledge, understanding and perceived self-efficacy and in some case increased self-esteem – a sense of value and worth – should lead to changed sexual behaviour. This raises two initial issues.

Levels of awareness and risk

First, although in many communities the understanding of HIV and AIDS issues is low, this is not always so in communities in which sport-for-development organisations operate. For example, in a study in Nairobi of participants and non-participants, Delva *et al.* (2010: 1017) found that 'attitudes towards avoiding risk behaviour, subjective norms on virginity and responsibility, and intention concerning condom use and faithfulness were not significantly different between study groups, as the median scores for these variables were very high in both groups'. They speculate that this could mean that there is a high awareness of the consequences of risky sexual behaviour and an acceptance of protective behaviour in the general population. In a 1998 study in Zambia, Hughes-d'Aeth (2002: 401–402) found that

> there was definite awareness of HIV and AIDS, even in areas remote from urban centres. Secondly, generalised knowledge of the virus and its symptoms was for the most part accurate amongst those interviewed. There was awareness of different modes of transmission, the dangers of multiple partners, the problem of sugar daddies, STD and HIV acquisition, infection through body fluids, etc.

In a study in Dar-es-Salaam, Coalter and Taylor (2010) found a rather mixed picture regarding the levels of knowledge and understanding between participants in a sport-for-development programme and non-participants, despite the fact that the sport-for-development organisation (EMIMA) had a major HIV and AIDS orientation and that most of the participants had been in the programme for about 18 months. Male and female participants did have a better understanding of certain key issues. For example, about two-thirds (68 per cent) of the females knew that *you can be infected with HIV when having sex for the first time*, compared to less than half (45 per cent) of non-participant females; about three-quarters (77 per cent) of participant males compared to two-thirds (66 per cent) of non-participant males. Also larger proportions of participant males and females knew that *condoms protect from HIV if used correctly*, with 80 per cent of participant females knowing this compared to only 52 per cent of non-participant females. Despite such important differences substantial proportions of *participants* still did not know the facts on these two key issues. Indeed, despite being part of the programme for some time, some had false ideas about HIV and AIDS. For example, participants were more likely than non-participants to believe that there was a *cure for HIV and AIDS*, that it is *possible to be infected via a mosquito bite* and that *sex workers are the only ones spreading HIV*, although in all cases the numbers were small

In Kampala the overall understanding of HIV and AIDS issues was better than in Dar-es-Salaam – possibly reflecting the major educational effort by the Ugandan government's long-running ABC campaign (abstain, be faithful, use condoms). Further, the understanding of participants who had been in the KCCC programme with a strong HIV and AIDS content for some time was slightly better than non-participants, although the understanding of non-participants was high on some issues (Coalter and Taylor, 2010). As in Dar-es-Salaam, a key difference related to the issue that *you can be infected with HIV when having sex for the first time*. Once again the non-participant females were poorly informed, with only 38 per cent knowing this, compared to 82 per cent of participant females; three-quarters of participant males knew this, compared to only 52 per cent of non-participants. All participant females and 96 per cent of males knew that *a healthy looking person can be HIV positive*, compared to 88 per cent of non-participant females and 78 per cent of males (the sample sizes were relatively small and the differences were only one or two individuals). However, 92 per cent of non-participant females and 87 per cent of males agreed that *condoms protect people from HIV if used correctly*, whereas only 63 per cent of participant males and 73 per cent of females agreed – this may or may not reflect the fact that the sport-for-development programme was run by a Catholic charity.

Clearly it is not possible to generalise from these two surveys, but they do illustrate that the level of understanding of relevant issues is not always as low as assumed and that participation in particular sport-for-development programmes, while clearly providing access to relevant information, does not guarantee a consistently high level and breadth of understanding. The conclusion is certainly *not* that HIV and AIDS education is not important, but that there is a requirement for more needs assessment and targetting among sport-for-development organisations. First, while those participating in sport-for-development programmes had a better aggregate understanding of some issues, non-participants were not wholly ignorant and on some key issues had a reasonable understanding – what population will have 100 per cent agreement or understanding of anything? The pedagogic implications of this relate to the assumption that all those joining sport-for-development organisations have equivalent low levels of understanding. For example, one South African community sports leader stated that most people had the information already and that they were bored with it, although such a reaction might disguise other fears and taboos (Coalter and Taylor, 2010).

Pisani (2008) makes a wider and more fundamental point by arguing that many programmes are not targeted at relevant high risk groups (e.g. sex workers; intravenous drug users; prisoners), often for ideological, political, moral or pragmatic reasons. For example, in Ghana 76 per cent of new infections still happen in commercial sex, but 99 per cent of funding goes to 'general population' interventions (Pisani, 2008). Further, given the approach of some sport-for-development organisations, it is worth noting Pisani's (2008) contention that abstinence drives boys to prostitutes, with an increased risk of HIV.

Hughes-d'Aeth (2002: 401) suggests that:

> The way an NGO defines infection risks influences the ways it attempts to modify that risk, thus targeting of groups and clarification of risks is part of the process of developing effective anti-HIV and AIDS messages. There is no single risk reduction message relevant to all.

Similarly UNICEF (nd: 25) argue that we need to acknowledge the

> tremendous variation in the personalities and circumstances of young people [which] drive their choices ... prevention responses must therefore be tailored to meet the wide-ranging needs of such a diverse group [and] quantitative and qualitative data is a prerequisite to identifying those young people who are most at risk ... and that if disaggregated by factors such as age, sex, marital status, wealth quintile and geographical location can drive better programming.

In earlier chapters we referred to the notion of environmental determinism and a deficit model – assuming general things about individuals in communities that might not be wholly accurate. In this area, perhaps not surprisingly, sport-for-development programmes tend to assume that the general level of HIV and AIDS awareness is low and that one major contribution of such programmes is awareness raising via participation in a collective programme. Clearly it is impossible to generalise about such issues – levels of awareness will vary widely between communities, other HIV and AIDS organisations might be working with various populations and there might be specific high-risk populations. However, in my experience such considerations were rarely taken into account, especially when this rationale would attract funding. The pressure of the MDGs on sport-for-development funding almost inevitably means that there will be such an emphasis, often in the absence of relevant information about the nature and distribution of local levels of knowledge, or more importantly the nature of risk. For example, Pisani (2008: 272) argues that "'[y]outh' is an especially popular focus for prevention efforts in Nigeria, even though HIV tests in several thousand recent students from technical college showed that just 1.2 per cent were infected – hardly an out-of-control epidemic'.

Information and changed sexual behaviour

The second assumption is that increased knowledge and understanding and perhaps increased perceived self-efficacy should lead to changed sexual behaviour. However, the World Health Organisation (2006) reports on a randomized community trial of a multi-component adolescent sexual health programme in rural Mwanza in Tanzania, which assessed behavioural and biological outcomes, including HIV incidence and the prevalence of sexually transmitted infections (STI). This found that:

> The intervention had a significant impact on knowledge about HIV, reported attitudes towards HIV and some reported behaviours, with variations occurring

by the sex of the participant, but it did not have a consistent impact in either direction on STI outcomes.

(World Health Organisation, 2006: 48)

Michielsen *et al.* (2010: 1200) in a systematic review and meta analysis of sub-Saharan African randomised and non-randomised trials for education for HIV prevention noted that:

> Youth did not significantly reduce sexual activity and condom use at last sex only increased notably among males. Only one study reported a positive impact on a biological outcome. This finding corresponds with other reviews, who find significant changes in knowledge and attitudes, but a small degree of risk reduction.

A South African systematic literature review (Delva and Temmerman, 2006: 128) found that

> although school-based programmes are usually associated with improved awareness, knowledge and attitudes, very few result in actual changes in risk behaviour. Only programmes dedicating ample time to communication skills, gender equality, self-esteem and self-efficacy training and role-plays showed an impact on sexual behaviour. In contrast, programmes based upon the belief that behaviour was the result of an informed choice failed to act beyond raising awareness and more positive attitudes and intentions.

Perhaps this is because, as Pisani (2008: 126) argues, 'sex is the least likely human activity to fit neatly into the blueprint of rational decision-making favoured by economists'. Consequently, given the weak and often tenuous relationship between information, knowledge and subsequent behaviour it is possible to argue that improved levels of knowledge are a rather limited test of performance and effectiveness when dealing with life-threatening behaviour.

Knowledge, self-efficacy, expressed intention and sex

However, few sport-for-development programmes rely solely on a simple, formal didactic approach and most use a variety of methods that seek to address some of the issues raised by Delva and Temmerman (2006) via a sport-plus approach. For example, the Grass Roots Soccer Foundation uses the notion of the educative potential of sporting role models and activity-based learning, using these to supplement formal classroom lessons. Locally and nationally known soccer players, viewed as recognised role models, are trained to deliver a classroom-based curriculum, plus action-based exercises and role-play. In an evaluation of one of these programmes, Botcheva and Huffman (2004) record significant short-term increases in certain areas of knowledge and attitudes. However, in a five-month follow-up they report a significant decrease in the percentage who agreed that condoms could prevent someone from getting AIDS and agreeing that support of a classmate with HIV and AIDS should be expressed. Further, they report that 'unexpectedly' the results indicate that the programme did not affect students' beliefs in their own ability to have control over HIV and AIDS – their perceived self-efficacy.

A more sophisticated approach is to use the malleability of sport to develop symbolic games of the type developed by Kicking Aids Out (nd) and widely used in the sector. This approach disseminates health-related messages via a peer-led, learning-by-doing approach using symbolic games adapted from both traditional and modern sports such as football and basketball (Banda and Mwaanga, nd; Mwaanga, 2002). For example, the Sugar Daddy Game is based on tag and emphasises the potential dangers of older rich men and child abusers. Or, the Sticks Relay in which two teams race up and down the playing area picking up 27 small sticks. The object is to win the race by lining up the sticks to construct the sentence 'AIDS is real'. Although some notion of self-efficacy underpins these programmes (Mwaanga, 2010) it is not well defined and seems to refer to skills derived from an understanding of the myths and reality about HIV, combined with some decision making and avoidance strategies (Banda and Mwaanga, nd).

This approach is undoubtedly popular and in interviews with South African community sports workers most regarded the games as an innovative and useful technique, with young people who would be resistant to formal didactic approaches (Coalter and Taylor, 2010). Interestingly, such a positive evaluation was offered by some who were also working in AIDS organisations. For example, one volunteer said that this approach was a more successful way of getting children to talk about the issues; another suggested that the physically active approach was more effective than a passive classroom approach.

An even more sophisticated approach, which reflects generic health education thinking about behaviour change, is to place more systematic emphasis on the development of perceived self-efficacy, rather than simply assume that it is inherent in the practice of sport, or can be taught via symbolic games, or resides in simply knowing about the risks of contracting HIV (Wight, 2007). For example, in their evaluation of Grassroots Soccer, Botcheva and Huffman (2004) speculate that pupils' failure to develop a belief in their ability to have control of HIV and AIDS might be due to the educational focus of the programme, with little conscious emphasis on perceived self-efficacy. This perspective acknowledges that relevant information must be accompanied by the systematic development of certain social skills, competencies and confidence in order to increase the probability of young people changing their behaviour – they must believe that they are capable of doing it (Mwaanga, 2010; Maro et al., 2009). Sport, or various elements of sports programmes, is often regarded as an effective medium for the development of perceived self-efficacy and self-esteem and these are regarded as essential to *potential* behaviour change and the development of safe-sex habits (Wight, 2007).

There is little systematic evidence about the relative effectiveness of such programmes compared to other approaches – as we have seen in Chapters 4 and 5, programmes vary in the impact that they have on participants, many of whom already have reasonable levels of self-belief. One of the few systematic and comparative evaluations of the effectiveness of a sport-for-development programme is provided by Maro *et al.* (2009) and Maro and Roberts (2012). This relates to a football-based programme (EMIMA) delivered by peer coaches that combined HIV and AIDS information with an explicit mastery-based approach designed to increase perceived self-efficacy. Two randomly allocated sports participant groups (one mastery orientation/ one non-mastery) were compared with a school-based HIV and AIDS education class and a non-school group. The authors claim that in terms of knowledge about HIV and AIDS there was no difference between the two sports groups, but they were higher than the school group and, not surprisingly, the non-school group. However, we are simply provided with an aggregate score rather than details of differential understanding of individual issues, although we are told that the two sporting groups were more likely to believe that having an exclusive sexual partner was protection against HIV infection and to intend to use condoms at first sexual intercourse. Their conclusion is that 'the use of peer coaches within the soccer coaching environment ... was effective in transmitting knowledge about HIV/AIDS and safe sex practices and was reliably more effective than the traditional HIV/AIDS education through the normal school system' (Maro *et al.*, 2009: 137).

This conclusion differs from other research that indicates that teachers were better at improving knowledge, although peer educators were better at influencing norms (Mellanby *et al.*, 2001). Further, UNICEF (nd: 7) states that 'there is important evidence that school-based sex education can be effective in changing the knowledge that leads to risky behaviour'. However, such findings are not in conflict – they simply reflect different contexts, processes, educational content and experiences and indicate how difficult it is to come to definitive conclusions about optimal ways to address such complex issues. In this case it is possible that the differences in knowledge reflect differences in programme content between the local school and the sport-for-development programme. However, we are not provided with this information.

More pertinent to our concerns with programme processes is their exploration of perceived self-efficacy. They claim that although those who took part in the mastery-oriented soccer coaching programme did not have better knowledge that the normal sports participants, they had *stronger intentions* to use condoms and perceived behavioural control in engaging in safe sex, although we are not provided with the vitally important sex breakdown of the impacts. They suggest that the motivational strategy 'increased the efficacy of the participants to utilise the safe sex strategies' (Maro *et al.*, 2009: 139), although this seems to be a confusion between perceived self-efficacy and *expressed intention*. However, other than a reference to 'coaching climate structural features' we are not provided with information to enable us to understand the differences in approach, social climate, relationships and participant experiences between the mastery and the traditional coaching approaches. Also, the measures used for efficacy seem to be rather limited – this is referred to as 'perceived behaviour control to condom use' but is simply presented as an aggregate score. This might simply reflect a degree of social desirability bias in a programme that consistently emphasises the importance of condom use. That this might be so is indicated in a later article about the same study (Maro and Roberts, 2012), which informs us that, although the mastery group had a higher mastery score than the regular group, the mean difference was not large. This was because the regular group had a relatively high mean for the mastery criteria because 'many of the peer coaches in the regular EMIMA programme used mastery enhancing strategies in their coaching without knowing specifically that they were' (Maro and Roberts, 2012: 18).

However, such an analysis tells us nothing about 'mastery' and its supposed impact on self-efficacy and intentions – consciously or unconsciously applied, the programme seems to have had largely the same effect. This limits greatly our ability to understand the processes and experiences that it is claimed led to more effective communication of information. So the precise nature and role of 'mastery' in the programmes and its impact on efficacy (defined in terms of intention to use condoms) remain unexplored and unexplained and therefore provide no understanding for other programme designers, nor the basis for comparison with other studies.

Further, while Maro *et al.* (2009) and Maro and Roberts (2012) provide interesting and thought-provoking findings about the relative effectiveness of a peer-led, mastery orientation in strengthening the *expressed intention* to use condoms, the conclusions drawn seem to be somewhat overstated. They claim that the results demonstrate that HIV and AIDS education using peer coaches in sport 'can effectively *reduce the risk* [emphasis added] of at-risk children from infection with HIV' (Maro *et al.*, 2009: 137). Further, in support of such an assertion we are offered the information that, '*anecdotally* [emphasis added] the records of EMIMA show that not one participant who had been through the EMIMA programme has been confirmed to contract HIV' (Maro *et al.*, 2009: 140). In addition to wondering what 'anecdotal' records are, surely the test of effectiveness would need to be the continuation of the comparative study and not simply rest on an 'anecdotal' record from a self-selecting population of participants – how did the school children fare?

One is struck by the surety of such claims in comparison with the concerns of experienced health and HIV researchers who admit 'how limited our understanding is of the mechanisms by which sexual health promotion does or does not work' (Wight, 2007: 23). Clearly improving knowledge and strengthening expressed intentions are positive impacts. However, the affirmation that risk is reduced simply ignores the known problematic relationship between knowledge, expressed intention and action. Although some programmes may be relatively more successful than others in providing relevant information and perhaps developing some degree of improved perceived self-efficacy, intentions are mediated by a wide variety of factors. For example, Wight (2005: 73) states that, 'while the weight of evidence shows that sex education does no harm and can do some good, the sexual behaviour of young people seems to be far more influenced by their family, their peers and the media'. Jeanes (2011) adopts a broadly similar approach to Maro *et al.* (2009) in suggesting that sport-for-development programmes may lead to the development of a 'critical consciousness', provide an experience of a power 'from within' and, via collaboration, a 'power with' others – all aspects of perceived self-efficacy. However, she is very clear that, in the absence of non-supportive or even antagonistic community structures and values, participants will fail to achieve 'power to' – i.e. to either abstain from sex or have safe sex. This is related to Ungar's (2006) point that while perceived self-efficacy is often viewed as an individual characteristic, research indicates that children linked issues of self-efficacy beliefs to relationships and in community and cultural contexts (see Chapter 4). We will return to this below.

As with any individual study, it is difficult to generalise its findings, especially when we are not provided with information about the processes and mechanisms that produced the claimed results – in fact two types of processes produced largely the same result. Maro and Roberts (2012) seem to recognise these difficulties by expressing rather confused comments about the generalisability of their research. For example, they admit that a wide variety of factors intervene between improved knowledge, expressed intention and action and conclude that 'the condom attitudes, beliefs, and intentions observed in the present study may be unique to this sample of at-risk children and should not be generalised to other children groups who engage in at-risk behaviours' (Maro and Roberts, 2012: 20). They also state that 'we are less certain whether the findings related to children from these disadvantaged communities may be generalised to children of the same age cohort from other communities in Dar-es-Salaam' (Maro and Roberts, 2012: 20). Despite this, they then state that 'we are confident that the results may be generalised to at-risk children in similar contexts in sub-Saharan Africa' (Maro and Roberts, 2012: 20).

However, despite rather confusing talk of efficacy, Maro *et al.* (2009: 141) conclude that the 'real message' does not relate to efficacy, but to the relative effectiveness of peer leadership. Not only did it prove to be more effective than the approach of the education system in Dar-es-Salaam, but such a programme 'should be implemented nationwide, even sub-Saharan Africa-wide. Simply put, using trained peer coaches through sport may effectively help to reduce the risk of infection with HIV among young people'.

The use of peer leaders is widespread in sport-for-development programmes and many generic health education initiatives – consequently it is not clear what aspect of this approach made the EMIMA programme so apparently successful. Before turning to a more detailed discussion of the theory and practice of peer leaders, it is worth considering briefly some additional empirical information about the relative effectiveness of programmes broadly similar to that reported by Maro *et al.* (2009), but which do not depend on expressed intention and 'anecdotal' records.

A study in Kenya of non-participants and participants in a peer-led sport-for-development programme asked about actual condom use. Despite the participant group having significantly higher condom use at first sex and with the current/last partner, levels of condom use remained 'disturbingly low' (Delva *et al.*, 2010: 1012). Only 30.9 per cent of the participants claimed to have used a condom at first sex and consistent condom use with their last/current partner was reported by only 23.2 per cent of participants. Further, in terms of dose response, they 'found that respondents who had been highly exposed to the programme were not more likely to use condoms than those who reported never having participated in the HIV and AIDS Prevention and Awareness programme' (Delva *et al.*, 2010: 1018). Their overall conclusion was that the sexual behaviour of the participants did not differ significantly from that of non-participants.

Stephenson *et al.* (2005) report on a two-year English study of the impact of teacher-led and peer-led sex education on unprotected first intercourse before age 16. In a cluster-randomised, non-blinded controlled trial of 8,156 pupils they found that the peer-led programme was well received and was more likely to have good knowledge of methods to prevent STD transmission. However, there was no significant difference between the groups, for either sex, for the outcomes of saying no to unwanted sex, no regret at first sex, use of contraception at first sex. Further, the peer-led pro-gramme did not reduce the proportion of boys or girls having unprotected first intercourse compared to the teacher-led programme.

Peer leaders: symbolism, efficiency or effectiveness?

We have noted Maro *et al.*'s (2009) assertion that using trained peer coaches in sport-for-development programmes may help to reduce the risk of infection with HIV among young people. The majority of sport-for-development organisations use a system of peer leaders and peer education and Jeanes (2011) notes that peer education has become one of the most frequently used strategies for HIV education. In fact, Nicholls (2009: 157) argues that 'sport-in-development is largely occurring on the backs of young people through peer education'. One core pragmatic reason for this is that young volunteers are essential for the financial viability and sustainability of poorly funded programmes and represent a major value added for funding agencies – they get more for their money. Second, they are frequently used to symbolise inclusiveness, empowerment and the effectiveness of such programmes, especially where the peer leaders are female.

More generally, Munro (2005: 4), the founder of the Mathare Youth Sport Associa-tion in Nairobi, emphasises the importance placed on indigenous and relevant role models by asking rhetorically: 'role models for youth: is anything more important in development?'. He argues that in most African countries the poor are the majority and youth constitute the majority of that poor majority and that 'among the many debilitating aspects of poverty is that the poor, and especially the youth, lack con-fidence and belief in themselves'. Consequently, 'after food, water, shelter, health and education, nothing is more important for future development than providing good role models for our youth' (Munro, 2005: 4).

In addition, the use of peer leaders is also based on several theories of education, learning and behaviour change (UNAIDS, 1999) and many sport-for-development programmes are based on such understanding, although this is often not fully articulated. Further, Payne *et al.* (2003) illustrate that, to be effective, role models must be 'embedded', based on the development of supportive, longer-term trusting relation-ships. In this regard it is worth noting that much learning theory related to role modelling raises significant questions about the effectiveness of the use of sports person-alities from different cultures and/or short-term volunteers from different cultures – approaches that are widespread in sport-for-development. We have already noted

Bandura's (1994) argument that if participants see the models as different from themselves in significant ways their perceived self-efficacy is not much influenced by such models (see Chapter 4).

In line with social learning and self-efficacy theory (Bandura, 1962) the two major factors underpinning the potential effectiveness of role models are the characteristics of the models and their perceived similarity to the learner. Learning is most likely to occur when there is a lack of social distance and a perceived similarity between the teacher and the learner. This may be especially important for females in cultures or communities with few public female role models. Saavedra (2005) emphasises the special importance of female role models in sport-in-development organisations – 60 per cent of Kicking Aids Out! peer leaders are female (Nicholls, 2009). In activities that seek to confront traditional, exploitative and often abusive social relations there is a clear need for embedded and relevant female role models.

This similarity also reinforces the fact that learning is more likely to occur when the learners perceive that they are capable of carrying out the behaviour/achieving the task – self-efficacy expectancy. This is strengthened by perceived similarities with the teacher – 'if she can do it, then so can I' – what Bandura (1994) calls 'vicarious experience'; and there is an *outcome expectancy* that the performance of the activity will have desirable outcomes, which can be affirmed and reinforced by the social climate of the programme. This is related to the theory *of reasoned action*, which states that one of the influential elements for behavioural change is an individual's perception of social norms or beliefs about what significant others do or think about a particular behaviour (Fishbein and Ajzen, 1975; UNAIDS, 1999). In addition, the *diffusion of innovation theory* (Rogers, 1983) posits that individuals who are opinion leaders within a community or social group act as agents of behavioural change by disseminating information and influencing group norms. The practice of peer education draws loosely from elements of each of these theories as it implicitly asserts that certain members of a given peer group (peer educators) can be influential in achieving attitudinal and behavioural change among their peers (UNAIDS, 1999). However, as we will see, not all peers are equal.

Arguments for peer education

Within the health education literature we can identify a number of frequently used justifications for adopting peer education (Turner and Shepherd, 1999; Hughes-d'Aeth, 2002; Wight, 2007) – although tellingly Turner and Shephard's (1999) article is entitled 'A method in search of a theory'. In addition to the not-to-be-underestimated cost-effectiveness and symbolic value, the various arguments are as follows:

- Peers are a credible source of information and, as they are embedded in communities, they can use already established means of sharing information and advice.
- Peers are more successful than professionals at changing attitudes. Because young people's attitudes are highly influenced by their peers' values and attitudes,

peer educators are more likely to be regarded as people who understand their experiences and concerns (YouthNet, 2005; Kerrigan, 1999). For example, a study comparing teacher-delivered and peer education found that, while teachers were better at improving knowledge, peer educators were better at influencing norms (Mellanby et al., 2001).

- Peers may be in a position to reinforce learning through ongoing social contact, rather than relying on a one-off talk or lesson. To be effective role models must be 'embedded' and able to develop supportive, longer-term trusting relationships (Payne et al., 2003). Again, this raises important pedagogic issues about the transitory nature of famous sports people and imported foreign volunteers.

- Peer education involves a form of empowerment. Campbell and Mzaidume (2002: 230) suggest: 'Peer education seeks to empower lay people through placing health-related knowledge in their hands. This increases the likelihood that people will feel they have some control over their health'.

- Kerrigan (1999), in discussing the role of peer educators in HIV and AIDS programmes, argues that the key to successful peer education lies in the fact that it makes possible a dialogue between equals and collective planning to adopt practices that are contextually and culturally relevant. UNAIDS (1999) notes that the theory of participatory education has been important in the development of peer education (Freire, 1970). Participatory or empowerment models of education posit that powerlessness at the community or group level, plus the economic and social conditions inherent to the lack of power, are major risk factors for poor health (Amaro, 1995). Many advocates of peer education claim that this horizontal process of peers (who are *presumed* to be equals) talking among themselves and determining a course of action is key to peer education's influence on behavioural change (World Health Organisation, 2006). For example, Wight (1999) suggests that if an intervention is delivered by members of the target group it might be more beneficial to the target group's self-esteem than having outside professionals exhorting them to change behaviour.

Peer education: who benefits?

An interesting and consistent finding, and one that may mislead observers as to the developmental nature of peer-led programmes, is that 'perhaps the clearest benefit of peer education of all kinds is the way it empowers and enhances the self-efficacy and self-esteem of the peer-educators' (Wight, 2007: 19). Pearlman et al. (2002: 31) found that 'over a 9-month period newly enrolled peer leaders had significantly higher mean scores for HIV and AIDS knowledge and perception of one's self as a change agent in the community than comparison youth'. Burnett (2010: 39) refers to 'an overwhelming belief that volunteering will enhance unemployed youths' opportunities to obtain employment by giving relevant experience and learning job related skills and values'. Hence the consistent use of peer leaders as symbols for the general success of sport-for-development programmes and as providers of testimonies for sport-for-development congregations.

It is hardly surprising that those specially selected, perhaps for being confident and articulate, and provided with specialist training will feel affirmed and be given a boost to their self esteem and perceived self-efficacy. Mwaanga (2003) illustrates that the level of participation in a sport-for-development programme was a key moderator of programme effectiveness, with the youth programme leaders most likely to benefit from their broader pattern of participation compared to ordinary participants. They were the most committed, having been selected and affirmed, gone through the various training programmes, had experience of decision making and perceptions of control and enjoyed the status of their positions as role models. For example, those selected for such training in the Indian programme were a distinctive group, with higher self-efficacy and self-esteem scores than the group from which they were selected (see Chapter 4). In interviews with South African community sports leaders all referred to the increased confidence derived from the training workshops and meeting new people with different perspectives (Coalter and Taylor, 2010). Further, the requirement to talk to other trainees and children *as a group* required some to overcome initial shyness and to develop the skill and confidence to do this. Related to this sense of self-efficacy, many referred to the development of *communication skills* as a key outcome. The training and learning components led to a feeling of *competence* – knowing what they were talking about in terms of sport and HIV – which led to a feeling of social *confidence*. Also the development of an understanding of elements of coaching, training, programme organisation and leadership and the opportunity to apply these skills led to an increased sense of confidence (a more detailed exploration of these issues in a UK context will be provided in Chapter 7).

The development of peer leaders, especially young women, can be viewed as a positive outcome of many sport-for-development programmes – selection, affirmation and concentrated training can achieve many of the impacts assumed by sport-for-development proponents. However, despite the relative success of some peer-leader training programmes in developing efficacy, esteem and aspiration (Mwaanga, 2003) this does not necessarily transfer into successful pedagogic practice and certainly cannot be taken to symbolise the more general effectiveness of the programmes.

Limitations of peer leadership: not all peers are equal

Health education researchers have identified a number of potential disadvantages associated with the use of peer educators. Such issues are rarely raised in sport-for-development research or promotional literature, where peer leaders are viewed as ideologically and symbolically central. Often peer leaders are offered as a potent symbol of the 'development' inherent in sport-for-development, irrespective of their pedagogic effectiveness, which has rarely been evaluated systematically (Kruse, 2006).

The various potential disadvantages serve to establish a framework for empirical investigation and analysis, rather than simply assuming that peer-led programmes are effective (however defined) and inherently 'developmental'. A number of problems and disadvantages can be identified (Wight, 1999; YouthNet, 2005; WHO, 2006).

On a practical level, it is often difficult to identify and recruit *appropriate* peer educators and the approach is highly dependent on this (YouthNet, 2005). The World Health Organisation (2006) recommends that a screening procedure should be used to select peer leaders to ensure that they are motivated and capable of taking on the required tasks. This is important because research indicates that similarity on age/gender/religion is not sufficient and that credible 'opinion leaders' are required as this determines their ability to act as role models (Wight, 1999). Such individuals need to be identified and trained, rather than selected on the pragmatic basis of availability and enthusiasm. Data collected in India indicate that the best peer leaders might not be those who exhibit the highest visible levels of confidence or self-esteem, as they might not be good listeners or sensitive to the needs and capabilities of more vulnerable participants (Coalter and Taylor, 2010). Related to this is the often unwarranted assumption of many peer education projects that school pupils or peer groups are socially homogeneous. Even in schools, most year groups have segregated friendship groups, with differing criteria of esteem and this is much more likely in communities, or large-scale programmes (Wight, 2007). Woodcock *et al.* (2012: 378) propose that various leadership items in their questionnaire could be used to identify those ready to receive training and that this could be combined with 'objective assessments on the same items, completed by existing leaders and/or peers, who are often clear about who they would "follow"'. Kerrigan (1999) emphasises the importance of appropriate, accurate and repeated training to ensure the consistency and accuracy of delivery. However, it is inevitable that there is a wide variation in the nature, quality and depth of training and the quality of peer leaders. In this regard Wight (2007) suggests that it is probably more difficult to train peer educators than adult teachers in the principles of a theoretically-based programme and the targeting of specific cognitions. For example, a South African community sports organiser said that an inability to say where HIV and AIDS 'comes from' undermined his credibility (Coalter and Taylor, 2010).

Wight (2007) and WHO (2006) argue that an extensive programme of consolidation and refresher courses is required to ensure the coherence of messages and to avoid misconceptions and this needs to be combined with a reliable monitoring system to pre-empt problem areas and ascertain effectiveness. For example, interviews with South African community sports organisers (Coalter and Taylor, 2010) indicated substantial variation in the delivery of HIV education programmes, based mostly on volunteers using their own experiences to address certain issues – a reformed drug addict and young mothers. For example, a young mother gave young girls the advice to 'stay away from boys' and 'just play sport'. Although personal experiences are potentially valuable, unless the lessons are articulated through and reflect the desired curriculum and are based on an understanding of pedagogical processes, it can lead to inconsistency in the information communicated, or even the articulation of personal prejudice. Simply talking about personal experiences, however heartfelt, may not be wholly appropriate. Further, some of the South African female leaders said that they preferred to play and have fun with children rather than adopt the required more formal coaching approach. Such variation in practice raises questions about the nature of such programmes as examples of 'sport-for-development'. Training peer leaders is one thing, ensuring the delivery of consistent, coherent, relevant and pedagogically effective programmes raises other issues. Such problems are exacerbated by the ongoing need to recruit and train new peer educators as existing ones grow out of an adolescent peer group. However, within some of the projects of which I am aware, the concept of 'peer' is stretched and high levels of unemployment ensure continuity, if not relevance or effectiveness.

While any sport-for-development organisation may be effective in raising the understanding of peer leaders/community sports volunteers about HIV and AIDS, this does not imply that the peer leaders will be effective communicators, or always know how to deal with varied and sometimes resistant audiences. For example, Wight (2005) quotes research on a peer leader project in which peer educators had greater difficulty in managing boys' behaviour than did teachers and consequently a large minority of pupils, particularly girls, had difficulty contributing to peer-led sessions. In interviews with South African community sports leaders some complained about the children's lack of commitment, lack of concentration, lack of respect and failure to attend practice and tournaments (Coalter and Taylor, 2010). In a Tanzanian programme the peer leader's attempt to provide information about HIV was greeted by the comment 'I came to play football and all you want to do is to frighten me'.

Although accepting the theoretical legitimacy of the peer educator approach, Kruse (2006) points to the lack of research on the nature and quality of such processes, arguing that there is a lack of information about the quality of the exchanges in particular contexts, the extent to which peer leaders and coaches are given sufficient training and the extent of supervision and support provided after initial training. In this regard Nicholls (2009: 170), a strong advocate of peer leadership, argues that 'the necessary support for peer educators is not always available in the resource-poor and donor-driven world of development through sport' – once again we are faced with questions about processes, mechanisms and consistency of delivery.

- Although peer education is viewed as a form of collective empowerment, some suggest that unless the peer educators themselves define the goals of the intervention, which is extremely rare, ultimately what they are doing is trying to put over adult messages to young people (Wight, 1999; Nicholls, 2009; Jeanes, 2011; Lindsey and Grattan, 2012). Others raise a more fundamental issue, arguing that formal peer education still involves a teacher–pupil hierarchy that does not empower those being educated. This can be particularly important in countries where the main form of education is highly didactic and authoritarian, as in sub-Saharan Africa (Warwick and Aggleton, 2004; Plummer et al., 2007).
- A central aspect of the concept of role modelling is that the role models should be observed competently carrying out the desired positive behaviour, not just providing information about it. For Wight (2007) this poses obvious problems in sexual health interventions, since most sexual behaviour is private.
- As the peer educators are, by definition, from the communities being targeted, it is likely that they will share some of the values and understanding that the intervention aims to change. HIV and AIDS education is rarely restricted to technical/medical

information, but is couched in a moral or religious discourse (e.g. the use of condoms; pre-marital abstinence; faithfulness; sexuality; circumcision; sex workers). Consequently it is unlikely that there will be a consensual view to be communicated in any simple way and many issues will be contentious and consequently may be ignored. For example, as many cultures and religions express strident opposition to homosexuality, which is illegal in 37 African countries, dealing with such issues may be extremely difficult or simply avoided. Studies have shown that male circumcision provides a 50–60 per cent reduction in the risk of HIV infection, but this is a highly sensitive issue in many communities – for example, in 2008 elders from Kenya's Luo community refused to endorse a plan to promote male circumcision (BBC, 2008). Within this complex social and cultural context, interviews with South African community sports leaders revealed a number of obstacles and difficulties:

(i) In some rural communities much of the information was regarded as taboo.

(ii) Parents did not want others talking to their children about sex and some felt that talking about condoms encouraged young people to have sex. This raises the complex issue of the extent to which sport-for-development organisations do, or should, seek parental permission to talk about such sensitive issues.

(iii) A young male stated that older people did not want to listen to him because of his age. This may be a significant issue in traditional communities and raises questions about the definition of a 'peer'. In this regard Jeanes (2011: 13) comments that 'due to the marginalised position of young people within Zambia, peer-led education may not be ideal for achieving these broader shifts in dominant cultural discourses'. She argues that although participants were confident that sports programmes were valuable for providing health information and developing young people's 'critical consciousness', they questioned their position as participants and leaders of these programmes to be the main agents of wider change within communities. Even participants of relatively high socio-economic backgrounds acknowledged that where there was resistance to certain health behaviours amongst community members, they as young people were unlikely to have the status to challenge damaging adult attitudes and beliefs (Jeanes, 2011).

(iv) Speaking about HIV could be taken to imply that the peer leader was HIV positive. For example, McNeill (2009: 4), writing about South Africa, argues that

> through the imposition of peer group education projects, current policies appear to have produced seriously counter-productive consequences. [The educators'] publicly expressed knowledge of AIDS is equated with an assumed experience of and implication in AIDS-related deaths. This has given rise to a widely held belief that peer group educators are vectors of the virus.

The above issues illustrate both general and specific factors related to the use of often poorly trained and relatively young people as both peer leaders and HIV and AIDS educators, perhaps selected for their ethusiasm, commitment and availability, rather than their socio-theoretical relevance to the role.

Such issues raise significant empirical questions and make any generalised claims about the effectiveness of peer-led programmes, such as that proposed by Maro and Roberts (2012), wholly unsustainable. Even if we had some robust data and some understanding of the variable nature of the mechanisms and processes involved, the wide variety of personal, contextual and cultural factors means that we need to be very circumspect about accepting some of the broad generalisations offered. Many of the affirmations about the value of such an approach seem to rest on its ideological centrality in programmes aimed at young people – peer leaders are viewed as symbolising the effectiveness and potential of youth development programmes. However, given the wide diversity of participants, the differing quality of peer leaders, the wide diversity in the nature and quality of their training, the variety of programme content and approach, the differing degrees of consistency of programme delivery, the variety of community contexts and the myriad cultural, ideological and religious factors, there is an urgent need for robust comparative evidence about processes and impacts.

Noises from beyond the touch line

However, even if such programmes are *relatively* successful in improving knowledge and understanding and in developing perceived self-efficacy and positive behavioural intentions, others offer more radical critiques. For example, Botcheva and Huffman (2004: 9) explain the limited long-term effectiveness of the Grassroots Soccer programme in part because of 'other contradictory messages that students receive from their teachers or religious institutions'. Clearly sport-for-development programmes are merely one source of information about HIV and AIDS and are, for most participants, rather limited influences on sexual and ethical mores – schools, parents, media, peers and religious organisations are all sources of often conflicting information. For example, in Kampala among respondents who has been in a sport-for-development programme for some time, although 91 per cent stated that the programme was one of their top three sources of information about HIV and AIDS, 60 per cent also nominated parents/relatives, 48 per cent referred to school and 46 per cent to the media. In Dar-es-Salaam, 94 per cent selected the programme in their top three, but 67 per cent also referred to the media, 36 per cent to school and 30 per cent to parents (Coalter and Taylor, 2010). Further, as the technical/medical information is always couched in some type of moral discourse, consensus is unlikely. In this regard Jeanes (2011: 13) notes that 'HIV and AIDS education programmes delivered through sport or other mechanisms are unlikely to be effective if targeting young people as if their health behaviour is played out within a social vacuum'.

Despite reporting positive participant experiences in a sport-for-development programme, Jeanes (2011: 11) concludes that 'participants were in agreement that peer-led education was unlikely to significantly influence behaviour if the values discussed and advocated within this setting were not replicated in young people's everyday lives'.

In this regard, Delva *et al.* (2010: 1018) argue that:

> Even though unprotected intercourse is the main mode of HIV transmission in sub-Saharan Africa, most intervention programmes use a reverse logic and assume that HIV-related knowledge and beliefs are the main determinants of sexual behaviour. However, many other factors on different levels influence sexual behaviour, including gender inequality, ethnicity, poverty, educational systems, policy and cultural practices.

In Tanzania an Anglican bishop in Arusha advocating condom use to prevent HIV and AIDS led to major protests. The church had to be closed and patrolled by armed guards during the six years of upheaval caused by the row (Avert, nd). In Zimbabwe slogans on walls informed us that condoms were part of an American conspiracy to destroy Africans and had been produced with miniscule holes to permit the transfer of fluids. In Kenya the Archbishop of Nairobi burned condoms in a public park – reflecting the widespread opposition of the Catholic Church to birth control. The extent to which HIV and AIDS education often goes to the core of traditional beliefs and power structures is illustrated by an example from my work in Senegal. A young man, who had taken part in a sports-based HIV education programme in Dakar returned to his village for a few days. On his return he entered the room of the tutor with a machete and tried to attack him because his village chief had told him that the information that he was being given was an attempt to destroy his culture and traditional beliefs.

More fundamentally, Delva and Temmerman (2006: 1260) suggest that the impact of programmes aimed at altering sexual behaviour and promoting condom use on incidences of HIV

> depends on the epidemiological context, indicated by the HIV prevalence in the target population, the prevalence of co-factors of HIV transmission (e.g. STI prevalence), mixing patterns between the target population and untargeted populations, and the sexual behaviour of the untargeted populations. In other words, merely proving that sport can reduce unsafe sexual practices would not be enough to ensure significant consequences in terms of averted HIV infections.

Michielsen *et al.* (2010: 1200–1201) in a systematic review and meta-analysis of randomised and non-randomised trials in sub-Saharan Africa found limited effectiveness, which stemmed from flawed assumptions underlying HIV risk-reduction interventions.

> Although the interventions varied markedly in the setting and delivery strategies they adopted, they predominantly focused on HIV and AIDS as a means of changing sexual risk behaviour. However, the existence of a direct causal link between sexual behaviour and HIV infection does not mean that the converse is true. From an ecological perspective, HIV and AIDS is only one factor among a great number of interacting factors which operate on different

levels to influence sexual behaviour. Seen from an ecological viewpoint, it is quite logical that interventions focusing on knowledge or attitudes to HIV and AIDS can only result in relatively small changes in sexual behaviour.

Consequently an over-concentration on young people and an individualisation of the issues – knowledge plus perceived self-efficacy – is viewed as limited, especially if the information and advice provided contradicts the family, community, cultural, peer and/ or religious norms. On the basis of interviews with participants, Jeanes (2011: 15) states that she is in agreement with Campbell and MacPhail's (2002: 334) argument that

> interventions should focus not only on changing the values and attitudes of young people, but also seek to develop 'health enabling communities' as a social and community context that enables or supports the negotiation of social identities and the development of empowerment and critical consciousness.

For example, UNICEF (nd: 11) argues that 'there must be increased community mobilisation, with the strong involvement of men, to address the factors that increase young women's risk of infection or potentially limit their ability to act'. Much of this is reminiscent of Ungar's (2006: 2) comment that 'aspects of children's lives that contribute to resilience are related to one another in patterns that reflect a child's culture and context' (see Chapter 4).

Gender, culture and the seeming paradox of sport

While UNICEF's concerns relate to major issues of male violence against females, there are other deeply rooted gendered cultural traditions that place females at risk. For example, in Malawi, Zambia and Kenya the custom of Utakaso requires the wife of a dead husband to have sexual intercourse with one of her husband's relatives, or a 'special person' in the community, to break the bond with his spirit and save her and the rest of the village from insanity or disease. In 2005 the *New York Times* (2005) reported on a survey by Women and Law in Southern Africa, which found that in at least one-third of the country's provinces, such sexual 'cleansing' persisted. The article states that 'even some Zambian volunteers who work to curb the spread of AIDS are reluctant to disavow the tradition'. It quotes one woman as stating that 'there is no way we are going to stop this practice because we have seen a lot of men and women who have gone mad' after their spouses died. Other customs in Zimbabwe and Zambia, where males prefer dry vaginal sex and women use potions such as toothpaste and fertiliser, increase the risk of lesions and therefore infection (Pisani, 2008).

The nature and scale of the issues are starkly outlined by UNICEF (nd: 8–9):

> Intergenerational sex and transactional sex often occur in the contexts of unequal power relations that inhibit women and girls' ability to make choices about safer sexual practices. Gender-based violence (GBV) is common in Southern Africa. Sexual violence can lead to HIV infection directly, as trauma

increases the risk of transmission. GBV also increases HIV risk indirectly. There is evidence of higher HIV risks among people with a history of gender-based violence and higher rates of GBV among those who have HIV. Reports in 2002 from Southern Africa showed that 18 per cent of women age 16–60 personally experienced violence in the previous 12 months. Further, some 40 per cent of women across the region said that they would have sex if their partner refused to use a condom and a similar proportion did not think that women had a right to refuse sex with their partner. One in every five youths age 12–17 said they had been forced or coerced to have sex, and one in 10 said they had forced sex on someone else.

In such circumstances, as Campbell *et al.* (2009) assert, fully empowering young women involves considerable shifts in male/female power relations, ultimately requiring men to relinquish their power to the benefit of women. Clearly such a task is not achievable solely via self-selecting, often institutionally marginal, sport-for-development programmes.

At first glance it seems paradoxical that such issues would be addressed in a sporting context. As Saavedra (2005) and Pelak (2006) note, much of the organisation of and participation in sport has been a hegemonic masculine enterprise. This has frequently reinforced gender distinctions and unequal power relations, with female participants often putting their femininity at risk. Saavedra (2005) points to four gendered obstacles to young women's participation in sport-for-development programmes: travelling to and from sessions exposes women to risk; traditional authority and power relations provides the possibility of abuse by coaches and trainers; a rigid economic and social division of labour and a constant struggle to meet basic needs places severe constraints on women and girls, requiring creative, and often collective, solutions to allow space and time for sporting activity; 'a woman or girl seen to dishonour her referent group or overstep gender boundaries may face physical and social punishment by family or retribution from elements within the community' (Saavedra, 2005: 5). However, Saavedra (2005: 1) argues that:

> Despite this and actually because of this, many view female involvement in sport as a potential radical and transformative process for women and girls, and possibly for the world of sport and society in general. Sport as an embodied practice may liberate girls and women from constraining hegemonic feminine ideals, empower them within their communities, provide positive health and welfare outcomes, and ultimately transform gendered notions leading to a more egalitarian world and unleashing the productive, intellectual and social power of women.

Applying such an analysis to South Africa, Pelak (2006: 387), while acknowledging the continued male-dominated and patriarchal nature of sporting organisations, argues that 'changes to local practices that incorporate women and girls are potentially empowering. ... women footballers are not only challenging historic boundaries within soccer but also contributing to the broader socio-political transformation of South Africa'. Clearly such issues involve deep-rooted and complex values and attitudes and it is not clear as to the extent of change that such programmes could aspire to achieve – certainly the two quotes above have a hint of evangelical hope, raise important questions about the relative social and cultural significance of sport-for-development programmes and, once again, present us with complex issues of possible displacement of scope (Wagner, 1964). Consequently, it is difficult to decide on how one would define precisely the 'effectiveness' of programmes and the timetable for such an assessment.

Influencing values and attitudes

Despite this, it is worth looking briefly at some survey data from mixed-sex sport-for-development organisations in Uganda and Tanzania, in which a series of questions about gender issues were agreed as being relevant to the programmes: responsibility for avoiding pregnancy, a female's right to choose a marriage partner, women's right to be active in politics, division of responsibilities for domestic labour, who should have the last decision in household matters, women's role in business, women's right to education, women's role in relation to the home and family (Coalter and Taylor, 2010). It was not wholly clear if such issues were dealt with via a formal systematic approach – e.g. workshops and discussions – or the assumption was that changes to values and attitudes would occur via the more diffuse 'hidden curriculum' contained in the provision of inclusive sporting opportunities, the use of female peer leaders and the encouragement of mutual respect and understanding between the sexes.

The data indicate that there were few clear and consistent differences between participants and non-participants (Coalter and Taylor, 2010). In fact, male participants in both programmes adopted more 'conservative' views than non-participants on some issues, especially that *the most important role for women is to take care of the house and family* and that *a man should have the last word about decisions in the household*. Female participants in a programme run by a Catholic charity were more likely to hold more 'traditional' views than non-participants on both these issues. The possible importance of religious beliefs is indicated by the fact that the majority Muslim participant sample in Dar-es-Salaam were more 'conservative' on these issues than the majority Christian non-participants from the same community; the female members of the Catholic Kampala programme had a tendency to have more conservative views than the female non-participants.

While it is acknowledged that such values and attitudes certainly do *not* relate to violence, the data illustrate several issues: the attitudes are complex, sometimes seemingly inconsistent; consensus is rare on significant cultural and moral issues; gender-related differences remained and that there was no consistent 'programme effect'. Just as participants were diverse in terms of their perceived self-efficacy and self-esteem, so they were diverse in their opinions about a variety of gender-related issues – and remained so after participating in the programmes, which was only one of a range of experiences and influences in their lives.

It seems clear that diverse programmes in different socio-cultural and religious settings that address such issues – frequently via an informal or hidden curriculum – are unlikely to have a strong or systematic influence on gender-related attitudes. On all issues there were substantial minorities of participants, sometimes majorities, who professed views that some might regard variously as 'traditional', 'reactionary' or 'sexist', although such evaluations need to be defended and such attitudes certainly do not inevitably lead to violence. Like perceived self-efficacy and self-esteem, participants in sport-for-development settings exhibited a wide variety of values and attitudes that were often not very different from other members of their community.

Such issues might be better dealt with via more permanent organisational settings than via limited or short-term sports programmes. For example, the Mathare Youth Sport Association has a consitition that requires equal male/female representation on all committees with annually rotating chairs and has recently appointed to the Board Gladwell Otieno, founder of the Africa Center for Open Governance and the former head of Transparency International in Kenya. Many of the issues chosen by the programmes for inclusion in the survey dealt with deep-rooted cultural attitudes and in some cases religio-moral beliefs. However, in the absence of organisational structural supports there was no obvious reason to believe that participation in these programmes would change traditional values and attitudes towards the family and gender-related responsibilities – in fact religious-based sport-for-development organisations may seek to reinforce them. Or it might be the case that some sport-for-development organisations would face strong opposition in highly religious and conservative communities if they sought to change such values. Perhaps more importantly any evaluation of the answers to such questions entails clear value judgements – in a sense such attitudes simply 'are' and to evaluate them implies a set of normative judgements that also need to be defended.

A minor league player?

The above issues and the dangers of viewing young people's lives in a social vacuum (Weiss, 1993; Ungar, 2006; Jeanes, 2011) are also complemented by some researchers' concerns about the relative isolation of sport-for-development organisations and individual peer leaders from mainstream HIV and AIDS organisations (Coalter and Taylor, 2010). Here it is interesting to note Pisani's (2008) generic concerns about the lack of integration and coherence in HIV and AIDS programmes and the difficulties in achieving such integration. In the area of sport-for-development Lindsey and Banda (2010: 102) comment on the marginal status of Zambian sport-for-development NGOs from mainstream HIV and AIDS policy forums and 'a lack of alignment between the programme outcomes of sport-for-development NGOs and those identified within the National HIV and AIDS Strategic Framework'. Whereas for the Zambian national HIV and AIDS funding, targets and monitoring 'were based upon measurable, quantitative outputs ... sport-for-development NGOs tended to focus on more nebulous outcomes in the form of personal and social development which were harder to measure quantitatively' ... and only very loosely related to HIV and AIDS prevention.

In the research that informs this book, interviews with community sports leaders in South Africa indicated that there was often a variety of AIDS organisations in communities and this could lead to confusion, even among the educators. For example, a volunteer who also worked for a mainstream AIDS organisation became confused because of the differences between the information provided by her organisation and that provided by the sport-for-development organisation (Coalter and Taylor, 2010).

In this regard UNICEF (nd) strongly advocates the need for a combination of prevention strategies and for the strengthening of links between prevention, voluntary testing and treatment. The World Health Organisation (2006: 280) argues for the need to 'build links between components of complex interventions (for example, referral systems and activities should operate across components)'. UNAIDS' (1999) view is that peer education needs to be undertaken as part of 'a larger, more comprehensive approach to HIV prevention that includes condom distribution, STI management, counselling, drama, and/or advocacy'. Reflecting these perspectives, Hughes-d'Aeth (2002: 401), reporting on evaluations of HIV and AIDS peer education projects in Zambia, concludes that peer education is an appropriate and effective strategy if used within a complex of mutually supportive activities including counselling, referrals, testing and orphan care. More pejoratively, Pisani (2008) refers to two false 'sacred cows': that NGOs do better at HIV prevention than governments and that the best people to provide prevention services were 'peers', people who themselves are members of the affected groups.

Conclusions

It is exceptionally difficult to establish the general effectiveness of peer-led sport-for-development programmes in addressing issues of knowledge, values, attitudes and, most especially, behaviour change. UNAIDS (1999: 33) notes that, in terms of evaluation,

> few of the evaluations of HIV and AIDS peer education programmes ... use rigorous research designs such as randomized controlled trials or STI/HIV incidence as outcome measures. Instead, many programmes collect only proxies of outcome measures, such as HIV-related knowledge, self-efficacy, and/or attitudes and beliefs, through the use of uncontrolled pre-test/post-test or post-test only research designs.

In terms of sport-for-development little seems to have changed (Lindsey and Banda, 2010) and, as outlined in Chapter 3, some researchers seem to have a radical aversion to such research (Lindsey and Grattan, 2012; Darnell and Hayhurst, 2012). Consequently, providers and researchers have limited understanding of the critical elements of *appropriate* peer selection, training and pedagogic practice in sport-for-development, within the context of a comprehensive HIV-prevention strategy (UNAIDS, 1999). In particular, UNAIDS (1999) indicates the need for more efficacy data from a variety of contexts and population groups to justify the allocation of resources and systematic and robust comparison of the effectiveness of peer educators with other communication channels such as health professionals, teachers or the mass media. Such data require-ments are clearly applicable to sport-for-development's claims about HIV and AIDS prevention.

However, Michielsen *et al.* (2010) indicate, via their systematic review and meta-analysis of randomised and non-randomised trials of HIV prevention initiatives in sub-Saharan Africa, that these issues are not associated solely with sport-for-development. They conclude that 'surprisingly little information was available on youth interven-tions' (Michielsen *et al.*, 2010: 1193). They also argue that, because there were few commonalities in study design and the nature of the interventions tested, this suggests 'that there is little consensus on the optimal approach to these interventions and that few studies have built upon previous knowledge in a linear fashion' (Michielsen *et al.*, 2010: 1193). The concern must be that if systematic, robust generic health-related AIDS research fails to identify robust evidence of successful interventions, or the mechanisms by which they might work, then the claims of sport-for-development's contributions to this area must be treated with some caution.

The limitations of peer-led sport-for-development interventions are best expressed by one of its foremost exponents and practitioners, Oscar Mwaanga, the founder of Edusport and Kicking-Aids-Out. Mwaanga (2010: 66) argues that

> to claim that sport can combat HIV and AIDS is not only to overstate the limited capacity of sport but also to dangerously ignore the complexity of HIV and AIDS ... the fundamental question that confronts us ... [is] how can we better understand the interplay between sport, with its limited capacity on one hand, and HIV and AIDS, in its full complexity, on the other.

However, we need to be clear about what we are saying. In many ways the claims about sport-for-development's ability to reduce the incidence of HIV and AIDS can be viewed as a reflection of the inflated promises associated with marginal policy areas and their attempts to establish relevance and gain access to a funding pot. As we argued in Chapter 3, such circumstances often produce 'inflated promises [with] goals lacking the clarity and intellectual coherence that evaluation criteria should have' (Weiss, 1993: 96) This seems somewhat similar to Pisani's (2008: 31) reference to the Millenium Development Goals and the associated 'AIDS funding honey pot' and the rapid expansion of UN agencies who discovered that HIV was part of their core mandate. Pisani's (2008: 271) ironic comments are worth quoting:

> The UN institutions are professional beggars and beggars go where the money is ... so you get 'culture and AIDS'; 'kids and AIDS'; 'fish and AIDS' ... there are only two issues really: 'sex and AIDS' and 'drugs and AIDS'. If you don't want to deal with those things ... then you'd better butt out of HIV prevention.

Consequently it is not uncommon for financially vulnerable organisations to suffer substantial mission-drift – in order to survive they depart from their core business in pursuit of funding. Of course, if their mission is simply to survive then there is little drift! Paradoxically sport-for-development in its pursuit of wider relevance, legitimacy, status and finance has exposed itself to potential failure in areas in which its actual contribution is still unknown, but will almost certainly be minor and necessarily in collaboration with other, more specialist, agencies.

However, to raise issues about sport-for-development's contribution to the reduction of the incidence of HIV and AIDS does not lead to a rejection of sport-for-development programmes and organisations. In this regard it is worth referring to the analysis of Delva *et al.* (2010) who found limited effectiveness of a sport-for-development programme. Despite such relative ineffectiveness they nonetheless conclude the other *potential* benefits such as proving equal sporting opportunities, a degree of social cohesion and the possible empowerment of members were sufficient to support such organisations.

7

'THERE IS LOADS OF RELATIONSHIPS HERE'

Developing a programme theory for sport-for-change programmes

Sufficient conditions and their commonality

As outlined in Chapter 2, the most consistent rationales underpinning public investment in sport and in sport-for-development have been based on the supposed moral component of sport and its ability to: teach 'lessons for life'; contribute to 'character building' (e.g. honesty, integrity, trustworthiness); develop self-discipline and deferred gratification and positive moral reasoning (President's Council on Physical Fitness and Sports, 2006); develop self-confidence, self-efficacy and self-esteem as a basis for changing values, attitudes and behaviour (Chapters 4, 5 and 6). Sport has consistently been promoted as having potential to contribute to crime prevention, the reduction of anti-social behaviour and the rehabilitation of recidivists, to promote social inclusion and contribute to the diffuse notion of 'development' (Coalter, 2007; Nichols, 2007; Collins and Kay, 2003) – it is as if 'sport' is viewed as consistently and inherently about development.

However, it is acknowledged that there are several unresolved issues with such interventions. First, evidence of their effectiveness is limited – either because robust and comparable monitoring and evaluation has not been undertaken consistently (Coalter, 2007; West and Crompton, 2001; Coakley, 2011), or that there are major and often inherent methodological difficulties in defining and measuring the impact of programmes (Coalter, 2007; Nichols, 2007; Nichols and Crow, 2004; Taylor, 1999; Hartmann and Kwauk, 2011). Second, sport is a summative term that hides more than it reveals. In Chapter 3 we noted the warning by the President's Council on Physical Fitness and Sports (2006) of the unhelpful nature of generalisations about 'sport' because of the varying rule structures, different types of social interaction, different developmental stimuli, varying subcultures and implicit moral norms and the probability that the experience of participants in the same programme may vary substantially.

Third, and reflecting this diversity, is the vital distinction between necessary and *sufficient* conditions and it is this issue that is the focus of this chapter. Clearly, participation in sport is a necessary condition to obtain any of the potential benefits supposedly associated with 'sport'. However, because such potential impacts are only a possibility (Svoboda, 1994) there is a need to consider sufficient conditions, i.e. the conditions under which the potential impacts might be achieved and by whom (Patriksson, 1995). Related to this is an emerging body of literature that takes Coalkey's (1998: 2) lead in viewing 'sports as *sites* for socialisation experiences, not *causes* of socialisation outcomes'. For example, Taylor *et al.* (1999: 50), summing up their evaluation of programmes using sport to reduce recidivism, state: 'All programmes agree that physical activities do not by themselves reduce offending. All agree that there are personal and social development objectives that form part of a matrix of outcomes'. Further, Hartmann (2003: 134) argues that 'the success of any sports-based social intervention program is largely determined by the strength of its non-sport components'.

Such comments indicate that, while 'sport' might provide the context for the development of positive experiences, the social *process* of participation is the key to understanding what is happening. For example, Fox (2000) emphasises the importance of 'attractiveness factors' in encouraging individuals to remain in programmes – e.g. the qualities of the leader, the exercise setting and relationships with other participants – and that these cannot be separated from the physical components of programmes in promoting self-esteem. Nichols and Taylor (1996) refer to voluntary participation, measured improvements to self-esteem and perceptions of fitness, the length of the course (the longer the better), involvement with a new peer group and access to employment-orientated training courses. In a similar vein, West and Crompton (2001), emphasise the importance of 'protective factors', drawn from an analysis of more generic youth work programmes (we will return to these below). Sandford *et al.* (2006: 262), in a review of research on the role of physical education programmes in re-engaging 'disaffected youth', note that 'it has been argued that the social relationships experienced during involvement in physical activity programmes are the most significant factor in effecting behavioural change'. Bailey *et al.* (2009: 1) in a review of the benefits of physical education and sport in schools, conclude that although many of the desired physical, affective, social and cognitive outcomes are possible, they are not automatic because they 'are mediated by environmental and contextual factors such as leadership and the involvement of young people in decision-making'. In England the Positive Futures initiative started as a sports-based national youth crime prevention programme funded by the Home Office to target and support ten to 19 year olds to prevent them being drawn into crime and drug and alcohol misuse. However, as it developed, there was a realisation that the achievement of their crime reduction goals was related to the ongoing personal and social development of participants. Consequently, the programme's objectives changed to 'widen horizons providing access to lifestyle, educational and employment opportunities within a supportive and culturally familiar environment' (Home Office, 2005: 4). Reflecting this, Crabbe (2000), who undertook the evaluations of the Positive

Futures programme, argues for the need to 'de-centre' sport in order to understand which sports work for what subjects, in what conditions. In a later paper he refers to such initiatives as 'cultural intermediaries' and identifies the need to consider concepts 'centrally concerned with the intimate dynamics of human relations' and the need 'to mobilise these concepts in a fashion which actively seeks to ... contribute to the design of the community sport project' (Crabbe, 2008: 34–35). He argues for the need to obtain 'a deeper understanding of the "complexities of participants" interactions and the often contradictory and fluid impact of initiatives'. The importance of the dynamics of human relations is emphasised by Morris *et al.* (2003: 72) who, in a review of 175 programmes (and 22 case studies) for at-risk youth, concluded that 'there is no significant relationship between program conception, delivery and intended outcomes in the *type of activity* [emphasis added] provided'. They concluded that *any* programme where there had previously been none was more important.

As we noted in Chapter 3, such socio-psychological emphasis on context, social and learning relationships and active cognition has similarities with social learning theories' emphasis on learners as active and interpreting agents (Bandura, 1994; Pajares, 2002). This is also similar to the realist evaluation approach of Pawson and Tilley (2004). This emphasises that social interventions 'work' by enabling participants to make different choices, although choice making is always constrained by participants' previous experiences, beliefs and attitudes, opportunities and access to resources. The making and sustaining of different choices requires a change in participants' reasoning (for example, values, beliefs, attitudes, or the logic they apply to a particular situation) and/or the resources they have available to them (e.g. information, skills, material resources, support). This combination of 'reasoning and resources' – the programme 'mechanism' – is what enables the programme to 'work'. As was argued in Chapter 3, we need to shift analysis and understanding from families of programmes (i.e. sports programmes) to *families of mechanism* – the processes, experiences and relationships that might achieve desired impacts (Coalter, 2007, 2011). This means that we need to understand better the middle-range mechanisms, which programme providers either assume or try to build into their programmes. For example, in programme design and daily practice across a range of seemingly different programmes, certain mechanisms or processes will result in the strengthening of (say) perceived self-efficacy by certain participants and not others. The identification of the *possible* communalities of such mechanisms across a range of interventions can assist in the development of, or linking with, broader theoretical and analytical frameworks, providing a much more robust and potentially generalisable version of what works, in what circumstances, for whom and why.

Many of the contexts and some of the issues that sport-for-development programmes seek to address may be 'new'. However, it is possible that most programmes that seek to change values, attitudes and behavioural intentions have similar middle-range mechanisms. The research used in this chapter and the interview data used to develop a programme theory are not from narrowly defined 'sport-for-development' projects, although all programmes sought systematically to change participants' values and attitudes. It is, of course, up to the reader to decide the relevance of the analysis and conclusions to the loosely defined and supposedly emergent area of sport-for-development. However, I have shared this data and analysis with programme designers of sport-for-development projects in India and South Africa and the reaction was 'this is what we do!' and 'I would love to test in on my programme'. Perhaps it is the latter reaction that is appropriate – what is presented here is a worked and working hypothesis for others to test in varying environments. I hope that it is also an illustration that other non-sporting areas of research may have a substantial contribution to make to the development of the supposedly new and under-researched field of sport-for-development.

From programmes to mechanisms

Tacon (2007) asserts that many sport-for-change projects have much in common with social work practice and the issue of the key mechanisms in generic youth work programmes for at-risk youth has been addressed by several researchers (e.g. Gambone and Arbreton, 1997; MacCallum and Beltman, 2002). Witt and Crompton's (1997) widely quoted analysis of the 'protective factors' essential to sports programmes for at-risk youth is derived from this literature. There is broad agreement about the required elements: safe and supportive environments; challenging and interesting activities; opportunities for youth to develop; adult caring role models and so on. Further, there is a general agreement that such programmes work via strong relationships between participants and *relevant* role models/mentors (see Chapter 5 on role models; Bandura, 1994; Lyle, 2006) and that the most effective programmes are those that develop long-term, supportive and reinforcing relationships. This again raises important questions about the effectiveness of short-term projects and the educational and developmental relevance of volunteers from other cultures. Gambone and Arbreton (1997) identified seven programme elements as part of approaches that focus on enhancing resilience, an issue central to many sport-for-development programmes (and analysed in Chapter 4):

- Opportunities that enable youth to develop a sense of safety.
- Challenging and interesting activities.
- Settings and experiences that help youth develop a sense of belonging.
- Social support from adults.
- Opportunities for input and decision making.
- Opportunities to develop leadership skills.
- Opportunities to undertake volunteer and community service activities.

The more widely known Witt and Crompton's (1997) *protective factors framework* contains most of the broadly agreed factors. This framework is derived from an examination of the factors in the lives of 'resilient' youth that enable them to avoid the negative consequences of multiple risk environments – i.e. those facets that moderate the impact of risk on behaviour and development. The protective factors approach shifts the focus from the risks to which young people are exposed to a concern that 'developing protective factors is central to promoting positive youth development in risk environments' (Witt and Crompton, 1997: 3). The factors that they suggest provide a framework for the structure and design of programmes are:

- Interested and caring adults.
- Sense of acceptance and belonging.
- Models for conventional behaviour.
- Like/perceived competence at a particular activity.
- Value placed on achievement.
- High controls against deviant behaviour.
- Positive attitudes to the future.
- Ability to work with others.
- Ability to work out conflicts.

Third, we draw on Pawson's (2006) conclusions from a realist review of published research on youth mentoring programmes for at-risk youth. From this research he identifies four broad stages through which the mentor/mentee relationship proceeds. These are mentoring as:

- Befriending. Creating bonds of trust.
- Direction-setting. Promoting self-reflection and the reconsideration of values, loyalties and ambitions.
- Coaching. Coaxing and cajoling mentees into acquiring the skills, assets, credentials required to enter the mainstream.
- Sponsoring. Advocating and networking on behalf of the mentee to gain requisite contacts and opportunities.

These various stages, in which progression is not guaranteed, are based on movement from emotional and cognitive gains into social and vocational skills and career gains. Given the self-selecting nature of many programmes, it is important to note that Pawson (2006) suggests that this progression is more likely for those who arrive in the programme with resilience and aspiration about moving away from their present status. This point is also made in Chapters 4 and 5 where the deficit model, on which much sport-for-development is based, is questioned.

This generic literature was drawn on to provide a broad theoretical framework for the in-depth interviews reported in this chapter and for the analysis and presentation of the data.

Methods

The research reported in this chapter is based on an evaluation of six sport-based projects in various parts of the UK that were funded by Comic Relief over a five-year period. The funded sports-oriented organisations had broad, diffuse and often ill-defined objectives. Their general targets were 'at-risk' youth in areas of deprivation and the programmes sought to reduce tensions, conflict and divisions based variously on territoriality, gang violence, racist and sectarian attitudes. They also sought to address issues relating to perceived lack of aspiration and ambition. A mixture of before-and-after surveys of participants in some programmes and retrospective in-depth interviews in others was used to evaluate the impacts of the programmes. Although work from all of the projects informs the analysis, the projects that are drawn on directly are:

- A soccer-based programme in a deprived inner city area in Liverpool (in the northwest of England) that has a long history of gang-related violence and high levels of unemployment. Recreational and competitive football programmes were provided to address broad issues relating to 'at-risk' youth and gang membership.
- A basketball-based project in several deprived areas of Glasgow in Scotland aimed at 'at-risk' youth and immigrants and asylum seekers. Recreational and competitive programmes were provided and there was a close link with a professional basketball team.
- A programme based in the East End of London using football (and other activities) to address issues of gang membership among Bengali youth.
- A sport-oriented project in Glasgow addressing issues of territoriality, gang membership and substance abuse. Recreational football was combined with other sporting activities, such as go-karting.

The programme personnel were asked to select a range of participants who were over 14 years of age and preferably had been in the programme for at least three years (this could include 14 year olds who joined at the age of 11). All those offered for interview were male, reflecting the nature of the programmes and their concerns with gang-related and criminal behaviour. While it is not possible to comment on the representativeness of these interviewees, they did contain a wide variety of young men, including those who were only ever 'at risk' largely via peer group membership, some who had been core gang members, some recovering addicts and at least one who had recently served time in a young offenders' institution for a serious assault (an offence committed while he was attending the programme, although the assault was committed elsewhere). Individual in-depth interviews were conducted with 37 participants whose ages ranged from 14 to 21 years of age. The interviews were semi-structured and explored behaviour prior to joining the programmes, reasons for joining and staying in the programmes, the most significant aspects of the programmes from the participants' perspective and the impact that they perceived that it had had on them. The interviews were 'informed', although not tightly structured, by the perspectives outlined above. Interviews were recorded and fully transcribed for analysis and the broadly similar perspectives of Witt and Crompton (1997), Gambone and Arbreton (1997) and Pawson (2006) were used to structure the analysis, identify categories of responses and interpret the data. Although the interviews were not directive and highly structured and were conducted in a variety of locations with different programmes, as will be seen below, most of the responses fell easily into the categories identified by previous researchers, although much of their work did not relate to sports projects. However, referring to the debate in Chapter 3, I make no claims for the liberating or empowering nature of these interviews.

The relative role of sport

Although all were funded as sports-based projects, the relative centrality of sport varied.

- Some were sports programmes in which young people played both recreational and competitive football and basketball. This might be in culturally or religiously mixed environments, with the hope that the collective act of participation in a supposedly neutral activity would break down barriers and lead to changed values, attitudes and behaviours.
- Some were *sport-plus* (Coalter, 2007) in which sport was viewed as an important context for changing values, attitudes and behaviour, but this was not left to chance. For example, some used a 'red card' approach in which on-field unacceptable behaviour was addressed immediately, or workshops were used to discuss a range of issues (e.g. anger management, territoriality, drug use, sectarianism, violence). This is very similar to many sport-for-development projects.
- Some were *plus-sport* (Coalter, 2007), youth-work organisations in which free access to sport was used as 'fly paper' to attract young people, or defined widely and used as a reward and a social context for intensive youth work practice and social bonding (e.g. go-karting).

In general, sport was only one of several activities in which participants took part and in such circumstances it proved to be very difficult to identify specific 'sports effects' – a problem common to most such interventions (Coalter, 2007; Hartmann and Kwauk, 2011).

Recruiting participants

Like most sport-for-development projects these programmes had diffuse ideas of a 'target group' – usually some type of supposedly 'at-risk' youth – and different ways of recruiting them. Such differences had implications for the extent to which programmes attracted target participants, how they sought to achieve desired impacts and outcomes and how they could assess success. We can identify three broad types:

- Open access, sports-only programmes in deprived areas and open to all young people. Crucially, such programmes deal with *self-selecting participants*. – as with many sport-for-development programmes. Consequently, it is possible that the key target groups of such programmes will not be attracted (if they actually exist). Those who provide such programmes often work with an implicit *deficit model* based on a form of *environmental determinism* – that all young people from areas designated as high crime, or recording racist attacks, will themselves be 'at risk', or will have racist attitudes, low self-confidence, weak self-esteem or low aspirations (see Chapters 4 and 5). Such assumptions are essential rationales and form the basis for funding applications, although the evidence from this and my sport-for-development research is that little systematic analysis of prior values, attitudes and behaviour is undertaken. There is a paradoxical danger of well-meaning projects being based on negative stereotypes of all young people from particular areas, with the attendant danger of misconceived provision and inappropriate performance indicators.

- Relatively open access, but with a targeting outreach approach to attract young people who were more obviously 'at risk'. Some programmes also regarded it as essential to recruit more widely in order not to stigmatise vulnerable young people and also to introduce them to 'ordinary kids' as part of the broader socialisation objectives.

- Versions of outreach youth work, in which young people were befriended and recruited to programmes aimed almost wholly at them. These programmes included an opportunity to take part in sport, but often as a social context for further youth work and as an incentive to stay with the programme. However, even in such focused programmes, it was felt necessary for participants to take part in supervised activity sessions with other young people from different areas.

A further significant distinction is between once or twice a week programmes – mostly open access – and more open-ended programmes with a permanent base where participants had ongoing 'drop-in' contact with staff. Such variations meant that participants were involved in a variety of social relationships and experiences, in which sport had a varied importance. All interviewees quoted are from types (ii) and (iii) above.

The role of sport

Witt and Crompton (1997) suggest that participants should be provided with the opportunity to take part in an activity that they like and for which they have a perceived competence; Gambone and Arbreton (1997) suggest that young people should be provided with challenging and interesting activities. It is clear that this is the presumed role that sport plays in such programmes. Despite this, football and basketball rarely featured in discussions about claimed changes in attitudes and behaviour. In fact, one respondent stated that he learnt more about football in his semi-professional team, but he attended his programme because the staff had more interest in him as a person, as did a skilled basketball player on another programme – the relationships with the coach/leader did not end at the touchline. Although some in the basketball programme saw sport as more central, this could reflect the programme's choice of interviewees, who were mostly skilled competitive basketball players, some of whom had aspirations for basketball-related scholarships. A refugee from the Balkans valued the opportunity to integrate by developing both verbal and social communication that was facilitated by the cooperative nature of teams:

> ... when you play in teams and you know ... the people who used to fight with ... it's just the friendship starts, starts to build up when you, oh he's passing to me, oh, I shouldn't have done that to him, you know.

For these immigrants, who were mostly skilled, competitive and regular players, the team environment facilitated a degree of social connection and the development of language skills. However, for most participants, who were drawn from broadly similar communities, the most important aspects of the programme related to more general issues about the social climate and social relationships. It is to these that we now turn.

The social climate: 'There is loads of relationships here'

Here Witt and Crompton (1997) list two key protective factors – interested and caring adults and a sense of acceptance and belonging. Similarly, Gambone and Arbreton (1997) refer to settings and experiences that help youth to develop a sense of safety and belonging, plus social support from adults. Pawson (2006: 124) identifies the basic stage of development as one in which the mentor's role is established via *befriending*, defined as 'creating the bonds of trust and the sharing of new experiences so that the mentee recognises the legitimacy of other people and other perspectives'. Others, influenced by aspects of social learning theory, have referred to the importance of a lack of perceived social distance in such relationships (e.g. Bandura, 1994).

'I tell him lots of things that I wouldn't tell my mum'

Although sport was an attraction and an important shared interest, the relationships established went beyond that of player and coach. The relative lack of social distance was part of the attraction: 'And he's great. He's like a mate to me. He's just like one of the lads. He's that close with us. He's just dead laid back'. Another referred to the coach as a trusted 'role model. ... He's like my best friend'. An interviewee who had played elsewhere, commented on a 'different approach to coaching':

> [T]hey wanted to know about you, they wanted to know what you wanted to achieve and they were there to help. Whereas with the other team I was with, were just really, 'you're good, we'll take you', ignore everybody else sorta thing.

For some this perceived lack of social distance was an important attraction and was the reason for staying in the programme:

> If you don't have a personal friendship with the coaches, then you're not gonna go along to sessions. If you don't know them on a personal level there's

not really any point in you going on because you're not gonna enjoy the session ... But if you know them and you like them, then you're gonna want to go back just for the fact they were friendly. Know what I mean?

In a programme solely for at-risk young men a participant appreciated the level of consultation about activities and said that the staff 'treat you like adults ... [unlike] teachers do to you, they don't control you. ... Teachers shout at you as if they are higher than you'.

Beyond the touch line

Other comments make it clear that diversion and rehabilitation work need to 'go beyond the touchline'. The level of intimacy is often re-enforced by a high level of access to staff, which the young men found impressive – 'they give you a lotta time, know what I mean?'

> [I]f you get yourself into trouble, like you can always come here and try and sort it out and talk to them and explain what's going on and see their point of view of what they're doing and get some advice what they would say. So yeah, it's just not football.

For others, the staff was regarded as family, or at least compensating for dysfunctional family relationships:

> It wasn't just [the programme which kept me out of trouble] but it helped. It helped a lot, especially, you see where you were talking about the friendship side of it ... that helped big time 'cos I actually fell out with my mother, so, and I turned to [...] more, I turned to them more than I did my dad. I couldn't talk to my dad. That's one of the things I've spoke to [...] about. Know what I mean? I just kinda looked up to them ... I treat them like family, aye. If there's anything, anything happens in life that gets me down or whatever, I can easily just turn round to them straight away and no, no hesitation.

Respect, trust and reciprocity: the key mechanism

These various aspects – closeness, support and accessibility – combine to underpin the most significant aspect of the programmes – the development of the closely inter-dependent factors of respect, trust and reciprocity. This has a wider influence on both behaviour and aspiration – 'We like not to disappoint them like but we don't want to let them down'. In a competitively oriented programme this 'friendship' relation-ship was based on a respect for the coach: 'They give you a lot of respect and they always, they always say to you, if I give you respect, you need to give me respect back ... They demand respect from you 'cos they're gonna give you respect'. In a targeted group, an ex-gang member, who claimed to have stopped 'daft gang fighting', felt that this was partly a result of being involved with the programme and his relationship with the leaders – 'I have got a lot of respect for the three of them'. In one programme access to tickets to professional basketball games served to consolidate programme-based relationships.

> They're interlinked with the [...] as well, so you can go to [...] games, which gives you something else to do as well, know what I mean ... It's more, 'do you want to come along with me to the games?' Know what I mean? It is a big family and you get a lot more friends as well.

Initial respect for the leader/coach and the fact that they 'give so much of their time' and treated them 'like adults', leads to the development of a relative closeness and trust that many did not have with other adults in their lives. This then underpins the ability of the leaders to influence values, attitudes and behaviour. This was aided by the growing sense of reciprocity in which various individuals wanted to give something back and not to disappoint the leader/coach and consequently began to change their attitudes and behaviour.

What if ... ?

Witt and Crompton (1997) list three protective factors relating to the understanding of consequences and changing behaviour: models for conventional behaviour; high controls against deviant behaviour; ability to work out conflicts. In Pawson's (2006) second phase of 'direction-setting', self-reflection is promoted via the discussion of alternatives to enable participants to consider their loyalties, values and ambitions.

Obviously a core concern of the programmes was to emphasise 'conventional behaviour' and we have already noted how the commitment and behaviour of the coaches/ mentors generated strong trust and respect and these acted as moral controls on behaviour. For example, when asked how behaviour is controlled within the programmes one respondent stated: 'They'll stop really 'cos everyone respects him, so everyone gets on together. It doesn't mess, it's like he says behave, everyone'll behave'.

However, in addition to the strong moral influences on behaviour, some programmes addressed issues directly and systematically. They stressed the need to be aware of the consequences of actions and to develop an ability to make mature choices – the need to move away from arbitrary risk-taking behaviour. Some interviewees referred to the phrase 'what if', which was used by staff to encourage them to think about the possible consequences if misbehaviour occurred in a less safe and supportive context. In another programme respondents stated that 'the words kinda stick in your head': ' ... likes if I do something stupid, like to [coach] or something, like arsing about, it's like what if like that goes wrong and what are the consequences that could happen. Like just stuff like that'. Some programmes used specific incidents during games to reinforce the need for self-control and the possible wider consequences of failing to do so. One incident in which the respondent lost his temper and left the pitch illustrates this.

> When I walked away, it was the coach who came up and spoke to us and he said 'if you're gonna do this at a job interview, if you're gonna do this when times get hard … you're not gonna have very much success in life'. So it makes you think … See the point when he tells you, you think, oh fuck, know what I mean, fuck you, fuck off and that and I did, I did walk away a few times but then when you go home and you're sitting on your bed at night, you think about it a lot more, you think about, you know, the way you're trying to make of your life, if you are gonna do that in life, know what I mean. Just the words kinda stick in your head, know what I mean. It doesn't just affect you on the court, it affects you when you go home as well. You don't want to be that same arsehole that you were 2 years ago.

'Go for your goal an' that!'

Witt and Crompton (1997) emphasise the need for programmes to place a high value on achievement and to promote positive attitudes to the future. Pawson's (2006) second stage of 'direction-setting' also includes the development of aspirations and his third 'coaching' stage is one in which participants are cajoled into acquiring the skills and assets required to enter the mainstream.

Issues of aspiration and goal setting were addressed via a mixture of support and exhortation. For one respondent the general message was 'don't let anyone put ye af it! … Go for your goal an' that!'. Many agreed that they had been hanging around street corners 'causing a nuisance to yourself' – and probably drifting into trouble. The impact of involvement in a programme is expressed succinctly: 'When I met [coach] … I actually started realising that I could do something with my life'. To reinforce and support such ambitions, some organisations provided access to subsidised or free coaching awards and First Aid courses. However, there was also a proactive approach to helping to find employment:I '[I]f you use [organisation] to its full strength, they really can like help you a lot, like CVs, help you write CVs out, getting your CVs around, getting you job interviews'. Some also offered assistance similar to Pawson's (2006) final stage of 'sponsoring', in which the mentor networks assisted the mentee to gain contacts and opportunities – a form of bridging social capital (Chapter 8). For example, one respondent appreciated the general assistance for job hunting:

> I'm not rich or nothing. So I've not got nothing and they helped me out by letting me use the computers in the office, letting me research some of the …

to get my job and that, and let me prepare for my meetings and stuff. So then they also helped me get a job as well. Know what I mean? I could research … so if they asked me questions when I went to the meeting, I could answer them straight off. I knew what I was talking about.

As part of Pawson's (2006) 'direction-setting' phase self-reflection is promoted via the discussion of alternatives to enable participants to consider their loyalties, values and ambitions. In this regard a key feature of the supportive, achievement-oriented environment was to give the opportunity to develop different values, attitudes and aspirations and change relationships with their previous peers. For example:

I kept going along, just started from there, just kept playing and playing, then I started becoming further away from my friends. Just became further apart from them 'cos I was going and playing basketball more, it kept me away from all the trouble. So then, you know, if you don't speak to people, then you know, you're not friends anymore. I've kinda broke away from it 'cos I was playing basketball so much.

Another who began to attend college and develop occupational ambitions, drew the more general conclusion that 'I probably would be still hanging around with that crew and wouldn't probably have no ambitions or like going to college, 'cos I don't think there would have been a need for it'.

Volunteering and 'a sense of being needed'

Witt and Crompton (1997) suggest that a key programme component should be the development of the ability to work with others. Gambone and Arbreton (1997) propose that programmes should provide opportunities to develop leadership roles and opportunities to undertake volunteer and community service activities.

Confidence and self-worth

In one programme the development of employment-related skills via Level 1 coaching was complemented and reinforced by the opportunity to coach on the programme.

The main one was interacting because it gave us a lot of confidence dealing with the younger ones, you know, like just interacting with them and just speaking to them, sharing about your experiences with all them and that.

Another stated that 'it gave me the sort of sense of importance I suppose, 'cos you're important to what they're doing. So it gave me that sense of being needed'. For others, it was not simply the experience of overcoming fear and developing self-confidence, but also passing on their experiences and helping younger ones to develop sporting skills – 'giving something back':

Q: Which is the proudest bit? Playing or coaching the kids?

A: I'd probably say coaching. See to help somebody else or pass on what I've learned from other guys, it's a big, big, big difference. See when you see some of the wee kids and you help them out with what he's doing or whatever, you take him aside and talk to him and he's back on and he seems happy, it's a big, big, big thing, because I tell you it changes your life.

For some the experience of volunteering and addressing their fears contributed to a growing maturity:

I think it's made me more mature really like because I think we just needed to grow up at the time but now that I've done like loads of voluntary work I can like talk to the younger groups and things like that. That's mainly one of the reasons that we're doing the voluntary work, so we can interact with the younger ones and like tell them how you shouldn't be like going, not tell them but advising them, showing your experience with theirs and all that.

It is clear that, for these individuals, such experiences and the opportunity to confront their fears and make a positive and useful contribution – give something back – led to an increase in perceived self-efficacy and increased self-esteem. This provides support to the earlier argument that peer leaders are the most likely to benefit from sport-for-development programmes (see Chapter 6).

Growing up safely

For many participants the organisations provided a safe, supportive, achievement-oriented environment in which they could mature. Many acknowledged their debt to the programmes and, especially, their close relationships with the staff and the way this *assisted* their growing maturity. Some believed that they would inevitably have matured over the time that they had been with the programme (reflecting a wider pattern of a decline in anti-social behaviour in later adolescence), but one acknowledged that the programme had quickened his maturity:

I think I probably would have matured later … and I would have kept doing that for a lot longer if basketball hadn't stopped me, you know. … the basketball stopped me in my tracks, it stopped me from going that far. … That's where it helped me personally, 'cos I was going down a really slippery slope but then basketball came in and it kinda cut me off from that. It sorta helped me change, you know.

Two steps forward …

Although we have identified a series of 'successes' associated with the programmes, we do not have data to enable us to go beyond the various interviewees to assess the *relative* effectiveness of such programmes – e.g. we have no interviews with those who dropped out, not all outcomes could be deemed to be a success and the projects did not keep systematic records of post-attendance behaviour (a widespread problem in this area). Further, Pawson (2006) illustrates that mentees' progress is often both halting and non-linear. He argues that many disadvantaged young people have frequent and repetitive battles with authority, bust-ups with family and brushes with the law and that the mentee/mentor relationship is characterised by a persistent element of 'fire fighting'. This is confirmed by our data, with some interviews indicating that dealing with such individuals can be a long-term and emotionally intense job, with some having slipped in and out of criminal or anti-social behaviour. Some inevitably continued to struggle with behavioural issues and lived in environments where there were constant pressures and temptations. In such circumstances changes in values, attitudes and behaviours occured as a result of a continuous process. For example, one interviewee remembered and valued the support provided by a staff member:

> He helped me in court … Gave me a reference and that and, eh, stood up and said stuff and, you know, said I was going to [a foreign trip] with them and I've been doing, eh, loadsa voluntary and things like that … So he helped [me] in court really from going to jail.

Part of the key to the relative effectiveness of the organisations was that the staff continued to support those who 'erred' and did not abandon them. This reflected and reinforced the relationship based on respect, trust and reciprocity at the heart of the *sport plus* and *plus sport* programmes. However, it also raises important issues about how the effectiveness of such organisations should be assessed and the extent to which they can compensate for wider economic, social and cultural influences on young people's attitudes and behaviour (see Spaaij, 2011). Some of the issues at stake are illustrated by Taylor *et al.*'s (1999: 50) summing up of their evaluation of programmes using sport to reduce recidivism: that personal and social development 'may, sooner or later, improve offending behaviour, but their impact is unpredictable in scale and timing. To expect anything more tangible is unrealistic'.

This is why, as argued in Chapter 3, a theory of behaviour change – a programme theory – cannot be assumed to be uni-linear, either in terms of its impacts (values, attitudes, perceived self-efficacy, self-esteem) or, more especially, behavioural outcomes. As Pawson and Tilley (2000) argue, the programmes work by offering participants a series of resources and choices, but choice making is always constrained by participants' previous experiences, beliefs and attitudes, opportunities and access to resources – the offer may be refused.

Sufficient conditions and programme theories

The above processes, issues and experiences illustrate Pawson *et al.*'s (2004: 5) contention that 'intervention chains are long and thickly populated. Interventions carry not one, but several implicit mechanisms of action'. They illustrate the need to move beyond the 'black box' (Scriven, 1994) view, much loved by policy makers, sports evangelists and conceptual entrepreneurs, that traditional short-term sport programmes can effectively change a range of deep-rooted values, attitudes and behaviours, with little understanding of the mechanisms via which this might be achieved. We have noted Coakley's (2004) contention that sports are *sites* for socialisation experiences, not *causes* of socialisation outcomes. Such perspectives shift analysis from families of programmes (e.g. sport and crime; sport and conflict; sport-for-development) to *families of mechanisms* – the processes, relationships and experiences that might achieve the desired impacts and, hopefully, outcomes.

In terms of investment decisions and programme development there is a need to clarify programme theories, or theories of behaviour change, which inform, or should inform, programme design and practice (Coalter, 2007, 2011). A programme theory is a sequence of *presumed* causes/actions/processes and effects (Weiss, 1997) and its utility is summed up by the World Bank (2004), which argues that it allows an in-depth understanding of the working of

> a program or activity. In particular it need not assume simple linear cause-and-effect relationships. ... By mapping out the determining or causal factors judged important for success, and how they might interact, it can then be decided which steps should be monitored as the progress develops, to see how well they are in fact borne out. This allows the critical success factors to be identified.

We will not repeat the defence provided in Chapter 3, but note that such an approach seeks to describe mechanisms, examine the theoretical underpinnings of programmes as a basis for evaluation and, most importantly, provide some basis for generalisation in order to inform future programme design. Weiss (1997: 154) suggests that shifting focus from activities to mechanisms by which change might be achieved permits a tracking of the unfolding of events and improves our ability to make causal attributions on the basis of demonstrated links. More radically she argues that if this is successful across a range of projects 'evaluation would not need randomized control groups to justify its claims about causality'. This is a very ambitious goal and the analysis presented here certainly does not make such a claim. However, it is hoped that it makes some contribution toward the achievement of such a goal.

A tentative programme theory

Given the diversity of participants, programmes, processes, relationships and desired impacts and outcomes it is not possible to develop a definitive or prescriptive programme theory – each programme may require its own programme theory to reflect its context, although intellectual progress requires a search for middle-range communalities. As in all forms of social intervention, the nature and extent of impacts and outcomes depend on the interaction of a variety of factors. Figure 7.1 illustrates that the variety of sport-for-change programmes can be placed on a continuum that includes a range of components. The vertical columns contain *possible* programme elements, although it is difficult to be definitive as progammes may contain particular combinations. However, the various elements are listed in a broadly hierarchical way, from relatively superficial components, which one might expect in all programmes, to more fundamental aspects dealing with issues of vulnerability and risk. The information from the evaluations and existing research indicates that the most effective interventions for those most at risk will contain most of the elements towards the bottom of the vertical columns and will not rely on a simple one-dimensional notion of the 'power' of sport.

Inputs 1: Methods of recruitment

There is a continuum of programmes, ranging from open access programmes that provide free or highly subsidised activities to self-selecting young people in the local community, to those that are aimed solely at those deemed to be at risk and recruited either via referral or targeted street work.

Inputs 2: The nature of participants

The method of recruitment has substantial implications for the nature of the participants and the extent, distribution and severity of the various social and personal issues that the programmes seek to address. Targeted programmes are likely to recruit participants who are characterised by the issues with which the programmes are concerned. However, there is a danger that open access, self-selecting programmes will be based on a vague mixture of a *deficit* view of participants and an *environmental determinism*, which assumes that young people from deprived communities are uniformly deficient. Without evidence of the nature and distribution of the issues that the programme is seeking to address it is not possible to establish meaningful performance indicators and to assess effectiveness. Even more importantly, the lack of such information limits greatly the ability to design and deliver appropriate programmes and often results in sports programmes that are simply assumed to be able to address often poorly understood issues (see Chapters 4, 5 and 6).

Outputs 1: The nature and type of programme: from sport to plus sport

There is a continuum of programmes based on the balance between sport and other programme components. Programmes can be viewed on a continuum:

- Those that simply provide sporting opportunities, assuming that unexamined 'inherent properties' of sport will address certain issues.

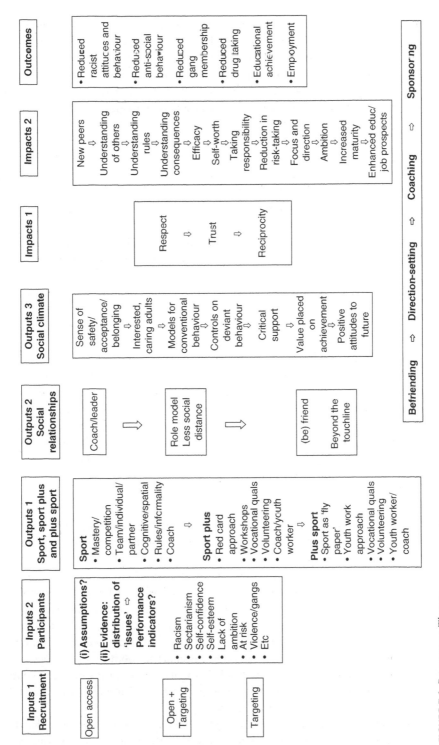

FIGURE 7.1 Programme Theory

- *Sport plus* programmes in which the processes involved in sport are supplemented by other activities that address directly the issue of concern (e.g. workshops on drug use; racism; sectarianism; HIV and AIDS; gender issues).
- *Plus sport*, where sport is a 'fly paper' to attract young people to programmes in which the main educational and developmental work is undertaken via a range of non-sporting and personally and emotionally intense activities.

Within these various contexts, the types of sport can also take various forms. Sports can:

- be individual, partner or team based, although relatively competitive football tends to dominate. Such sports involve different types of social relations and experiences, which may or may not be relevant to the issues being addressed (President's Council on Physical Fitness and Sports, 2006);
- emphasise individual task/mastery or competition. In this regard much research points to the effectiveness of a mastery orientation for vulnerable young people. In this approach participants' skills are matched with the challenges they face and they are provided with positive encouragement, thus facilitating experiences of personal success and support (Biddle, 2006);
- be norm based (i.e. subject to external judgements) or criterion based (personal judgements of progress);
- be based on spatial skills (e.g. football) or motor skills (e.g. gymnastics);
- emphasise rules or informality. While it is often assumed that part of the positive impact of sport is the experience of rule-governed behaviour, research suggests that some adolescents reject organised, competitive sport because it contains components similar to those that they have previously failed to resolve – adherence to formal rules and regulations, achievement of externally defined goals and competitive situations – and prefer games with fewer and less specified rules, with fewer requirement for conformity (Sugden and Yiannakis, 1982; Coalter, 2007).

The choice of sport and the manner in which it is delivered will have a major influence on the experience of participants, the nature of the social relationships and the potential for skill development and personal change.

Despite these issues, many programmes fail to think much about 'sport' – taking a 'black box' approach, in which outcomes are regarded as inevitable and the contents of the box (i.e. processes and experiences) are taken for granted. In many programmes there is a need to think much more deeply about the 'sport' that is being provided, the extent to which it will deliver the experiences assumed and contribute to the desired impacts. Such considerations are essential for both sports coaches with little or no youth work training (who are likely to take 'sport' for granted) and youth workers with an interest or some expertise in sport, who may not understand the full potential of particular approaches to delivery.

Finally, some programmes, mostly *sport plus*, offer the opportunity to undertake coaching qualifications and also to volunteer within the programmes. As our data illustrate, these experiences are highly valued by young people and contribute substantially to the achievement of some of the impacts (see the analysis of peer leaders in Chapter 6).

Outputs 2: Social relationships

The combination of types of programmes and types of personnel who deliver them are central to the predominant types of social relationships within a programme – which research and our evidence identify as a key factor in effectiveness.

The coach/leader role, which is the predominant one in open access sports programmes, is a relatively impersonal one that tends to be confined to the organisation and delivery of the sessions, with limited ability to develop personal relationships with relatively large numbers of participants. On the other hand, the various forms of the (be)friending role (Pawson, 2006), in which a degree of trust and intimacy is developed and often goes 'beyond the touchline', is much more characteristic of some of the *sport-plus* approaches and all *plus-sport* approaches. As has already been suggested, this is the approach most likely to be effective with the most vulnerable and at-risk.

Outputs 3: Social climate

The nature of the activity and the social relationships are fundamental to establishing the ethos – or social climate – of the programmes. Some may simply rely on sport's presumed inherent properties – team work, rule-governed behaviour, the development of social skills, learning to respect and cooperate with others – although such experiences and impacts are not inevitable, as the sporting environment varies widely, as do participants' reactions.

More generally, most programmes seek to provide an environment where young people feel a sense of safety and acceptance. Although they would be unlikely to continue to participate if this was not the case, it also provides the context for developmental work. Within this context, interested and caring adults are able to construct positive social relationships with young people, although the emotional intimacy of these will vary with the nature of the relationships implied in Outputs 1 and 2. Also, reflecting the variety of contexts and relationships, the coaches/leaders/youth workers can act with varying effectiveness as role models, mentors and (be)frienders. Within these contexts, varying types and degree of control on deviant behaviour are exercised – ranging from formal sanctions, or even expulsions, to a high level of self-control based on respect and reciprocity.

Contexts in which a high value is systematically placed on achievement and positive attitudes to the future are more likely to be those characterised by a *sport plus* and (be)friending and mentoring approach. This also relates to *direction setting*, in which self-reflection is promoted via the discussion of alternatives to enable participants to consider their values, loyalties and ambitions (Pawson, 2006).

Impacts 1: Laying the basis for changed attitudes and behaviour

The various social relationships, the social climate and the components of direction setting may lead some participants to develop the basis for changing their values, attitudes and behaviours. In the data collected for this evaluation it was clear that the development of *respect* for the leader/role model/mentor was a key building block for the development of trust and then a degree of reciprocity – the desire not to disappoint the leader/mentor and to conform to his/her expectations. The development of such relationships and attitudes are most likely to occur in the smaller scale and more intensive *sport plus* and *plus sport* programmes, where such intimate role modelling is often central to the programme approach.

Such relationships and attitudes are likely to be reinforced via Pawson's (2006) 'coaching stage', in which participants are mentored, encouraged and persuaded to acquire the skills and assets required to pursue education, training or employment.

Impacts 2: Changing values and attitudes

The precise nature of the desired positive individual impacts – various changes in values, attitudes and behaviour – will vary between programmes. Further, the ability to achieve some of them will be dependent on the mixture of the inputs, outputs and personal impacts outlined above. Many programmes hope to promote a better understanding of other communities, cultures or religions and some hope to enable participants to make new friends – either from other communities, or to remove them from criminal or 'at risk' cultures. As part of this, development programmes seek systematically to emphasise the need for participants to understand the implication of certain negative behaviour in sporting and non-sporting contexts and, more importantly, to reflect on and accept responsibility for their actions. It is hoped that this mixture of formal and informal 'coaching' will lead to a general reduction in risk-taking behaviour.

Such changes in attitudes and behaviour might also reflect psychological changes in perceived self-efficacy and self-esteem, although such changes are more likely to be systematically promoted and supported in *sport plus* and *plus sport* organisations. Such organisations are most likely directly to encourage and support an increased focus and sense of direction and to provide opportunities that enhance educational and employment prospects.

It is inevitable that young people who participate in programmes for some years will mature and it is often difficult to identify precisely the contribution of the programmes to this process. However, it is clear that, for those who stay in such programmes over a three–five year period, at the very least they are offered a safe and supportive environment in which to grow up and this was acknowledged by several interviewees.

In some cases the vital connection with education or the labour market is provided via *sponsorship* (Pawson, 2006) – i.e. the organisation's personnel use their networks to assist the mentee to gain relevant contacts and opportunities. There is a continuum of such sponsorship and few of the organisations in this evaluation (or the sport-for-development organisations in Chapters 4 and 5) had strong and direct links with employers, although they provided strong encouragement and support and references. However, if the aim is to enable young people to enter the 'mainstream', programmes based on an overly individualised version of this process, ignoring the fact that the wider context in which they live, may not provide the full support that many young people need (Ungar, 2006; Jeanes, 2011). Programmes that aim simply to strengthen individuals' self-efficacy or self-esteem, or encourage ambition, may underestimate the difficulties that many at-risk young people face in continuing in education, or entering the labour market.

Outcomes

Given the variety of contexts and programmes, the desired strategic outcomes will necessarily vary. For example, similar to many sport-for-development programmes, the programmes in this evaluation had a wide variety of vaguely formulated, desired strategic outcomes – ranging from changing presumed racist attitudes, via developing presumed weak aspirations to ending gang-related violence.

Reading Figure 7.1

This tentative broad programme theory is most certainly not presented as definitive, but is an attempt to provide a template to permit those designing and delivering such programmes to 'situate' themselves, or to think about issues of design and delivery. In terms of theoretical interrogation and practical development it is offered simply as a first step in seeking to understand programme processes and mechanisms – perhaps to 'de-reify' sport-for-development (Crabbe, 2000; Coakley, 2011; Hartmann and Kwauk, 2011). The broad thinking underpinning this can be illustrated via two examples (working from left to right in Figure 7.1).

Open-access programmes

These will broadly:

- Attract self-selecting participants who may or may not be characterised by the issues that the programme seeks to address, with the attendant dangers of environmental determinism and an unwarranted deficit view of participants. This is a fundamental issue and is rarely addressed in sport-for-development programmes, yet it raises the core issue of the nature of the desired 'development' and of relevant measures of effectiveness.
- Depend mostly on the supposed inherent properties of sport to achieve desired outcomes – a sports programme rather than *plus sport* or *sport plus*.
- Be provided by a sport coach/leader, rather than those trained to deal with issues of vulnerable youth and/or 'development'.

- Participants and coaches will be unlikely to develop intense personal relationships based on trust and reciprocity.
- Such programmes will have an inconsistent and probably weak impact on values, attitudes and aspirations as participation will only be one of a range of, often more influential, activities and experiences.

Targeted programmes

These will broadly:

- Adopt at least a *sports plus* approach, or may see sport as a 'fly paper' to attract participants to youth work-type programmes.
- Adopt a role model or even a befriending or mentoring approach. This also contains the possibility of using peer leaders although, as outlined in Chapter 6, there are a number of considerations to be made about their relevance and effectiveness.
- Place a strong and systematic emphasis on attitude change, behavioural modification and achievement. This can be reflected in the hidden curriculum and/or via various workshops and discussions.
- Develop relationships of respect, trust and reciprocity as a basis for behaviour change.
- Assist in, and systematically promote, the development of self-worth, ambition and direction among participants. Again, such impacts will not be left to the supposed 'power' of sport.

Programme notes

As argued in Chapter 3, Figure 7.1 *cannot* be read as implying a simple uni-linear path from recruitment to the achievement of the desired impacts and outcomes. Following Bandura (1994) and Pawson and Tilley (2004), central to the process of personal change is the requirement that participants make choices and change their reasoning. This, in part, depends on participants' previous experiences, beliefs and attitudes, opportunities and access to various types of resources. The key assumption underpinning a programme theory approach is that the various activities, processes, relationships and experiences that constitute a programme are designed and delivered in such a way as to maximise the possibility of participants making what are regarded as positive choices. In a sense programmes need to start with the desired strategic outcomes and impacts and work backwards (this is the logic underpinning Witt and Crompton's [1997] protective factors framework). What are the elements in the programme that will change sectarian attitudes? What are the experiences that will lead to an end to gang membership? In other words such outcomes have to be formulated within an appraisal of what each programme can realistically seek to achieve. For example, it is unlikely that open access, self-selecting traditional sports programmes can have realistic aims of improving the educational achievement or employment prospects of all or most participants. The more fundamental changes in values, attitudes and behaviours that underpin crime reduction, reduced drug taking or improved employment prospects are more realistically related to more intensive *sport plus* and *plus sport* approaches. Depending on the degree of social vulnerability, or at-risk status, such outcomes tend to be achieved via particular social climates, longer-term social relationships and forms of direction setting and coaching.

This is presented as tentative and others are invited to interrogate, disagree and/or develop the proposed progamme theory through practice and research. Finally, the data from this evaluation serves to illustrate and reinforce Pawson *et al.*'s (2004: 7) contention that:

> It is through the workings of entire systems of social relationships that any changes in behaviours, events and social conditions are effected. ... Rarely if ever is the 'same' programme equally effective in all circumstances because of the influence of contextual factors.

8

SOCIAL CAPITAL

A social good or for the social good?

Introduction

In launching the International Year of Sport and PE the United Nations (2005: 1) stated that although it had previously collaborated with a range of organisations in the commercial, public and voluntary sectors, 'what was missing, however, was a systematic approach to an important sector in civil society: sport'. This is followed by the assertion of the need to 'ensure that this powerful and diverse element of civil society becomes an active and committed force in the global partnership for development'. In an earlier document the United Nations (2003: 15) stressed the centrality of volunteering in sport and argued that it contributes to 'social welfare, community participation, generation of trust and reciprocity, and the broadening of social interaction through new networks. Consequently, volunteerism creates social capital, helping to build and consolidate social cohesion and stability'. Here the themes of this chapter are identified – civil society, social capital and the role of sport-for-development organisations.

The UN turns to civil society and sport's opportunity

The World Bank (nd) defines civil society as:

> [T]he wide array of non-governmental and not-for-profit organizations that have a presence in public life, expressing the interests and values of their members or others, based on ethical, cultural, political, scientific, religious or philanthropic considerations. Civil Society Organizations (CSOs) therefore refer to a wide of array of organizations: community groups, non-governmental organizations (NGOs), labor unions, indigenous groups, charitable organizations, faith-based organizations, professional associations, and foundations.

As outlined in Chapter 2, the United Nation's turn to civil society was a culmination of a more general increased interest in the 1980s, which accelerated in the 1990s and reflected a broader shift in the 'aid paradigm' (Renard, 2006). This new paradigm is illustrated in the World Bank's increased emphasis on the potential of social capital, community and social relations to contribute to various types of social development and economic growth. Woolcock and Narayan (2000) argue that the new emphasis on civil society and social capital reflected a recognition that the concentration of development policy on the economic dimension was too narrow, often dismissing various aspects of traditional social relations and networks as being obstacles to development, rather than potential resources. In fact, Portes and Landolt (2000) suggest that the new emphasis represented an attempt to repair the damage done by previous policies, with their emphasis on market forces, increasing income disparities, atomization and the erosion of communal normative controls. However, the precise nature of civil society in non-industrialised societies has been the subject of debate (Pollard and Court, 2005) with some commentators raising questions about the utility of the term. Comaroff and Comaroff (1999) suggest that the notion of a 'vacuum' to be filled by NGOs – or sport-for-development organisations – is misplaced and that the concept of civil society needs to be broader and include involuntary membership and kinship relations. For example, a NORAD report (2002: 3) on civil society in Mozambique concluded:

> An estimated 60 per cent of the population lives according to traditional norms and structures with little notion of the state, formal laws and their rights. Governance is in the hands of indigenous/"non-state"/"non-system" leaders and structures that exist in many if not most areas, the leaders have legitimacy in that their position and their powers are accepted by the local communities and there is a degree of formality, structure and division of responsibilities. They have important functions in the distribution of resources (especially land), the resolution of conflicts, and in some cases even impose "taxes".

Van Rooy (2004: 26) suggests that within development policy the concept of civil society has become an 'analytical hatstand' on which donors can opportunistically hang a range of ideas around politics, organization and citizenship. Further, Renard (2006: 18) suggests that the broader vision of civil society in this paradigm is largely 'non-conflictive and not overtly political' – being based on a rather romanticised communitarianism (Woolcock and Narayan, 2000). There is a strong similarity between this non-conflictual, non-political communitarian paradigm and the sports evangelists' representation of sport as a 'neutral' social space where all citizens, or so-called 'sports people', meet as equals in an environment regarded as an 'unambiguously wholesome and healthy activity in both a physical and moral sense' (Smith and Waddington, 2004: 281). However, in various policy documents the concepts of civil society and social capital remain untheorized and, to extend Kruse's (2006) comments, are intriguingly vague and open for several interpretations. When combined with the vague notion of sport-for-development, they present substantial issues for analysis and evaluation.

We will return to these themes below, but within the new paradigm the notion of social capital is seen to hold 'the promise of a ground-up alternative to the top-down policies promoted by international financial organisations in the recent past' (Portes and Landolt, 2000: 530). The hope is that, where national and local states are weak or non-existent, organisations in civil society and the degrees of trust and reciprocity they are presumed to engender can provide informal social insurance, increase community participation, strengthen democracy and facilitate various types of social development and economic growth. For example, The World Bank (2010) argues that civil society organisations are important because they:

- Give voice to stakeholders, particularly poor and marginalized populations, and help to ensure that their views are factored into policy and programme decisions.
- Promote public sector transparency and accountability and contribute to the enabling environment for good governance.
- Promote public consensus and local ownership for reforms, national poverty reduction, and development strategies by building common ground for understanding and encouraging public–private cooperation.
- Bring innovative ideas and solutions, as well as participatory approaches to solve local problems.
- Strengthen and leverage development programs by providing local knowledge, targeting assistance, and generating social capital at the community level.
- Provide professional expertise and increase capacity for effective service delivery, especially in environments with weak public sector capacity, or in post-conflict contexts.

This broad shift from top-down economic aid to an increased emphasis on aspects of civil society and bottom-up community development, from economic capital to social capital, provided a major opportunity for the sport-for-development lobby and permitted it to argue for sport's contributions to aspects of the new aid paradigm (Coalter, 2008). For example, Hognestad (2005: 23) illustrates that the Norwegian government's *Action Plan for the eradication of poverty in the South 2015* emphasises the connections between poverty and cultural conditions and the significance of securing cultural rights as an important part of the fight against poverty. Further, while the concept of social capital is not explicitly stated, it is clearly implied by the UN statement that

> [l]ocal development through sport particularly benefits from an integrated partnership approach to sport-for-development involving a full spectrum of actors in field-based community development including all levels of and various sectors of government, sports organisations, NGOs and the private sector. Strategic sport-based partnerships can be created within a common framework providing a structured environment allowing for coordination, knowledge and expertise sharing and cost-effectiveness.
>
> *(United Nations 2005: 7)*

Consequently there is a need to promote partnerships that enable resource mobilisation 'both for and through sport' as 'effectively designed sports programmes ... are a valuable tool to initiate social development and improve social cohesion' (United Nations, 2003: 20, 12).

Sport-for-development and social capital

A feature of much writing and research in this area is its descriptive nature. Further, a normative communitarian sentiment often informs research – even the critics seem to believe in the essential communitarian properties of sport, which are compromised by top-down impositions by so-called neo-liberal, neo-colonialist funders (Lindsey and Grattan, 2012; Darnell and Hayhurst, 2012). For example, Okada and Young (2012) provide an analysis of the relative failure of a Cambodian programme to promote collegiality and harmony among hotel staff and encourage friendship and respect between the staff of rival hotels. Although they conclude that notions of sport for social development should be 'viewed through the lens of caution and circumspection' (Okada and Young, 2012: 23) they nevertheless feel the need to refer to 'the genuine human spirit of optimism and hope ... [and] the basic value of sports – such as teamwork, effort and achievement' (Okada and Young, 2012: 23, 22).

Such perspectives can lead to the illustration of the existence of some degree of social cooperation, emotional mutuality and understanding as being taken to be indicative of the presence of an imprecisely defined 'social capital'. This is viewed as 'inherently good, the more the better, and its presence always has a positive effect on a community's welfare' (Woolcock and Narayan 2000: 229). For example, Driscoll and Wood (1999) explore the role of Australian rural sport and recreation clubs in periods of social and economic change and their contribution to development of social capital. They conclude that such sports clubs have the 'potential' to perform wide-ranging socio-cultural functions, including leadership, participation, skill development, providing a community hub, health promotion, social networks, community identity and a local sense of control. However, their definition of the term social capital – 'a collective term for the ties that bind us' – is vague, with limited theoretical and analytical utility. Burnett (2001) draws on her extensive work in South African townships to argue for a range of potential impacts associated with the Australia–South Africa Sport Development Programme. Reflecting the difficulties of working in such circumstances, small samples, the absence of some pre-and post-intervention measurements and the adaptation of questions, no meaningful quantifiable triangulated conclusions could be drawn. However, Burnett (2001) suggests that the following were outcomes of the programme:

- Mutual acceptance and trust among age cohorts (e.g. within and between different sexes).
- Development of an attitude of care.
- Development of social conscience and active citizenship.
- Increased intra-group cohesion, although this relates to coaches/volunteers.

- Access to networks (e.g. schools, local government, facilities).
- Empowerment (e.g. accredited education and training).

Importantly, Burnett (2001) emphasises that any assessment of the impact of a programme can only be properly understood against the backdrop of poverty, lack of resources (financial, facilities, educational) and associated behaviours (e.g. apathy, violence and interdependent functioning). As we will see, this raises significant issues about the validity of using the concept of social capital to describe such relationships.

If we take as our starting point Szreter's (1998) assertion that social capital is not just a public good in and of itself, but is *for* the public good, then it is essential to view social capital in terms of the nature of the resources it contains, gives access to and the actions that it facilitates. The description of mutual acceptance and trust, increased inter-group cohesion and access to networks and facilities (Burnett, 2001) or 'ties that bind us together' (Driscoll and Wood, 1999) or 'meaningful, purposeful, pleasurable socialization experiences' (Spaaij, 2012: 1535) could be regarded as insufficient to define fully the nature of social capital and its potential contribution to 'development'. This is because, as we will see, aspects of apparently positive social capital can be non-inclusive, non-developmental and networks can be resource poor. For example, Burnett (2001: 55) in her analysis of a sport-for-development initiative in South Africa remarked that 'neither the schools nor the households, which were subjected to a subsistence level of existence, could contribute meaningfully to provide material resources to implement the programme'. Consequently they were unable to mobilise resources *for* sport, never mind through sport (United Nations, 2003). To explore some of these issues it is necessary to look more closely at the theorists of social capital.

Which social capital?

There are three main theorists of social capital: two sociologists – Bourdieu (1997) and Coleman (1988–9: 1994) and one political scientist – Putnam (2000). All three would broadly accept the general definition of social capital as referring to social networks based on social and group norms, which enable people to trust and cooperate with each other and via which individuals or groups can obtain certain types of advantage. However, there are significant differences between the three perspectives related to their assumptions about the nature of society, human motivation, social relationships, power, the basis of trust and the nature and purpose of social capital – issues frequently ignored in the description of forms of social relationships, sociability and communality. In terms of our concerns with sport-for-development and the rather vague way in which social capital is applied, Coleman and Putnam are the most relevant.

Coleman, social capital and human capital

Although Coleman (1994) is rarely quoted in discussions about sport-for-development, his concerns with the relationship between social capital and the development of human capital (education, employment skills and expertise) are directly relevant. Field (2003: 33) argues that because Coleman (1994) draws on individualistic rational choice theory, 'social capital was a means of explaining how people manage to cooperate', with it representing social processes resulting from the free choice of individuals to further their self-interest. Coleman (1994) views social capital as largely neutral aspects of social structure and social relationships that facilitate actions and he stresses the conscious actions of individuals in the development and use of social capital. In this context social capital is viewed as

> the set of resources that inhere in family relations and in community social organisation and that are useful for the cognitive or social development of a child or young person. These resources differ for different persons and constitute an important advantage for children and adolescents in the development of their human capital.
>
> *(Coleman, 1994: 300)*

Further, as Johnston and Percy-Smith (2003) illustrate, Coleman identifies three essential social and structural aspects of relations of social capital: (i) obligations, expectations and trustworthiness of structures; (ii) information channels; (iii) norms and effective sanctions, which facilitate 'closure' of such networks and ensure that obligations are met and 'freeloaders' are expelled. The importance of such sanctions and norms lies in the expectation of reciprocity and the fact that an individual's 'investment' (e.g. time, effort) is not made for altruistic reasons, but in the strong expectation that it will pay future dividends – the favour will be returned. Coleman's (1994) ontology – rational choice theory that assumes that individuals act to balance costs against benefits to maximise personal advantage – is an ontological position at odds with the often populist communitarian rhetoric of sport, underpinned by team metaphors. Further, as this implies that the nature of such relationships is contingent on ongoing and negotiated mutuality, it raises significant issues for the rather rose-tinted cross-sectional descriptions of positive social relationships.

Coleman (1988–9: S117) places his analysis within an historical context by referring to the decline and eventual disappearance of 'the voluntary and spontaneous social organisation that has in the past been the major source of social capital available to the young'. In this regard Portes (1998: 10) notes that Coleman (1988–9) laments the decline of the 'close or dense ties' associated with 'primordial' institutions based on the family and emphasises the need to replace these with 'rationally devised material and status incentives'. In this regard it is worth noting that many sport-for-development organisations place a strong emphasis on the need for young people to remain in education and some provide financial support for them to do so. Further, there is a widespread emphasis on the development of various aspects of human capital (e.g. transferable social and organisational skills), trust and collective responsibility, accompanied in many cases by rationally devised material and status incentives – educational grants for voluntary work, the possibility of foreign travel. However, theory and evidence would suggest that permanent organisations with stable memberships, rather than sports teams or short-term sports projects, are more able to develop the necessary 'close or dense ties' (we will return to this below).

Putnam and social capitals

Putnam's (2000) version of social capital is the one that tends to inform the rather vague assertions in the policy rhetoric of sport-for-development. Putnam (2000) places much less emphasis on kinship relations, closure, instrumentalism and more or less conscious choice. His appeal to policy makers is that he is more interested in the role of organised voluntary associations and collective outcomes – a form of communitarianism that fits well with ideologies of sport. From his perspective social capital can be regarded as a public good, which serves to bind communities together – clearly attractive to those who place emphasis on inclusion, cooperation and collective action as a path to 'development'. Social capital is viewed as an essentially neutral resource that is a property of collectives – communities, cities, regions. For Putnam (2000: 18–19) 'the core idea of social capital is that social networks have value ... [it refers to] connections between individuals – social networks and the norms of reciprocity and trustworthiness that arise from them'.

Communities with high levels of social capital are viewed as being characterised by three main components – strong social networks and civic infrastructure, which are characterised by strong social norms (i.e. informal and formal rules about personal and social behaviour) and associated sanctions for transgression, which both support and reinforce mutual trust and reciprocity among members of a community. Putnam (2000) views the civic engagement, associational life and volunteering associated with social capital as important because they improve the efficiency of communities by facilitating coordinated actions, reducing transaction costs (e.g. high levels of trust facilitate commerce via less dependency on formal contractual agreements) and enabling communities to be more effective in pursuit of their collective interests. Its potential value for development is indicated by Woolcock and Narayan (2000: 23) who state that 'social capital includes norms and values that facilitate exchanges, lower transaction costs, reduce the cost of information, permit trade in the absence of contracts and encourage responsible citizenship and the collective management of resources'.

Putnam (2000) distinguishes between two types of social capital – bonding and bridging. The former refers to networks based on strong social ties between similar people – people 'like us' – with relations, reciprocity and trust based on ties of familiarity and closeness. Putnam (2000: 33) refers to this as a type of 'sociological superglue', whose function is to enable people to 'get by' and which works to maintain a strong in-group loyalty and to reinforce specific identities. Many writing within the mainstream development literature acknowledge that for people living in highly deprived communities, such networks are a key resource and an important basis for cooperation and survival. However, for many analysts development depends on *bridging social capital*, which refers to weaker social ties between different types of people – more 'colleagues' than family and friends. This is less of a glue than 'a sociological WD40' (Putnam, 2000: 23) and facilitates 'getting ahead' via, for example, the diffusion of information, employment opportunities and resources not available via the more closed and resource-poor networks of bonding social capital.

Whereas bonding and bridging social capital tend to be concerned with horizontal social relationships, Woolcock (2001) proposes the additional concept of 'linking social capital', which refers to vertical connections between different social strata, including those outside the community. As this type of social capital offers access to wider networks and the potential to leverage a broader range of resources, it seems a key link to development and we will return to it below.

Most of the descriptive research in sport-for-development seems to be based on some version of bonding social capital – 'a collective term for the ties that bind us' (Driscoll and Wood, 1999; see also Burnett, 2001; Tonts 2005). Certainly, aspects of bonding social capital could be regarded as part of the historic role of sports clubs as a form of mutual self-help. Like-minded people, often from similar economic circumstances, ages, educational backgrounds, sex, social class, race and religion, come together to produce and consume a common interest – a particular sport. If we move beyond the simple use of the terms 'sport' and 'participation', and begin to conceptualise the issues around more formal and stable clubs and organisations, it is clear that, to varying degrees, they are capable of developing forms of bonding social capital that provide a basis for resource mobilisation for sport and, to a certain extent, *through* sport (United Nations 2003).

To illustrate some of these issues we turn to a case study of the Mathare Youth Sport Association (MYSA). The MYSA example also serves to illustrate a central premise of the book – that if 'sport' is to make any contribution to 'development' then this is most likely to be achieved via a stable, bottom-up and embedded organisational setting, than via isolated teams or short-term projects dominated by non-indigenous volunteers.

The Mathare Youth Sport Association

Mathare, in northeast Nairobi, is one of the largest and poorest slums in Africa, with a population of about 500,000 living in an area of two kilometres by 300 metres (1.2 miles by 0.2 miles). It is a maze of low, rusted iron-sheeting roofs with mud walls. Housing is wholly inadequate, with most houses measuring about eight feet by six feet and holding up to ten people. Few houses have running water, open gutters of sewage run throughout, the road infrastructure is extremely poor, refuse and litter dominate the area and the local authority provides few services (www.mysakenya. org; Brady and Kahn, 2002; Willis, 2000). MYSA was established by Bob Munro (a Canadian United Nations environmental development officer) in 1987 as a small self-help project to organise soccer. The concentration on soccer is explained by the high levels of local interest, low-skill entry levels and basic facility and equipment costs. It is now the largest youth sports organisation in Africa, with more than 1,000 teams and about 20,000 members. MYSA's teams range from under ten to 18 years of age, organised in 16 zones – the biggest league in Africa. MYSA also has two male semi-professional teams, Mathare United A and B. These teams were established to provide a top of the sports development pyramid, provide motivation and relevant role models for junior players and to provide a source of collective pride and identity. In light of the analysis to be presented below it is essential to remember that MYSA is a highly successful *sports development* programme – in 2009 Mathare United supplied 11 players for Kenya's African Nation's Cup squad, plus its manager and coach and they have won both the Moi Cup and the Kenyan Premier League title.

Producing citizens

MYSA initially attracted young males who played on waste ground in the slums with juwalas – footballs made of recycled plastic bags and twine. The attraction of MYSA was threefold: first, access to real footballs (not to be underestimated in conditions of such poverty); second, organized and structured games, which simulated the professional game; third, an ordered and protective environment, which was especially important for the many street children attracted to MYSA. However, it soon developed into a much more complex and ambitious *sport plus* project, whose ultimate ambition is to produce citizens – 'the leaders needed for building the new Kenya' (Munro 2005: 5). Consequently, soccer is an entry point – a flypaper – to a comprehensive, interdependent programme – almost a small community – in which all elements are mutually reinforcing in order to produce a form of social capital. Some of these elements are outlined by Munro (2005) as follows:

- Youth are owners and decision makers. They are elected from zonal league committees to the Sports Council/Community Service Council and then to the MYSA Executive Council. The constitution requires equal male/female representation. As with all such organisations, recruitment and retention of young women presents difficulties. However, Brady and Kahn (2002) state: 'Girls' participation can begin to change community norms about their roles and capacities. In this way, sports may be a catalyst for the transformation of social norms'.
- To help youth to help themselves by helping others. Reflecting a key component of bonding social capital, Munro argues that 'when you are poor, cooperation and sharing are crucial for survival'.
- To help young leaders to stay in school. This is achieved via a points-based educational scholarship system, with points being awarded for volunteer activities such as coaching, refereeing and community service – an example of Coleman's (1988–9) rationally devised material and status incentives.

These various organisational philosophies and practices clearly reflect components of definitions of social capital – social networks based on social and group norms, which enable people to trust and cooperate with each other and via which individuals or groups can obtain certain types of advantage. Further, this is clearly a form of bonding social capital as it is based on strong social ties of familiarity and closeness between people who share very similar social, cultural and economic circumstances –

many members refer to MYSA as a 'family'. This is reinforced by the fact that all full-
and part-time employees are recruited from MYSA members, who are all residents of
the Mathare slum and who appear to possess a deep sense of responsibility to act as
positive role models. The sense of involvement, responsibility and values of active
citizenship are reinforced by members' involvement in decision making at all levels,
with a strong emphasis on mutual self-help – stated succinctly by Munro (2005) as
'you do something, MYSA does something. You do nothing, MYSA does nothing'.
This ethic of reciprocity, which serves as a form of closure thereby reducing the
problem of freeloaders, is especially important in a wider society where there is
widespread corruption. In this regard, although the numbers are small, MYSA has
imposed sanctions and expulsions on those who have failed to conform to the social
and group norms.

Sport plus: rationally devised material and status incentives

However, from the perspective of sport-for-development, it is essential to understand
that MYSA does not depend on any simple view of 'sports participation' to maximise
the possibility of achieving desired impacts and outcomes. For example, the rules of
soccer have been amended and during games anyone other than the captain who
speaks to an official can be sent off (a substitute player is permitted). However, punishment is accompanied by learning-by-doing, with the player required to referee ten
junior matches to put him or herself in the place of a referee before being permitted
to play again. Henry Majale, a current member of MYSA's senior management team
experienced this punishment and views it as having been a highly positive experience!
In addition, a green card is awarded by the referee to the most sporting player and
this is accompanied by the award of educational scholarship points – fairness brings its
rewards. As part of its commitment to helping young people to stay in school, MYSA
has about 400 annual leadership awards. Although schooling is free up to the age of
14, many schools require pupils to wear uniforms – prohibitive for many of those
living in poverty – and in the post-14 schools fees are required. The awards are paid to
the school of the winners' choice and are used to pay for tuition, books and uniforms.
Points towards these awards are also linked to volunteering, peer leadership and
coaching work. It is interesting that older players often accumulate these points for
their younger brothers or sisters, illustrating an important aspect of social capital – that
the social relations/networks provide access to significant resources and advantages. In
addition, MYSA provides small libraries and study rooms to compensate for the lack
of study space in overcrowded dwellings. An interesting illustration of the MYSA
philosophy is that when I initially visited on a project funded by UK Sport to look at
sport-for-development, the first place to which I was taken was a small and cramped
library filled with very studious young people sat around a large table in a very small
room. At first I thought that they had mistaken me for someone from UNICEF, but
it was a clear indication that educational and personal development rather than sport
was at the centre of their philosophy.

A more general commitment to community service is required. The aim of the work is to increase environmental awareness and entails a weekly 'clean up', in which teams clear drains, cut grass and remove litter. Although this work makes little overall impact on the overwhelming environmental problems of Mathare, the core value being emphasised is that of collective responsibility and reciprocity – 'if you get something from the community you must put something back into the community' (Munro, 2005). The extent of programme integration and the re-enforcement of values are emphasised by the fact that each completed clean-up project earns a soccer team three points towards its league standings – sporting success is a combination of sporting talent and social responsibility.

Rather than reflecting Putnam's (2000) somewhat 'organic' view of social capital, the MYSA approach seems to be closer to Coleman's (1994) 'rationally devised material and status incentives' (Portes, 1998: 10) that he saw as compensating for the weakening of family, community and local government structures. It also illustrates aspects of Coleman's (1994) perspective about the close relationship between social capital and the development of human capital and his greater emphasis on the more conscious and self-interested aspects of social capital and their importance for children's education and development. For example, initial parental resistance to girls' participation is often overcome once parents realise the educational and other benefits to be obtained. Further, issues of reciprocity and trust are clearly and regularly articulated and reinforced within the organization, rather than simply assumed, or illustrated via sanctions for transgression.

Consequently, MYSA's importance and effectiveness goes well beyond any simple definition of 'sport', or the traditional functions of most sporting organisations (Coalter, 2007). In effect, it operates in a number of areas in civil society, seeking to compensate for major failures of the local and national states' welfare provision – facilitated and given coherence by soccer and soccer-related programmes. Although MYSA is a particularly sophisticated example of a *sport plus* organisation, it is also based partly on an approach that is characteristic of many sport-for-development organisations – the development and use of volunteer youth peer leaders, educators and coaches.

Volunteering plus

We have noted the United Nation's (2003) assertion that volunteerism creates social capital and helps to build and consolidate social cohesion and stability. This mirrors Putnam's (2000) emphasis on civic engagement, associational life and volunteering. In traditional sports development programmes leaders and coaches are simply inputs – qualified sports development officers who use their professional expertise to develop programmes for local communities. However, by adopting a youth peer-leader approach, many sport-for-development organisations involve young men and women at various levels of planning, implementation and decision making, providing important experience of control, empowerment and a sense of collective responsibility, via the much emphasised and important status of 'role models'. In other words, people or 'responsible citizens' are a major output and input of many such organisations. They are central to their financial sustainability and precede the programmes whose broader impacts are often the subject of assertion or, sometimes, evaluation. (See Chapter 6 for a critical evaluation of the concepts of role models and peer leaders.)

Consequently, volunteer peer leaders, teachers and coaches are at the centre of such organisations and programmes – both practically and symbolically (Nicholls, 2009). We have already noted in Chapter 6 that peer leaders are a vital resource for financial sustainability; are an attractive value added for aid agencies; their use is based on sound (if usually implicit) educational and learning theory (Bandura, 1962); to be effective, role models must be embedded, have perceived similarities to, and limited social distance between them and the learner; learning is based on the development of supportive, longer-term trusting relationships (see Bandura, 1962; Payne *et al.*, 2003). In addition, Saavedra (2005) and Brady and Kahn (2002) emphasise the special importance of female role models in sport-for-development organisations, most of which seek to confront traditional, exploitative and often abusive social relations.

Social capital: motivation and differential distribution

In this regard a better understanding of how such organisations work might be gained by adopting a less romanticised communitarian view of sport, or sporting organisations, and explore the potential range of motivations – from those motivated by Putnam's (2000) civic/democratic/moral values to more Coleman-like instrumentalism (Gaskin and Smith, 1995; Portes, and Landolt, 2000). In my experience there appears to be a substantial ethos of altruism, sense of belonging and collective responsibility among many youth peer leaders. However, in many cases this is accompanied and reinforced by rationally devised material and status incentives – access to educational scholarships, foreign travel to competitions, status within the organisation and community, increased employability – which appear to be closer to Coleman's (1994) more instrumental and self-interested approach. This is wholly understandable in conditions of extreme poverty, but the nature of motivations and incentives has clear implications for the design and use of sport-in-development programmes and for our understanding of the nature and stability of the social capital that they produce.

The issues of motivation and meaning also raise another important issue when discussing social capital and sport-for-development – the possible differential distribution of benefits, which is referred to by Fukuyama (2001: 2) as the 'radius of trust'. For example, where an organisation's social capital produces positive externalities (e.g. via MYSA's clean-up activities and educational scholarships) then the radius of trust can be larger than the group – an outcome clearly implied by much policy rhetoric in sport-for-development. However, while it is clear that there are collective benefits as a result of the ability of the organisation to mobilise and maximise the use of sporting resources (e.g. access to limited playing space), there is also likely to be a differential distribution of social capital and its benefits *within* the organisation – the collective strengths of social capital inevitably benefit some more than others. Fukuyama (2001) suggests that it is probable that trust-based and cooperative norms are strongest among the organisations' leadership and permanent staff. For example, those most actively involved over time will be those most likely to benefit via the development of their human capital, social networks and increased employability (Seippel, 2006; Skidmore et al., 2006). To presume that this happens to all participants, whose participation might be both erratic and short term, seems wholly unwarranted. For example, this widespread and seemingly inevitable situation is used by Spaaij (2012) to criticise Melbourne sports clubs for failing to offer Somalis opportunities to develop 'linking capital'. In a small qualitative study of the Edusport organisation in Zambia, Mwaanga (2003) illustrates that the level and intensity of participation were key moderators of programme effectiveness – not surprisingly the youth peer leaders were more likely to benefit than ordinary participants. They are the most committed, have gone through the various training programmes, have experience of decision making and perceptions of control and status and are highly conscious of their positions and responsibilities as role models, both in the organisation and the community (see Chapter 6).

Such comments are not criticisms – to produce a cadre of highly committed and responsible youth peer leaders (especially female) in such difficult economic and cultural circumstances is clearly an achievement. Rather, the comments simply emphasise the need to reject easy generalisations about sport-for-development and 'social capital'. There is a need to more systematically understand how certain types of organisations work, the extent to which they produce which type of social capital, the nature and extent of the 'radius of trust' and if rather simple sport-for-development 'projects' have any meaningful role to play in mobilising resources both for and *through* sport and improving social cohesion (United Nations, 2003). For example, Woodcock *et al.* (2012: 378) suggest that 'a range of impacts is likely to increase positively as the organisation becomes established in a local area' and that there is a need 'to provide continuity ... in order for community members to trust and respect the organisation'.

If we accept Coleman's (1994) perspective, there are clearly identifiable structural and social components of organisations or communities that produce and sustain certain types of social capital – these are issues for empirical investigation rather than theoretical assertion.

Bonding capital and the economy of affection

MYSA illustrates the potential of sport-for-development organisations to compensate for certain aspects of the wider failures of national and local states, weak civic structures and disintegrating families. However, it must be emphasised that this analysis is based on stable, complex organisational *sport-plus* structures and not on short-term simple sport-focused programmes, nor is it claimed to apply community wide. Such *organisations* have the potential to develop, consciously and systematically, forms of social capital by providing young men and women with rare opportunities to participate in decision making, confront exploitative gender relations, encourage and support ambition, recognise the value of education, develop relationships based on trust and reciprocity and provide opportunities for the development of aspects of human capital. In this regard Woodcock *et al.* (2012: 378) found that 'there are clear and significant impacts of membership duration' and that 'improvement in psychological constructs such as well-being, self-esteem, quality of life, safety and resilience, may be more a result of the development of a positive enabling culture within a *project community*' (emphasis added). Simply playing sport regularly or irregularly may or may not have its benefits, but its ability to develop such forms of social capital – i.e. more than simple sociability – must be doubted, unless evidence illustrates otherwise.

However, academics and policy makers concerned with various forms of community development express reservations about the limitations of bonding social capital – especially for contributing to wider policies of social and economic regeneration or development. They urge caution and suggest that strong bonding capital can have substantially negative effects, with Woolcock and Narayan (2000) referring to bonding social capital as a 'double-edged sword'.

Putnam (2000) acknowledges that there may be a 'dark side' to bonding capital if it acts to impose conformity and downward levelling and excludes 'outsiders'. This is partly illustrated by Tonts' (2005) analysis of the role of local sports clubs in the development and maintenance of social capital in relatively isolated rural communities in Western Australia that are suffering economic and social decline. Because of a lack of alternative social provision the clubs played a central role in sustaining social networks, fostering social interaction and providing a sense of place and community. It is proposed that the clubs also made a contribution to bridging capital by overcoming community social and cultural barriers, which was necessary in order for the clubs to survive. The clubs are wholly dependent on volunteers for fundraising and facility maintenance and the author emphasises the trust, altruism and reciprocity central to these activities, which are increasingly stressful in communities with declining populations. However, the author also refers to 'sporting tribalism' and to 'social sorting' and refers to evidence of class and ethnic fractures in the running of the supposedly egalitarian Australian Rules football club. Further, there were issues relating to the status of, and attitude towards, Aboriginal people, raising questions about the ability of sport to build longstanding and meaningful social capital across different racial groups. The author also raises issues about sex-based exclusions and the sense of social exclusion felt by some non-sports participants.

Second, Forrest and Kearns (1999: 1) argue that while it is possible that social capital can assist in community bonding, cohesion is not necessarily positive and may lead to 'defensive communities' – linking disadvantaged individuals together, but effectively excluding them from the wider society and its resources and opportunities and effectively restricting routes out of poverty and reinforcing exclusion. For example, Hyden (1983: 8) refers to 'the economy of affection', which is defined in terms similar to bonding social capital – 'a network of support, communications and interaction among structurally defined groups connected by blood, kin, community or other affiliation, for example, religion'. The importance of this is that it is often 'so strong that it easily subverts conventional modes of development based on state or market' (Hyden, 2006: 2). This is because greater emphasis is placed on social reproduction and subsistence than on production, investment and profit and the culture has a strong emphasis on financial, social and political reciprocity. Calderisi

(2007: 83) puts it rather bluntly, referring to 'the tyranny of family loyalty', which means that 'if someone succeeds, however modestly, relatives will often insist on sharing in the fruits of that accomplishment'. The economy of affection can lead to what many might regard as nepotism. In one sport-for-development organisation the chief executive appointed a number of staff on the basis of family connections rather than relevant skill and expertise. While this is an understandable expression of family loyalty and the economy of affection, it almost inevitably leads to dysfunctional organisations.

Portes and Landolt (2000) provide examples that go beyond family and where community closure combines with an economy of affection to prevent the success of business initiatives by enforcing excessive claims on entrepreneurs. They quote Geertz's example of how successful businessmen in Bali 'were constantly assaulted by job and loan-seeking kinsmen on the strength of community norms enjoining mutual assistance' (Geertz, 1963: 522). This resulted in stunted investment and growth and eventual bankruptcy. They also quote an example from the Ecuadorean highlands where many cloth and leather artisans converted to Protestantism:

> The reason has little to do with their religious convictions or affinity to the 'Protestant ethic', but with the need to escape the host of obligations enforced by the Catholic *cofradias*. For these hard-working artisans, negative social capital comes in the form of repeated requests to finance religious festivities and bear the cost of food and drink for the rest of the community.
>
> *(Portes and Landolt, 2000: 522)*

Can we go beyond the touchline?

Related to Forrest and Kearns' (1999) concern about the linking together of disadvantaged individuals is the widespread danger that 'equating social capital with the resources acquired through it can easily lead to tautological statements' (Portes, 1998). In other words many networks will be internally and externally 'resource poor'. For example, Fernández-Kelly (1995: 217–218), reporting on a study of the African-American community of West Baltimore, argued that 'social capital generated by their families can only be parlayed into resources existing in their physical surroundings. Because these resources tend to be of poor quality, the advantages derived from social capital are few'. Consequently, in all approaches to the identification and analysis of social capital we need to address the implications of Szretzer's (1998) assertion that social capital is not simply a social good, but it is *for* the social good. While sport-for-development organisations may manage to promote many positive aspects of bonding social capital, there is a danger of failing to recognise that such networks are usually resource poor. They may have the ability to mobilise resource *for* sport, although Burnett (2001) provides an example of where they did not. However, their ability to mobilise resources *through* sport for 'development' will be much more limited – developing sport may be easier than sport-for-development. For example, Burnett (2010: 36) referring to her research in South Africa, found that the dependency on the 'external' provision of resources for programme implementation and events, timely education and training, dependency on leadership for strengthening institutional capacity and a competitive environment to forge meaningful relationships beyond the social realm of the community, are indicative of the relative delicateness of sustaining bridging and linking ties.

The significance of this again relates to our concern with displacement of scope in that 'local-level cooperation alone cannot overcome macro-structural obstacles to economic stability, autonomous growth, and accumulation' (Portes and Landolt, 2000: 542). Portes and Landolt (2000) agree that the development of forms of social capital is a very attractive proposition for aid agencies, because they can increase the yield of aid and investment (e.g. via volunteer labour and greater openness and accountability). However they caution:

> One must not be over-optimistic about what enforceable trust and bounded solidarity can accomplish at the collective level, especially in the absence of material resources. Social capital can be a powerful force promoting group projects but ... it consists of the ability to marshal resources through social networks, not the resources themselves. When the latter are poor and scarce, the goal achievement capacity of a collectivity is restricted, no matter how strong the internal bonds ... social capital is not a substitute for the provision of credit, material infrastructure and education.
>
> *(Portes and Landolt, 2000: 546)*

Further, we have already noted Renard's (2006) comment that the vision of civil society often tends to be overly communitarian, underplaying politics and conflicts of interest. In this regard Woolcock and Narayan (2000: 235) point to the limitations of civil society organisations in contexts where there is 'rampant corruption, frustrating bureaucratic delays, suppressed civil liberties, and vast inequality'. They refer to the *institutional view* of the role of social capital in development – that civil society organisations are not simple substitutes for the state and can only really thrive to the extent that the state actively encourages them. In other words, in the absence of what they refer to as 'civic and government social capital' such well-intentioned efforts will have limited general impact. (For an example of the negative impacts of corruption in a governing body of sport on a sport-for-development organisation, see Munro, 2006.) Similarly Black (2010: 125) argues that

> development practice, as a process of far-reaching change or even 'creative destruction' at both micro and macro levels, will encounter suspicion and resistance by those who occupy positions of relative privilege and power, whether at the 'grassroots' community level or within national governments.

Here it is worth noting Moyo's (2010: 59) somewhat provocative analysis of the impact of aid on social capital, arguing that by thwarting accountability mechanisms, encouraging rent-seeking behaviour, siphoning off scarce talent from the employment pool and removing pressures to reform inefficient policies and institutions, aid guarantees that in the most aid-dependent regimes social capital remains weak. ... in a world of aid there is no need or incentive to trust your neighbour. ... Thus aid erodes the essential fabric of trust that is needed in any functioning society.

Such analyses raise significant questions about displacement of scope and de-contextualised assertions about sport's ability to develop social capital and mobilise resources *through* sport in order to contribute to 'development'.

Such limitations might be moderated partially by the development of the other forms of social capital – bridging social capital and linking social capital. A study in Japan (Okayasu, Kawahara and Nogawa, 2010) illustrates that cross-generational comprehensive community sports clubs, which include non-sporting activities, were more likely to produce bridging social capital than less inclusive traditional community sports clubs. This is because the majority of traditional community sports clubs' memberships consist of people from the same school and university and from the same generation.

Connected and isolated clubs

Whereas bonding and bridging social capital are concerned with horizontal relationships, linking social capital, (Woolcock, 2001) refers to vertical connections between different social strata, including those entirely outside the community, thereby offering access to wider networks and the potential to leverage a broader range of resources. In fact, Skidmore, Bound and Lownsborough (2006: viii) suggest that policies to promote community participation in governance are usually concerned with linking social capital, because by 'being involved in the governance of services, participants build relationships with public institutions or officials which give their community access to valuable external resources like money, support or political leverage'. In this regard it is worth noting Seippel's (2006) distinction between *connected sports organisations* (i.e. members have ties to members of other associations) and *isolated organisations*, which focus solely on their sport and the local community. The latter may be a vehicle for the mobilisation of resources *for* sport and may achieve certain impacts supposedly associated with participation in sport (e.g. perceived self-efficacy, self-esteem) and develop certain forms of bonding social capital, with varying 'radii of trust'. However, the United Nations' (2005: 7) aspiration for an integrated approach to sport-for-development 'involving a full spectrum of actors in field-based community development including all levels of and various sectors of government, sports organizations, NGOs and the private sector', obviously relates to connected clubs or organisations. Clearly, the extent to which clubs can develop both bridging and linking capital will vary by a range of factors: competitive or recreational; sport or *sport plus*; isolated or connected; size and stability of membership and personnel; longevity and location (e.g. urban or rural). Nevertheless, in some cases they are part of a wider 'sports community', in which participation in leagues, competitions and governing bodies may provide theoretical opportunities for the development of forms of bridging and linking social capital. However, the extent to which this is restricted to 'sporting social capital' – i.e. mobilisation of resources *for* sport, largely within the sports community – is an important empirical question in relation to their potential to contribute to broader processes of development.

Woolcock and Narayan (2000: 231) refer to the combination of bridging and linking social capital as the *networks view,* arguing that 'strong intra-community ties and weak extra-community networks are needed to avoid making tautological claims regarding the efficacy of social capital'. However, the networks view seems to be closer to Coleman's (1994) individualistic perspective than to Putnam's (2000) more communitarian views and returns us to the questions relating to the beneficiaries of forms of social capital – with substantial implications for development. For example, Woolcock and Narayan (2000: 234) suggest that 'this view minimises the "public good" nature of social groups, regarding any benefits of group activity as primarily the property of the particular individuals involved'. Leonard (2004) offers a similar analysis about the potential conflict between strong bonding social capital in Catholic communities in Belfast (as a result of inter-community violence) and the need for small businesses and individual entrepreneurs to develop bridging and linking capital in order to develop and expand their businesses. Whereas bonding social capital may provide a basic collective support and insurance network for the poor, for development to occur it needs to be weak enough to permit the individual poor to gain access to wider and more formal institutions and a more diverse stock of bridging and maybe linking social capital – MYSA's citizens must leave eventually and Ecuadorean artisans must convert to Protestantism.

Some sport-for-development *organisations* (rather than teams or short-term projects) have the potential to gain access to forms of both bridging and linking social capital, although their relationships with national governing bodies, government sports organisations, larger NGOs and local and national government departments vary widely. In particular, the burgeoning international sport-for-development networks provide access to such networks and the funding and resources that accompany them. However, in some cases these relationships are antagonistic and they may be regarded as competitors for limited resources and influence. In this regard Renard (2006) suggests that there may be a conflict at the heart of these relationships in the new aid paradigm – between largely locally determined poverty reduction strategies (or in our case, sport-for-development strategies) and externally imposed Millennium Development Goals, which may skew programmes and not reflect local issues and needs. Renard (2006) posits two contrasting sets of relationships, which can be regarded as forms of linking social capital.

One set of relationships involves donors and recipients pursuing similar policy objectives, based on consensus and trust. It might be hypothesized that this refers to aid given to existing sporting organisations by sporting organisations in a spirit of relative altruism, in order to promote and develop sport and international sporting solidarity (Kidd, 2008; Burnett, 2001). Such aid is nearly always for a *sports plus* approach (at least in terms of the accompanying rhetoric), concerned with sports development and the strengthening of the sporting infrastructure, but always accompanied by a strong implicit belief in the positive impacts supposedly associated with sport.

Renard's (2006) second set of relations is based on the possibility that donors and recipients may have differing agendas. This is more likely where sport's 'fly paper' properties are emphasised and sports organisations are funded, or even specifically constructed, with the purpose of achieving defined, non-sporting social and/or developmental goals. In this regard concern has been expressed about the possible consequences of external aid to such civil society organisations. Some have argued that the rapid growth in influence of locally non-accountable NGOs represents new forces of neo-colonialism, with their main leadership and strategies being formulated in the West they are viewed as promoting new forms of dependency. With regard to sport, Giulianotti (2004) has raised questions about the exporting of overly functionalist views of sport by sports evangelists and questions the nature of the dialogue between donors and recipients and the extent to which empowerment is a goal. As discussed in Chapters 2 and 3 this is a position that has grown in writing on sport-for-development and many argue that this is the predominant relationship – although the generality of much of this critique raises the possibility that it is derived from first principles rather than based on empirical investigation (Darnell, 2007; Lindsey and Grattan, 2012; Darnell and Hayhurst, 2012). It is certainly the case that donors often have unrealistically high and vague aspirations for the contribution of sport to 'development' and that these encourage organisations wholly dependent on external aid to include objectives and programme elements in funding applications that they might not otherwise have contemplated. The necessity to compete for limited resources frequently leads to projects being developed to fit the funding criteria, with the potential to compromise beneficiaries' needs, promote organisational mission drift and the acceptance of donor targets with insufficient implementation capacity (Howells, 2007). However, this is an empirical question as the relationships will vary and it is important to at least consider the possibility that 'exploitation' may not always be one way – if the mission is simply to survive, then there is little drift! Certainly such issues cannot be reduced to abstract theoretical assertions based on vague terminology such as 'neo-colonialism', the 'Global North' and 'Global South' – these owe more to ideology than to robust empirical research.

The nature of such donor/client relationships is important because of a desire to promote forms of social capital, and the more general concerns that 'the essence of social capital is that it consists of activities and relationships freely engaged in by individuals' (Field, 2003: 118). For example, Fukuyama (2001: 18) warns that excessive (state) intervention 'can have a serious negative impact on social capital'. Field (2003) refers to Coleman's (1994) doubts about the ability of constructed forms of organisation to provide the required normative cohesion and network closure central to the effective working of social capital – although this is clearly a matter for empirical investigation. It is worth leaving the last word on this to Bob Munro (2005) who stated that 'the best thing that happened to MYSA was that nobody was interested for the first five years'. The implication of this is that the absence of aid dependency, or the availability of aid, permitted the establishment of locally based aims, objectives, principles and processes – whether these are viewed via the lens of Coleman or Putnam. This also raises significant questions about the possible differences between bottom-up, organic community-based initiatives, those formed rather opportunistically in response to aid opportunities, or those encouraged by the initiative of external aid agencies. The relationships between the so-called Global North and Global South might not be as homogeneous as is asserted.

From ideology to sociology

There are obvious analytical and policy dangers in decontextualised, romanticised, communitarian generalisations about the supposed 'power of sport' to generate 'social capital'. Much of the research and analysis seems to be based on Putnam's (2000) concept of bonding social capital, with the notions of communality and mutuality conveniently reflecting the ideologies of teamwork explicit in sporting ideology. Some research indicates that in small and often isolated communities, sports clubs and organisations can provide a community focus, contributing to sociability and communality – although the research indicates that this has its limits. However, although these can be regarded as positive outcomes, it is reasonable to ask about the extent to which such relationships can be regarded as 'social capital' in an analytical rather than a descriptive sense. Both Coleman (1994) and Putnam (2000) view social capital as a *facilitating* resource – not just a public good, but *for* the public good. In such circumstances cohesion and mutuality are not viewed as developmental ends in themselves, but as means to ends. For example, both emphasise the importance of the nature of the *resources* contained in social networks and that these vary substantially between contexts and between bonding, bridging and linking social capital. In this regard many writers have pointed to the strong possibility that networks of bonding social capital contain limited resources and stress the limitations of what enforceable trust and bounded solidarity can accomplish (Hyden, 1983, 2006; Fernández-Kelly, 1995; Portes and Landolt, 2000; Kruse, 2006).

Putnam (2000) is aware of the 'dark side' of bonding social capital and the potentially non-developmental effects of defensive communities, the exclusion of outsiders, the enforcement of conformity and downward levelling – often expressed via the economy of affection (Hyden, 1983). Further, even where positive relationships are identified, they may be contingent on ongoing and negotiated mutuality. Such dynamism raises significant issues for the rather rose-tinted, cross-sectional descriptions of positive social relationships and access to sporting resources. The importance of sanctions and norms and the possibility that individuals act as if they were balancing costs against benefits to maximise personal advantage is an ontological position at odds with the rather organic communitarian and populist rhetoric of some sport-for-development evangelists.

Two recent studies point to the limitations of the integrative potential of sport – although, as always, context is a significant mediator. Okada and Young (2012: 23) in their analysis of a Cambodian programme to promote collegiality among hotel staff conclude that making a case for an unfettered 'sport-equate-to-social-development argument is uncompelling, and that any promise sport offers communities in either a micro or macro sense should be viewed thorough the lens of caution and circumspection'. Spaaij (2012: 1535), in a study of the failure of Melbourne sports clubs to integrate Somali immigrants, warns that 'the role of sport participation as a means of social capital and social integration should be neither overstated nor over-generalised' and, more fundamentally, that it is 'substantially secondary to other avenues of integration – employment, education, housing and health'.

The MYSA case study illustrates that some types of sport-for-development *organisations* can be organised systematically to develop forms of human and social capital. However, this is much closer to Coleman's (1994) rationally devised material and status incentives than Putnam's (2000) more organic communitarian perspective. Such organisations can offer compensation for aspects of weak civic structures, disintegrating families and inadequate education systems. They can develop forms of social and human capital by providing some young people with opportunities to participate in decision making, confront exploitative gender relations, encourage ambition and recognise the value of education, develop relationships based on trust and reciprocity, provide opportunities for the development of aspects of human capital – especially via volunteer youth peer coaches and educators.

However, there is a wide variety of types including relatively stable organisations, short-term projects and relatively isolated teams – all seemingly encompassed by the term 'sport-for-development'. It is not 'sport' that produces and sustains certain types of social capital, enters into partnerships and mobilises sporting and possibly non-sporting resources, but certain types of *social organisation,* characterised by certain types of internal and external social relationships and which contain certain types of resources. In considering the role of sport-for-development organisations in civil society and their contribution to the formation of social capital there are a number of key theoretical, policy and practical issues that need to be clarified: the types of social capital being assumed; the difference between simple communitarianism and social capital; the extent to which social capital is necessarily positive in terms of development, however defined; the nature of the limitations of resource-poor networks; the precise meaning of resource mobilisation *through* sport, rather than simply for sport (United Nations, 2003); the nature of programmes or organisational structures and their stability over time; the extent to which organisations are connected or isolated in meaningful ways (Seippel, 2006); the nature of the distribution of bridging and linking social capital *within* organisations and communities; the radius of trust (Fukuyama, 2001) and the relationships with broader development agencies and strategies.

Consequently we are left with questions about how to understand the relationships between forms of sport, forms of organisation, types of social capital and forms of development, or the extent to which such relationships can exist (Kruse, 2006). Certainly, in the area of sport-for-development we can see the truth of Pawson's (2006: 5) assertion that 'social interventions are always complex systems thrust amidst complex systems'. This is frequently ignored in policy rhetoric and the evangelical call to arms so beloved of some conference speakers.

Finally, as sport-for-development rushes to embrace the opportunities seemingly offered by the new emphasis on social capital, it is worth considering Portes' (2000: 5) comment that social capital is the 'latest culprit' in a long line of theories identifying the supposed 'missing element' in impoverished areas – the inability of the inhabitants to act together. Portes (2000: 5) argues that 'reasoning retroactively the idea is that the poor are poor because they lack the collective spirit and solidarity found among more successful communities'. However, reflecting the concerns of Weiss (1993) and Ungar (2006), he refers to a series of studies that indicate that 'the problem in poor areas … is not that people do not know each other or help each other, but that the resources to do so are meagre and the social ties so insulated as to yield meagre returns' and concludes that 'poverty causes social pathology – not vice versa' (Portes, 2000: 5).

To better understand the issues we need to take the issue of displacement of scope more seriously and develop a theoretically and analytically robust empirical sociology of sport and social capitals, rather than promulgate a politically convenient ideology.

9

CONCLUSIONS

Hope is not a plan

How new is new?

Earlier I questioned the extent to which sport-for-development could be viewed as a 'new field' in its 'formative stage' (Kay, 2009: 1177; Woodcock *et al.*, 2012). While such a position might provide legitimation for the conceptual entrepreneurs and the establishment of new journals, academic courses, websites, organisations, conferences and congregations and sources of research funding, it seems an odd claim for several reasons.

First, the claims of sports evangelists are based firmly on long-standing traditional assertions about the nature and contribution of sport – the legitimacy claimed by sports evangelism is based on the fact that it is *not* new. It is based on assertions about the supposedly inherent developmental potential of 'sport', which one presumes is based on some assumption that evidence exists for such claims, beyond the individual success of the 'celebrity diplomats' (Black, 2010: 126; Kidd, 2008).

Second, a striking aspect of this area is the widespread ignoring of a large body of research evidence about personal and social developmental aspects of sport. While I accept that context is a significant factor in understanding impacts and, especially, outcomes, I am not convinced that there is *nothing* of value in such research. Perhaps it is ignored because it raises difficult questions about many of the claims made by the conceptual entrepreneurs of sport-for-development (President's Council on Physical Fitness and Sports, 2006; Coalter, 2007; Coakley, 2011; Hartmann and Kwauk, 2011; Value of Sport Monitor, nd). It might be argued that the widespread use of *sport plus* approaches indicates a recognition of the developmental limits of 'sport', although such subtleties are difficult to detect in evangelical rhetoric.

Third, the claim that sport-for-development is a new field also serves to narrow the definition of 'relevant' research and this is recognised by a number of researchers. Coakley (2011) highlights the need to look outside the limited field of sport-for-development; Tacon (2007) correctly argues that many sport-for-change projects have much in common with social work practice; Witt and Crompton's (1997) analysis of the 'protective factors' essential to sports programmes for at-risk youth is derived from this youth work literature (see Chapter 7). Throughout this book I have drawn on research and analysis from outside sports research to explore issues relating to perceived self-efficacy, self-esteem, peer leadership, HIV and AIDS education, social capital and the middle-range mechanisms of sport-for-change programmes. For example, although some place peer leaders at the symbolic heart of sport-for-development programmes, there is little systematic evidence about their effectiveness (Kruse, 2006). Drawing on a wider range of robust research and theory serves to de-mystify the role that they have been accorded and also sets out an agenda for research. It is of course up to the reader to decide if such borrowing is useful.

Fourth, the implicit view seems to be that sport-for-development requires an accumulation of impact studies to address the supposed 'evidence deficit' (Woodcock *et al.*, 2012) – whether this is via decolonising, feminist-oriented, participatory action research (Lindsey and Grattan, 2012), the simple accumulation of 'neo-colonialist' quantitative impact studies, or the accumulation of well-selected 'heartfelt narratives' (Hartmann and Kwauk, 2011: 286), which are rarely representative of participants' experience and are qualified by the strong possibility of social desirability bias. There seems to be a desire to seek to illustrate the value of sport-for-development via the identification of 'exemplary cases' or 'best buys' (Pawson, 2001a). It could be argued that the research by Maro *et al.* (2009) and Maro and Roberts (2012) explored in Chapter 6 is an example of that approach. However, other than an affirmation that peer education is relatively effective (a claim that many in other academic fields dispute), we are provided with little detail of programme processes and their claims for generalisation appear to be confused – a major limitation of all such studies.

Programme theory and necessary conditions

Because of the above, there is a need to consider the implications of Pawson's (2006) and Weiss' (1997) emphasis on middle-range mechanisms. Such perspectives shift our focus from *families of programmes* (sport and crime; sport-for-development; sport and education) to *families of mechanisms*, with apparently diverse interventions possibly sharing common components. Although Pawson *et al.* (2004: 7) argue that 'rarely if ever is the "same" programme fully effective in all circumstances', he also suggests:

> There are probably some common processes (e.g. how people react to change) and thus generic theories (about human volition) that feed their way into all interventions. If synthesis were to concentrate on these middle-range mechanisms, then the opportunities for the utilisation of reviews [of research] would be much expanded.
>
> *(Pawson, 2006: 174)*

A concern with mechanisms reflects a more general shift from an emphasis on politico-epistemological purity to 'a logic of inquiry' (Pawson, 2006: 178). This means embracing a loose amalgam of theories of behaviour change (Foster *et al.*, 2005; Bailey *et al.*, 2009), realist evaluation (Pawson and Tilley, 2000; Pawson, 2006; Nichols and Crow, 2004; Tacon, 2007) and theory-based evaluations to seek to understand the nature and theoretical robustness of the assumptions underpinning interventions, the policy-makers and practitioners' understanding of the presumed 'mechanisms' and consequently to provide a framework for their evaluation (Coalter, 2006; 2007). Weiss (1997: 520) argues that one of the clearest arguments for the development of programme theories and theory-based evaluation is 'when prior evaluations show inconsistent results' – clearly applicable to most sports programmes seeking to promote personal and social change (Coalter, 2007). The concentration on middle-range mechanisms would also enable a broader view of the world of evidence and draw on a wide range of generic research and practice. It should also lead to conceptual clarification and improved programme design and, probably, increased ability to achieve the desired impacts – outcomes raise deeper issues. Even more ambitiously, Weiss (1997: 154) suggests that theory-based evaluation 'can track the unfolding of events, step-by-step, and thus make causal attributions on the basis of demonstrated links. If this were so, evaluation would not need randomized control groups to justify its claims about causality'.

There are two broad and inter-connected approaches to developing programme theory. The first is for programme providers to outline systematically the various components and mechanisms and how, via a *presumed* series of causes and effects, they might lead to desired impacts. A second approach is to derive a programme theory from relevant research and theory and to design a programme that contains the mechanisms and elements that have been identified as maximising the potential to achieve the desired impacts. The approach in Chapter 7 sought to combine both via interviews with participants. The supposed relative dearth of relevant research in sport-for-development is not a major constraint, as the concern would be with relatively generic mechanisms that have been identified as contributing to value, attitude and behaviour change – substantially broadening the definition of relevant research. For example, *perceived self-efficacy* is known to be affected by factors such as mastery experiences, role modelling, verbal persuasion and social support. In fact, some knowledge of such research and theory is necessary in order to evaluate critically the providers' programme theories. As illustrated in more detail in Chapter 3, such an approach has a number of significant advantages (Coalter, 2009):

- It emphasises the critical distinction between necessary conditions and *sufficient conditions* required to maximise the potential to achieve desired impacts.
- It requires a systematic reconsideration of the individual deficit model.
- It identifies and seeks to resolve different programme theories held by programme providers, policy makers and funders.
- It assists in the formulation of theoretically coherent and realistic impacts related to programme processes.
- It provides the basis for formative, rather than summative evaluation – it moves beyond a concern with *what* should happen to a consideration of *how* and *why*.

M&E becomes developmental, as formative evaluations are concerned with ways of improving the implementation and management of interventions.

- It helps evaluators to focus on key questions/mechanisms and it provides feedback about which chain of reasoning breaks down and where it breaks down.
- It contributes to capacity building, to developing a greater sense of ownership, understanding and integration and developing an organisational ability to reflect on and analyse attitudes, beliefs and behaviour.
- It maximises evaluators' ability to identify possible generic mechanisms. Such mechanisms provide the basis for careful generalisation and possibly the development of sport-for-development.

Such an approach can address the liberationists' concerns about inclusion and dialogue, although perhaps not their apparent aversion to programme improvement. Both Weiss (1986) and Pawson (2006) argue that a theory-based approach moves beyond simple 'political arithmetic' and 'partisan support' to a situation in which 'the influence of research on policy occurs through the medium of ideas rather than data' (Pawson, 2006: 169). It is interesting to note that the data produced by Lindsey and Grattan (2012) and Kay (2009) seem to indicate that there is little difference between the 'oppressed' and the 'oppressors' with regard to assumptions about possible impacts and outcomes. It would be even more interesting to know if they share the same programme theories and theories of behaviour change. In my experience the robust and deeply ingrained commonsense ideologies of sport held by many tend to make such conversations rather difficult and sometimes threatening to all involved. However, such conversations are still necessary.

Cognitive, affective and normative dimensions: an imbalance

It is obvious that I have little sympathy with the liberation methodologists, however well meaning they are. Positioning themselves firmly on the side of the oppressed leads to a potent mixture of issues of ontology, epistemology, methodology and methods combined in rather incendiary ways with diffuse notions of politics, power and liberation. This results in the designation of the type of quantitative research reported in this book as being unavoidably part of neo-colonialist hegemonic repression and contributing to the reproduction of unequal power relations – if only research was that important!

As was argued in Chapter 3, the symbolic weight attributed to sport-for-development and certain approaches to evaluation, as signifying neo-colonial oppression, seems to be a form of ideological over-reach. It could be argued that all that is being said is that qualitative research has a role to play, or even more mundanely that it is good manners to ask people what they think. Further, despite the strident promotion of 'decolonising, feminist-oriented, participatory action research' (Lindsey and Grattan, 2012) this seems to have produced rather predictable data that some of these critics admit has rather limited analytical value. Whatever the issues, it feels as if an ideological sledge hammer is being used to crack a rather straightforward methods nut.

My response to this is that of Hammersley (1995: 19), who argues that 'philosophy must be not be seen as superordinate to empirical research ... research is a practical activity and cannot be governed in any strict way by methodological theory'. Allied to this is Sugden's (2010: 267) advocacy of a form of critical pragmatism that 'places emphasis on theoretical development and refinement through critical, practical, empirical engagement, rather than fixating upon abstract debate and unmoveable theoretical principles'. Or, as Burnett (2001) argues on the basis of her extensive fieldwork experience, there is a need to be pragmatic and flexible.

Craib (1984) argues that social theory has three dimensions and that theorists are doing three different things simultaneously, with varying balances between them. The *cognitive dimension* seeks to establish objective knowledge about the social world. The *affective dimension* is one in which elements of the theories embody the experience and feeling of the theorist, which means that any debate involves more than rational argument. The third dimension is *normative* – any theory of the way that the world is, is also based on assumptions about the way that the world ought to be, what sort of actions are possible or desirable. It seems to me that too often the cognitive element is compromised in sport-for-development. For example, even the critics of certain supposedly neo-colonialist policies and practices retain an affective and normative belief in the inherent developmental potential of sport. In this regard Hartmann and Kwauk (2011: 289) refer to the functionalist view of sport, which underpins much sport-for-development, as being based on 'the normative vision of social life, social change, and the status quo embedded in this dominant vision'. They also suggest that 'given its history and ideology, sport is easily understood by the dominant class as a socially beneficial and culturally normative "character builder"' (Hartmann and Kwauk, 2011: 292). Coakley (2011: 309) refers to the fact that commitment to neo-liberal ideas 'runs deep in ... the global social problems industry funded primarily by North Americans and Northern Europeans', reinforced by the cult of the individual used as a marketing tool by corporate sponsors and media companies. The importance of this is that:

> When organized into interpretive perspectives, these ideas constitute widely shared visions of how social worlds could and should be organized – much like other interpretive frameworks inspired by ideology more than research and theory. When combined with similarly shared emotions, identities, and dominant narratives, they tend to resist change, even when evidence contradicts them.
>
> *(Coakley, 2011: 309)*

Although the tensions between normative, affective and cognitive perspectives are inevitable, within sport-for-development they are sub-optimally confused among those whose imperative is 'to make a difference' (Black, 2010). The combination of neo-liberal assumptions, the claim making of conceptual entrepreneurs, the faith and beliefs of the sports evangelists, the cloistered environment of incestuous amplification, organisational self-interest, liberation methodologists and the notion that sport-for-development is 'new' makes this a difficult research terrain. The truth of Pisani's

(2008: 300) assertion that 'doing honest analysis that would lead to programme improvement is a glorious way to be hated by just about everyone' was never truer than in sport-for-development.

Fred's survival and deficit models

Despite the lack of clarity and precision relating to the definition of 'development' it seems legitimate to assume that a core assumption of, and rationale for, sport-for-development programmes is that poor communities automatically produce deficient people who can be 'developed' through sport. Such assumptions seem to be essential rationales and usually form the basis for funding applications, although my experience suggests that there is little systematic analysis of prior values, attitudes, knowledge and behaviour. There is a paradoxical danger of well-meaning projects being based on negative stereotypes of all young people from particular areas, with the attendant danger of misconceived provision, inappropriate performance indicators and subtle forms of racism.

I would argue that, despite their admitted limitations, the data in Chapters 4, 5 and 6 at least raise some legitimate questions about such assumptions, as does the comment that 'Fred, you would not survive three days here'. The young people in these programmes were not homogeneous groups and there was a range of self-evaluations, with many expressing quite strong self-belief in their own efficacy and most within an accepted 'normal' range of self-esteem – although these are open to some debate about meaning and cultural relevance and the data indicate the existence of interesting cultural variations. It seems to be a reasonable assumption that living in such deprivation means that many have to develop certain levels of *perceived* self-efficacy and self-worth in order to remain positive and to survive. Of course it is possible that some of these evaluations reflect a certain self-protective element, with a degree of denial and suppression (Jenkins, 1997; Hunter, 2001). We have no way of knowing from our data, although their relative consistency across several cultures seems to indicate otherwise. The data in Chapters 4 and 5 certainly cannot be regarded as representative of the Global South/Majority World (Kay, 2011)/low income countries – politically correct terms that seem wholly inappropriate to issues of empirical research. However, at the very least, the data raise questions about the extent to which respondents can be regarded as relatively normal young people living in often dreadful circumstances. It also raises questions about the extent to which decolonising, feminist-oriented, participatory action research can provide sufficient analytical depth and conceptual discrimination.

The data raise questions about overly generalised deficit models, which ignore the fact that the nature and extent of impacts on participants will depend not only on the nature of the experience, but also on the nature of the participants and their response to the various aspects of the programmes – the key mechanism. To ignore this contains obvious ideological and pedagogic dangers. It raises important questions about how 'need' and 'development' are conceptualised and how desired impacts and behavioural outcomes are defined and measured. The need for greater clarity is also emphasised by the apparent diversity among the Global South/Majority World/low income participants – both between the East African participants and, most especially, between them and the Indian participants. This is a complex diversity not easily captured via qualitative research. In such circumstances the universalising anti-neo-colonialist analysis contains the danger inherent in the 'the know-it-all tendencies of normative theory' (Pawson, 2001b: 11).

Displacement of scope and going beyond the touchline

The concept of displacement of scope (Wagner, 1964) – wrongly generalising micro-level effects to the meso and macro levels – seems very appropriate for sport-for-development with its universalising mythopoeic approach to sport and the lack of precise definitions of development. Wagner (1964: 582) argues:

> the problem of differentiated scope is inherent in the tremendous range of sociological subject matter itself. In other words, it imposes not only theoretical but also methodological tasks upon sociologists who are concerned with the micro-macro-sociological continuum as a whole.

In part this relates to long-standing debates within social science about the relationship between structure and action, between the individual and the social, or even between values, attitudes, intentions and behaviour. The fact that issues of displacement of scope are inherent in the range of sociological subject matter can clearly be applied to sport-for-development. If I may slightly extend Wagner's (1964) idea, the most basic questions related to sport-for-development programmes seem to be:

- In what ways are the participants in need of 'development'?
- Does participation positively affect the combination of values, attitudes, knowledge and aptitudes contained in a notion of 'development', for all or some?
- How does the programme achieve such impacts and for whom?
- Does this result in an intention to change specific behaviours, for all or some?
- Does this lead to an actual change in behaviour, for all or some?
- Does the participants' environment enable desired changes in behaviour (Mwaanga, 2003; Jeanes, 2011; Ungar, 2006)?
- If not, how does this contribute to broader processes of social and economic development?

Such questions clearly relate to an individualistic perspective of development that many argue is the dominant ideology of sport-for-development (Black, 2010; Kidd, 2008; Coakley, 2011; Darnell and Hayhurst, 2012; Jeanes, 2011). The questions bring to mind Weiss' (1993) concern with a 'blame the victim approach', which ignores structures and seeks to deal with long-standing broad-gauge problems via limited-focus programmes of behavioural change. In a similar vein Ungar (2006) comments that it might be better to 'change the odds' rather than try to resource individuals to 'beat the odds' in environments that frequently do not support behaviour change, or offer opportunities for 'development'. While it is clear that some sport-for-development programmes can strengthen the perceived self-efficacy of some participants, Ungar's (2006) concern with the resilience of *environments* rather than individuals raises important questions about the extent to which we can 'go beyond the touchline', or the manner in which this is possible.

From childhood to livelihood

Such limitations have been recognised by Magic Bus, whose long-term programme (seven to 18 years of age) has been given the ambitious strapline 'from childhood to livelihood'. Magic Bus is the leading sport for-development organisation in India and, as far as I know, the largest in the world and has adopted a much more holistic approach to its work than is usual in this sector. Its key aims relate to improving healthy eating, health knowledge and encouraging the use of health facilities; improving perceptions of the value of education and encouraging school attendance and addressing issues of gender equity. These are included in the programme curriculum via a traditional *sport-plus* approach. However, the programme does not depend on individualised programme-based approaches. Parents are intimately involved via initial meetings and a subsequent programme of meetings and events – their values and attitudes are addressed in parallel with the young people's. Further, the programme addresses issues of the local opportunity structure – schools and health services – and works with relevant partners and parents to provide access and to encourage use. In addition, reflecting Pawson's (2006) framework of coaching and sponsoring (see Chapter 7), Magic Bus has a programme called Connect, which seeks to improve the employability of their Community Sports Coaches via a series of work-oriented training modules and work placement – i.e. building on the wider understanding that peer leaders are the most likely to benefit from such programmes. Overall, the programme seeks to address Ungar's (2006) concern with 'navigation' – an individual's capacity to move towards resources that are available and easily accessed – and 'negotiation' – the provision of resources in ways that are meaningful to individuals and 'health enhancing'. This also reflects an attempt to address Black's (2010: 127) clear and unambiguous warning that:

> DTS [development through sport] interventions will not be successful or sustainable for most participants in the absence of a much wider range of interventions, changes and improvements. DTS practitioners must themselves be persuaded to transcend the 'myth of autonomy' to learn from, and collaborate much more systematically with, the diverse panoply of development agents.

Such comments also relate to another claim about sport-for-development's ability to go beyond the touchline – its supposed ability to develop social capital.

Social capital: not always for the public good

Frequent, if imprecise, claims are made about sport-for-development's ability to form partnerships that can enable resource mobilisation not only for, but *through* sport (United Nations, 2003). Here the ideologies of sport as a neutral, non-political space characterised by communality, mutuality and teamwork combine with often decontextualised, romanticised, communitarian generalisations about the supposed 'power of sport' to generate 'social capital' – usually based loosely on Putnam's (2000) concept of bonding social capital. Some research indicates that in small and isolated communities, sports clubs and organisations can provide a community focus, contributing to sociability and communality. However, four issues need to be addressed.

First, as with the deficit model underpinning much sport-for-development rhetoric, the implications of Portes' (2000: 5) reference to the type of 'retroactive reasoning' that concludes that the poor are poor because they lack collective spirit and solidarity needs to be considered before wholeheartedly embracing the seeming opportunity provided by the politics of social capital. Second, much current work in sport-for-development is cross-sectional and ignores the fact that such relationships are often dynamic and contingent on ongoing and negotiated mutuality. Such a view does not sit well with the rather organic communitarian and populist ontology of sport-for-development evangelists. Third, it is reasonable to ask to what extent the processes and outcomes described can be regarded as 'social capital' in an analytical or developmental sense. Both Coleman (1994) and Putnam (2000) view social capital as a *facilitating* resource – not just a public good, but *for* the public good (Szreter, 1998). In such circumstances cohesion and mutuality are not viewed as developmental ends in themselves, but as possible means to ends. Consequently, the nature of the *resources* contained in social networks is a major, but frequently ignored, issue. For example, Burnett (2001) illustrates that certain South African communities were unable to mobilise resources *for* sport, never mind through sport, and faced great difficulty in sustaining bridging and linking ties. Further, Hyden (1983, 2006) and Calderisi (2007) emphasise that the 'economy of affection' – a form of bonding capital – can obstruct organisational efficiency and economic development. In addition, raising issues of displacement of scope and the often ignored distinctions between bonding, bridging and linking social capital, Portes and Landolt (2000) stress the limitations of enforceable trust and bounded solidarity. As with issues of individual behaviour, collective action is usually only successful in receptive, supportive and non-corrupt environments. Fourth, as the MYSA case study illustrates (Chapter 8), it is not 'sport' that produces and sustains certain types of social capital, enters into partnerships and mobilises sporting and maybe non-sporting resources, but certain types of *social organisation*.

The contingent nature of impacts: stating the obvious … for some?

Reflecting previous research (Fox, 2000) the data in Chapters 4 and 5 indicate a *general tendency* for those with the weakest or lower-than-average scores for perceived self-efficacy and self-esteem to increase their evaluations. In two East African samples the increases in average self-efficacy scores were statistically significant, with no change in the Indian sample. In only one, questionable, case was the increase in self-esteem statistically significant. This reflects research that has found little systematic relationship between sports participation and global self-esteem (Zaharopoulos and Hodge, 1991; Bowker *et al.*, 2003) and emphasises the wide range of social factors beyond the touchline that influence self-esteem. Further, with regard to the traditional sports hypothesis that strengthened perceived self-efficacy will lead to increased self-esteem, the data indicate that the relationship is contingent and unpredictable. Although the all-female EMIMA sample had the most statistically robust increases for both perceived self-efficacy and self-esteem, the relationship between the *changes* in both measures was weak. The Kids' League produced a clear relationship for males, but not for females; in Magic Bus there was a strong relationship for the very small group of females, but not for males.

However, the most important finding relates to the view that participation in sport-for-development programmes inevitably leads to 'personal development'. This over-simplifies the differential impact of such programmes and the strength and direction of the impacts – the mixture of increases, decreases and no change in self-evaluations calls into question the meaning and diagnostic value of the selective 'heartfelt narratives' (Hartmann and Kwauk, 2011), presented as evidence to various congregations. As it is likely that *any* social interventions will produce individual successes, such testimonies tell us little about *how* various programmes operate and why they have differential impacts.

For example, the activity may be much less important than the 'attractiveness factors' that encourage people to stay with such programmes (Fox, 2000; Biddle and Mutrie, 2001; Sandford *et al.*, 2006). More fundamentally, Morris *et al.* (2003) suggest that *any* programme where there had previously been none may be the most important factor. The data in Chapter 7 indicate that the nature of the social climate and the social and emotional relationships are as, if not more, important than the activity itself. Once again we are drawn to a concern with middle-range mechanisms and Coakley's (1998) distinction between sports as *sites* for, but not necessarily causes of, socialisation outcomes and Hartmann's (2003: 134) assertion that 'the success of any sports-based social intervention program is largely determined by the strength of its non-sport components'. In this regard it is worth noting that the literature reviews by the International Working Group on Sport-for-development and Peace – not the likeliest of critics – concluded that 'the evident benefits appear to be an indirect outcome of the context and social interaction that is possible in sport, rather than a direct outcome of participating in sport' (SDPIWG, 2008: 4).

Given these perspectives, it is not surprising that, despite certain tendencies in the data, there was no clear and systematic 'sport-for-development effect' – I find it rather odd and somewhat naive that I even have to state this. When we move beyond the universalising rhetoric of the conceptual entrepreneurs this is hardly a surprise – the presumption of such a general effect could only exist in the rhetoric of the incestuous amplifiers. As in all forms of social intervention, the nature and extent of impacts were contingent and varied between programmes, participants and cultural contexts. In addition, as few sport-for-development organisations seek to achieve their desired impacts and outcomes solely through 'sport', the nature and experience of such programmes will vary widely. More generically, the data illustrate Pawson et al.'s (2004: 7) contention that:

> It is through the workings of entire systems of social relationships that any changes in behaviours, events and social conditions are effected. ... Rarely if ever is the 'same' programme equally effective in all circumstances because of the influence of contextual factors.

In this regard, despite the liberatory and symbolic significance attributed to peer-leader approaches, especially in relation to HIV and AIDS education, there is no systematic evidence about their relative effectiveness. Further, wider and more robust research raises significant issues about the universalising rhetoric expressed by some in sport-for-development. One is struck by the almost absolute conviction about this approach by some in sport-for-development compared to the much more measured and often sceptical analyses found in the more robust health-related research (Michielsen et al., 2010; Wight, 1999, 2005). The pedagogic effectiveness of such approaches is a matter for empirical investigation and cannot rest on affirmation rooted in normative and affective liberation theory – this is owed to the participants in the various programmes.

Of course, even where programmes lead to improved self-evaluations and increased knowledge or even intention to change behaviour, we are still left with the question as to what this has to do with 'development'.

Hope is not a plan: a defence of scepticism

In the Introduction I quoted Gramsci's comment about the need to combine pessimism of the intellect with an optimism of the will and said that this provides a succinct summary of the dilemmas that I have faced since my initial visits to Mathare, Dharavi and Bombay Port Trust. However, the source of my pessimism is not the many ever-optimistic, innovative and generous practitioners from whom I have learnt an immense amount about both programmes and humanity. Rather, my pessimism relates to two issues: (i) the sheer scale of the issues implied by the amorphous and ill-defined term 'development' and the failure to address systematically issues of displacement of scope; (ii) more significant are the evangelists, the self-interested conceptual entrepreneurs and the atmosphere of incestuous amplification in which research is reduced to the role of confirming what they already think that they know and where agnostics and atheists are banned from a narrow church. It is also disappointing that some academics also seem to work within the normative and affective perspectives of the evangelists. Certainly, on the basis of this book, I do not expect to be invited to any of their congregations in the near future.

In this regard I agree with Emler (2001a: 3) that 'we should be suspicious of any convenient convergence of self-serving interests with the greater good'. I accept that evaluation is, or should be, a rational exercise that takes place in a political context (Weiss, 1993). I also acknowledge that rhetoric partly reflects processes of lobbying, persuasion, negotiation and alliance building. I understand that in marginal policy areas such processes frequently produce inflated promises, unrealistic desired impacts and outcomes that lack the clarity and intellectual coherence that evaluation criteria should have. This is especially so if survival is the key objective for financially vulnerable organisations and raises interesting questions about the real meaning of 'mission drift'.

However, a major result of this has been that 'in its contemporary manifestation, the SDP [sport-for-development-and-peace] emphasis on practice has come, for the most part, at the expense of critical and theoretically-informed reflection' (Black, 2010: 122). From my perspective this does not imply that sport-for-development needs more cross-sectional descriptive studies of limited generalisability, more heart-felt narratives or even decolonising, feminist-oriented, participatory action research – noble and well mannered as this might be. Rather, as others have suggested, there is a need to step back and to reflect critically on what we and, most especially, others might already know (Tacon, 2007; Crabbe, 2008; Coakley, 2011). I have tried to make a small contribution to this by drawing on more generic research and analyses on aspects of the processes, impacts and outcomes often claimed by sport-for-development – to try to de-reify sport-for-development and to raise questions about its supposed 'newness'. I hope that this approach makes a small contribution to the development of theoretical robustness and of a more systematic and theoretically informed research agenda. As I have said, it is for others to decide if this is a relevant or useful contribution.

Further, if we soften Gramsci's pessimism to scepticism, I strongly believe that this is a core requirement of academic practice and the pursuit of cognitive under-standing – albeit struggling with the affective and normative components present in all social theorising, which are sometimes reinforced by the temptations of research funding. Some might argue that the contents of this book reflect Oscar Wilde's defini-tion of a cynic – someone who knows the price of everything and the value of nothing. I do not think that this is my position. Since my first visit to Mathare I have been privileged to meet some of the most generous, innovative and optimistic people that I have ever met and I am privileged to continue to work with, and learn from, them. However, I believe that it is the duty of an academic to bring a degree of informed scepticism to the claims of sport-for-development. For example, Portes (2000: 4) in his 1999 Presidential Address to the American Sociological Association referred to the 'trained skepticism' of sociologists and argued that 'gaps between received theory and actual reality have been so consistent as to institutionalize a disciplinary skepticism in sociology against sweeping statements, no matter from what ideological quarter they come'. Berger's (1971) main interest lay in the sociology of religion – oddly relevant to sport-for-development – and he sought to promote a humanistic sociology, not dissimilar to the liberation methodologists. Nevertheless, he argued:

> the sociological perspective, with its irritating interjection of the question *'says who?'* ... introduces an element of sober scepticism that has an immediate

> utility in giving some protection at least against converting too readily … [and] makes us a little less likely to be trapped by every missionary band we encounter on the way.

Consequently, while it is not possible to escape the affective and normative aspects of social theory, academics can contribute by working to privilege the cognitive – and there are signs that this perspective is beginning to emerge (e.g. Crabbe, 2008; Spaaij, 2011; 2012; Jeanes, 2011). Such an approach can contribute to the intellectual and practical development of sport-for-development by placing it within a much wider world of knowledge and research and by theorising its limitations as well as outlining its 'potential'.

As many regard 'academic' as the longest four-letter word in the English language – especially where research is also regarded as a 'dirty word' (Smith, 1999) – I will finish by seeking intellectual support for my position from one of the original practitioners of sport-for-development – although without his express permission. Mwaanga (2010: 66) argues:

> To claim that sport can combat HIV and AIDS is not only to overstate the limited capacity of sport but also to dangerously ignore the complexity of HIV and AIDS … the fundamental question that confronts us … [Is] how can we better understand the interplay between sport, with its limited capacity on one hand, and HIV and AIDS, in its full complexity, on the other.

While this is related to HIV and AIDS, for me it serves as a general comment on sport-for-development. Further, it echoes Pawson's (2006: 35) more generic comment that 'social interventions are always complex systems thrust amidst complex systems' – a complexity not admitted by conceptual entrepreneurs, but an essential requirement for academics, researchers and practitioners. One is reminded of Daniel Patrick Moynihan's (nd) comment and warning that 'it is quite possible to live with uncertainty, with the possibility, even the likelihood that one is wrong. But beware of certainty where none exists. Ideological certainty easily degenerates into an insistence upon ignorance'.

Leaving development to hope and 'sport' is a poor strategy.

REFERENCES

Adler, N. and Stewart, J. (2004). 'Self-esteem', John D. and Catherine T. MacArthur Research Network on Socioeconomic Status and Health. www.macses.ucsf.edu/Research/Psychosocial/notebook/selfesteem.html (accessed 20 August 2012).

Amaro, O. (1995) HIV/AIDS prevention program evaluation report, prepared for the Massachusetts Primary Prevention Group and the Massachusetts Department of Public Health.

Armstrong, G. and Giulianotti, R. (eds) (2004) Football in Africa: Conflict Conciliation and Community, Basingstoke: Palgrave Macmillan.

Avert (nd) Averting HIV and AIDS, www.avert.org/ (accessed 21 December 2012).

Bailey, R., Armour, K., Kirk, D., Jess, M., Pickup, I., Sandford, R. and the BERA Physical Education and Sport Pedagogy Special Interest Group (2009) 'The Educational Benefits Claimed for Physical Education and School Sport: An Academic Review', Research Papers in Education, Vol. 24, No. 1: 1–27.

Banda, D. and Mwaanga, O. (nd) Dunking AIDS out, York: York St John University.

Banda, D., Lindsey, I., Jeanes, R. and Kay, T. (2008) Partnerships involving sports-for-development NGOs and the fight against HIV / AIDS, York: York St John University.

Bandura, A. (1962) Social Learning through Imitation, Lincoln, NE: University of Nebraska Press.

——(1986) Social Foundations of Thought and Action: A Social Cognitive Theory, Englewood Cliffs, NJ: Prentice-Hall.

——(1994) 'Self-efficacy', in V.S. Ramachaudran (ed.) Encyclopedia of human behaviour, Vol. 4, New York: Academic Press, pp. 71–81.

——(1997) Self-Efficacy: The Exercise of Control, New York: Worth Publishers.

Baumeister, R.F., Campbell, J.D., Krueger, J.I. and Vohs, K.D. (2003) 'Does high self-esteem cause better performance, interpersonal success, happiness, or heathier lifestyles?', Psychological Science in the Public Interest, Vol 4, No. 2: 1–44.

——(2005) 'Exploding the Self-Esteem Myth', Scientific American, Vol. 292, No. 1: 84–92.

BBC (2008) 'Kenyans reject circumcision plan', 18 July, http://news.bbc.co.uk/1/hi/7514431.stm (accessed 21 December 2012).

Berger, P. (1971) Invitation to Sociology, London: Pelican.

Beyond Sport (nd) www.beyondsport.org (accessed 21 December 2012).

Biddle, S. (2006) 'Defining and Measuring Indicators of Psycho-social Well-Being in Youth Sport and Physical Activity', in Y. Vanden Auweele, C. Malcolm and B. Meulders (eds) Sports and Development, Leuven: Lannoo Campus, pp. 163–84.

Biddle, S. and Mutrie, N. (2001) Psychology of Physical Activity, London: Routledge.

Biddle, S., Gorley, T. and Stensel, D.J. (2004) 'Health-Enhancing Physical Activity and Sedentary Behaviour in Children and Adolescents', Journal of Sports Sciences, Vol. 22, No. 8: 679–207.

Black, D. (2010) 'The ambiguities of development: implications for "development through sport"', Sport in Society, Vol. 13, No. 1: 121–129.

Blascovich, J. and Tomaka, J. (1991) 'Measures of self-esteem', in J.P. Robinson and P.R. Shaver (eds), Measures of personality and social psychological attitudes, San Diego, CA: Academic Press, pp. 115–160.

Bosscher, R.J. and Smit, J.H. (1998) 'Confirmatory factor analysis of the General Self-Efficacy Scale', Behaviour Research and Therapy, Vol. 36: 339–343.

Botcheva, L. and Huffman, M.D. (2004) Grassroot Soccer Foundation HIV/AIDS Education Program: An Intervention in Zimbabwe, White River Junction, VT: Grassroot Soccer Foundation.

Bourdieu, P. (1997) 'The Forms of Capital', in A.H. Halsey, H. Launder, P. Brown and A. Stuart Wells (eds), Education, Culture, Economy and Society, Oxford: Oxford University Press.

Bowker, A., Gadbois, S. and Cornock, B. (2003) 'Sport Participation and Self-Esteem: Variations as a Function of Gender and Role Orientation', Sex Roles, Vol. 49, No. 1/2: 47–58.

Brady, M. and Kahn, A.B. (2002) Letting Girls Play: The Mathare Youth Sports Association's Football Program for Girls, New York: Population Council.

Brown, J., Cai, H., Oakes, M. and Deng, C. (2009) 'Cultural Similarities in Self-Esteem Functioning. East Is East and West Is West, But Sometimes the Twain Do Meet', Journal of Cross-Cultural Psychology, Vol. 40: 1140–1157.

Bulmer, M. (1982) The Uses of Social Research, London: Allen and Unwin.

Bulmer, M. (ed.) (1980) Social Research and Royal Commissions, London: Allen and Unwin.

Burnett, C. (2001) 'Social Impact Assessment and Sport Development: Social Spin-offs of the Australia–South Africa Junior Sport Programme', International Review for the Sociology of Sport, Vol. 36, No. 1: 41–57.

——(2006) 'Sport-for-development: The impact of the Australia–Africa 2006 Initiative on South African Communities', in Y. Vanden Auweele, C. Malcom and B. Meulders (eds) Sport and Development, Leuven, Lannoocampus, pp. 185–197.

——(2010) 'Sport-for-development approaches in the South African context: a case study analysis', South African Journal for Research in Sport, Physical Education and Recreation, Vol. 32, No. 1: 29–42.

Calderisi, R. (2007) The Trouble with Africa: Why foreign aid isn't working, New Haven, CT: Yale University Press.

Campbell, C. and MacPhail, C. (2002) 'Peer education, gender and the development of critical consciousness: participatory HIV prevention by South African youth', Social Science and Medicine, Vol. 55, No. 2: 331–345.

Campbell, C. and Mzaidume, Y. (2002) 'How can HIV/AIDS be prevented in South Africa? A social perspective', British Medical Journal, Vol. 324, No. 7331: 229–328.

Campbell, C., Gibbs, A., Nair, Y. and Maimane, S. (2009) 'Frustrated potential, false promise or complicated possibilities? Empowerment and participation amongst female health volunteers in South Africa', Journal of Health Management, Vol. 11, No. 2: 315–336.

Cantley, C. (1992) 'Negotiating Research', in J. Vincent and S. Brown (eds) Critics and Customers: The control of social policy research, Aldershot: Avebury.

Coakley, J. (1998) Sport in Society: Issues and Controversies, 6th edition, Boston, MA: McGraw Hill.

Coakley (2004) Sport in Society: Issues and Controversies, 8th edition, Boston, MA: McGraw Hill.

Coakley, J. (2011) 'Youth Sports: What Counts as "Positive Development"?', Journal of Sport and Social Issues, Vol. 35, No. 3: 306–324.

Coalter, F. (2006) Sport-in-Development: A Monitoring and Evaluation Manual, London: UK Sport.

——(2007) Sport a wider social role: who's keeping the score? London: Routledge.

——(2008) 'Sport-in-development: Development for and through sport?', in R. Hoy and M. Nicholson (eds) Sport and Social Capital, London: Elsevier, pp. 36–67.

——(2009) 'Sport-in-development: accountability or development?', in R. Levermore and A. Beacom (eds) Sport and international development, Basingstoke: Palgrave Macmillan, pp. 55–75.

——(2011) Sport, conflict and youth development, London: Comic Relief.

Coalter, F. and Taylor, J. (2010) 'Sport-for-development impact study', London: Comic Relief, UK Sport and International Development through Sport, www.uksport.gov.uk/docLib/MISC/FullReport.pdf (accessed 21 December 2012).

Coleman, J.S. (1988–9) 'Social Capital in the Creation of Human Capital', American Journal of Sociology, Vol. 94: 95–120.

Coleman, J.S. (1994) Foundations of Social Theory, Cambridge, MA: Belknap Press.

Collins, M. and Kay, T. (2003) Sport and Social Inclusion, London: Routledge.

Collins, M., Henry, I., Houlihan, B. and Buller, J. (1999) Sport and Social Inclusion: A Report to the Department of Culture, Media and Sport, Institute of Sport and Leisure Policy, Loughborough: Loughborough University.

Comaroff, J. and Comaroff, J. (eds) (1999) Civil Society and the Political Imagination in Africa: Critical Perspectives, Chicago, IL: University of Chicago Press.

Crabbe, T. (2000) 'A Sporting Chance? Using Sport to Tackle Drug Use and Crime', Drug Education, Prevention and Policy, Vol. 7, No. 4: 381–91.

Crabbe, T (2008) 'Avoiding the numbers game: Social theory, policy and sport's role in the art of relationship building', in M. Nicholson and R. Hoye (eds) Sport and Social Capital, London: Elsevier.

Craib, I. (1984) Modern social theory: From Parsons to Habermas, Brighton: Wheatsheaf Books.

Darnell, S. and Hayhurst, L. (2012) 'Hegemony, postcolonialism and sport-for-development: a response to Lindsey and Grattan', International Journal of Sport Policy and Politics, Vol. 4, No. 1, March: 111–124.

Darnell, S.C. (2007) 'Playing with race', Sport in Society, Vol. 10, No. 4: 560–579.

Davis, P. (2004) Is evidence-based government possible? Jerry Lee Lecture. 4th Annual Campbell Collaboration Colloqium, Washington. Copies from FC.

Delva,W. and Temmerman, M. (2006) 'Determinants of the effectiveness of HIV prevention through sport in Vanden Auweele', in C. Malcom and B. Meulders (eds) Sport and Development, Leuven, Lannoocampus, pp. 125–134.

Delva, W., Michielsen, K., Meulders, B., Groeninck, S.,Wasonga, E., Ajwang, P., Temmerman, M. and Vanreusel, B. (2010) 'HIV prevention through sport: the case of the Mathare Youth Sport Association in Kenya', AIDS Care, Vol. 22, No. 8: 1012–1020.

Department for International Development (2005) Guidance on Evaluation and Review for DFID Staff Evaluation Department, London: Department for International Development.

Driscoll, K. and Wood, L. (1999) Sporting Capital: Changes and Challenges for Rural Commities in Victoria, Melbourne: Victoria Centre for Applied Social Research, RMIT University.

Dweck, C. (1999) Self-theories: Their role in motivation, personality and development, Philadelphia: Taylor and Francis.

Ekeland, E., Heian, F. and Hagen, K.B. (2005) 'Can Exercise Improve Self-Esteem in Children and Young People? A Systematic Review of Randomised Control Trials', British Journal of Sports Medicine, Vol. 39: 792–798.

Emler, N. (2001a) Self-Esteem: The Costs and Causes of Low Self-Worth, York: Joseph Rowntree Foundations.

——(2001b) Commonly-Held Beliefs about Self-Esteem are Myths, Warns New Research Review, www.jrf.org.uk/pressroom/releases/281101.asp (accessed 21 December 2012).

Feltz, D,. and Magyar, M. (2006) 'Self-efficacy and adolescents in sport and physical activity', in F. Pajares and Y. Urdan (eds) Self-efficacy Beliefs of Adolescents, Charlotte, NC: Information Age Publishing, pp. 161–179.

Fernández-Kelly, M.P. (1995) 'Social and Cultural Capital in the Urban Ghetto: Implications for the Economic Sociology of Immigration', in A. Portes (ed.) The Economic Sociology of Immigration: Essays in Network, Ethnicity, and Entrepreneurship, New York: Russell Sage, pp. 213–247.

Ferron, C. (1997) 'Body Image in Adolescence: Cross-Cultural Research-Results of the Preliminary Phase of a Quantitative Survey', Adolescence, Vol. 32: 735–745.

FIFA (2005) Football for Hope: Football's Commitment to Social Development, Zurich, www.fifa.com/mm/document/afsocial/worldwideprograms/51/56/34/football_for_hope_brochure_2010_e.pdf (accessed 21 December 2012).

Field, J. (2003) Social Capital, London: Routledge.

Fishbein, M. and Ajzen, I. (1975) Belief, Attitude, Intention, and Behavior: An Introduction to Theory and Research, Reading, MA: Addison-Wesley.

Forrest, R. and Kearns, A. (1999) Joined-up Places? Social Cohesion and Neighbourhood Regeneration, York: YPS for the Joseph Rowntree Foundation.

Foster, C., Hilsdon, M. Cavill, N., Allender, S. and Cowburn, G. (2005) Understanding participation in sport and physical activity amongst children and adults, London: Sport England.

Fox, K.R. (1992) 'Physical Education and the Development of Self-Esteem in Children', in N. Armstrong (ed.) New Directions in Physical Education, Vol. 2, Towards a National Curriculum, Leeds: Human Kinetics.

——(1999) 'The Influence of Physical Activity on Mental Well-Being', Public Health Nutrition, Vol. 2, No. 3a: 411–418.

——(2000) 'The Effects of Exercise on Self-Perceptions and Self-Esteem', in S.J.H. Biddle, K.K. Fox and S.H. Boutcher (eds) Physical Activity and Psychological Well-Being, London: Routledge, pp. 88–117.

Freire, P. (1970) Pedagogy of the oppressed, New York: Herder and Herder.

Fukuyama, F. (2001) 'Social Capital, Civil Society and Development', Third World Quarterly, Vol. 22, No. 1: 7–20.

Gambone, M.A. and Arbreton, A.J.A. (1997) Safe havens: The contributions of youth organizations to healthy adolescent development, Philadelphia: Public/Private Ventures.

Gaskin, K. and Smith, D. (1995) A New Civic Europe? A Study of the Extent and Role of Volunteering, London: Volunteer Centre UK.

Geertz, H. (1963) 'Indonesian Cultures and Communities', in R. McVey (ed.), Indonesia, New Haven, CT: Yale University Press, pp. 24–96.

Gilligan, R. (2001) Promoting resilience: A resource guide on working with children in the care system, London: British Agencies for Adoption and Fostering.

Giulianotti, R. (2004) 'Human Rights, Globalization and Sentimental Education: The Case of Sport', Sport in Society, Vol. 7, No. 3: 355–369.

——(2011) 'Sport, peacemaking and conflict resolution: a contextual analysis and modelling of the sport, development and peace sector', Ethnic and Racial Studies, Vol. 34, No. 2: 207–228.

Glasner, P.E. (1977) The Sociology of Secularisation, London: Routledge & Kegan Paul.

Graham, S. and Weiner, B. (1996) 'Theories and principles of motivation', in D.C. Berliner and R.C. Calfee (eds) Handbook of educational psychology, New York: Simon & Schuster Macmillan, pp. 63–84.

Gramsci, A. (1994) Letters from Prison, Vols 1 and 2, F. Rosengarten (ed. and trans.), New York: Columbia University Press.

Granger, R.C. (1998) 'Establishing Causality in Evaluations of Comprehensive Community Initiatives', in K. Fulbright-Anderson, A.C. Kubisch and J.P. Connell (eds) New Approaches to Community Initiatives, Vol. 2, Theory, Measurement and Analysis, Washington, DC: Aspen Institute, www.aspenroundtable.org/vol2/granger.htm (accessed 21 December 2012).

Grissom, J.B. (2005) 'Physical Fitness and Academic Achievement', Journal of Exercise Physiologyonline (JEPonline), Vol. 8, No. 1, February: 11–25.

Gruber, J. (1986) 'Physical Activity and Self-Esteem Development in Children: A Metaanalysis', American Academy of Physical Education Papers, Vol. 19: 30–48.

Hammersley, M. (1995) The Politics of Social Research, London: Sage.

Hammersley, M. and Gomm, R. (1996) 'Exploiting Sociology for equality?', Network, British Sociological Association, No. 65 May: p. 1.

Harter, S. (1988) 'Developmental Processes in the Construction of the Self ', in T.D. Yawkey and J.E. Johnson (eds) Integrative Processes and Socialisation: Early to Middle Childhood, Hillsdale, NJ: Erlbaum, pp. 45–78.

——(1990) 'Self and Identity Development', in S. Feldman and G.R. Elliott (eds) At the Threshold: The Developing Adolescent, Cambridge, MA: Harvard University Press, pp. 352–388.

——(1999) The Construction of the Self: A Developmental Perspective, New York, Guildford Press.

Hartmann, D. (2003). 'Theorising sport as social intervention: A view from the grassroots', Quest, 55: 118–1140.

Hartmann, D. and Kwauk, C. (2011) 'Sport and development: An overview, critique and reconstruction', Journal of Sport and Social Issues, Vol. 35, No. 3: 284–305.

Hewitt, J. (1998) The Myth of Self-esteem: Finding happiness and solving problems in America, New York: St Martin's Press.

Hognestad, H. (2005) Norwegian Strategies on Culture – and Sports Development with Southern Countries, a presentation to the Sports Research Forum, Australian Sports Commission, Canberra, 13–15 April.

Home Office (2005) Positive Futures Impact Report: Staying in Touch, London: Home Office.

Howells, S. (2007) 'Organisational Sustainability for Sport and Development', paper presented at the 2nd Commonwealth Sport for Development Conference, Glasgow, 12 June 2008.

Hughes-d'Aeth, A. (2002) 'Evaluation of HIV/AIDS peer education projects in Zambia', Evaluation and Program Planning, 25: 397–407.

Hunter, J. (2001) 'A cross-cultural comparison of resilience in adolescents', Journal of Pediatric Nursing, Vol. 16 No. 3: 172–179.

Hyden, G. (1983) No Shortcuts to Progress: African Development Management in Perspective, Berkeley: University of California Press.

——(2006) 'Introduction and Overview to the Special Issue on Africa's Moral and Affective Economy', African Studies Quarterly, Vol. 9, Nos. 1 & 2: http://web.africa.ufl.edu/asq/v9/v9i1a1.htm (accessed 21 December 2012).

James, W. (1890) Principles of Psychology, New York: World.

Jeanes, R. (2011) 'Educating through sport? Examining HIV/AIDS education and sport-for-development through the perspectives of Zambian young people', Sport, Education and Society, June 13 (iFirst online): 1–19.

Jenkins, J. (1997) 'Not without a trace: Resilience and remembering among Bosnian refugees', Psychiatry, 60: 40–43.

Johnston, G. and Percy-Smith, J. (2003) 'In Search of Social Capital', Policy and Politics Vol. 31, No. 3: 321–334.

Kay, T. (2009) 'Developing through sport: evidencing sport impacts on young people', Sport in Society, Vol. 12, No. 9: 1177–1191.

——(2011) Sport in the service of international development: contributing to the Milennium Development Goals, paper presented to 2nd International Forum on Sport for Peace and Development, Geneva, 10–11 May.

Kay, T., Jeanes, R., Lindsey, I., Fimusamni, J., Collins, S. and Bancroft, J. (2007) 'Young people, sport development and the HIV-AIDS challenge', Loughborough: Institute of Youth Sport, Loughborough University.

Kerrigan, D. (1999) Peer Education and HIV/AIDS: Concepts, Uses and Challenges, Washington, DC: Horizons/Population Council.

Kicking Aids Out (nd) www.kickingaidsout.net (accessed 21 December 2012).

Kidd, B. (2008) 'A new social movement: Sport for Development and peace', Sport in Society, Vol. 11, No. 4: 370–380.

Krueger, J. (1998) 'Enhancement bias in the description of self and others', Personality and Social Psychology Bulletin, Vol. 24, 505–516.

Kruse, S.E. (2006) Review of Kicking AIDS Out: Is Sport an Effective Tool in the Fight Against HIV/AIDS?, draft report to NORAD, unpublished.

Leith, L.M. (1994) Foundations of Exercise and Mental Health, Morganstown, WV: Fitness Information Technology.

Leonard, M. (2004) 'Bonding and Bridging Social Capital: Reflections from Belfast', Sociology, Vol. 38, No. 5: 927–944.

Levermore, R. (2008) 'Sport: a new engine of development', Progress in Development Studies, Vol. 8, No. 2: 183–190.

Lindner, K.J. (1999) 'Sport Participation and Perceived Academic Performance of School Children and Youth', Pediatric Exercise Science, Vol. 11: 129–143.

Lindsey, I. and Banda, D. (2010) 'Sport and the fight against HIV/AIDS in Zambia: A "partnership approach"?', International Review for the Sociology of Sport, Vol. 46, No. 1, 90–107.

Lindsey, I. and Grattan, A. (2012) 'An "international movement"? Decentering sport for development within Zambian communities', International Journal of Sport Policy and Politics, Vol. 4, No. 1: 91–110.

Luszczynska, A., Scholz, U. and Schwarzer, R. (2005) 'The General Self-Efficacy Scale: Multicultural Validation Studies', The Journal of Psychology, Vol. 139, No. 5: 439–457.

Lyle, J. (2006) Sporting Success, Role Models and Participation: A Policy Related Review, Research Report No. 101, Edinburgh: sportscotland.

MacCallum, J. and Beltman, S. (2002) Role models for young people: What makes an effective role model program? Hobart: National Youth Affairs Scheme.

Mangan, J.A. (1998) The Games Ethic and Imperialism, London: Frank Cass.

Maro, C. and Roberts, G. (2012) 'Combating HIV/AIDS in sub-Saharan Africa: effect of introducing a mastery motivational climate in a community-based programme', Applied Psychology: An International Review, Vol. 61: 699–722.

Maro, C., Roberts, G. and Sorensen, M. (2009) 'Using sport to promote HIV/AIDS education for at-risk youths: an intervention using peer coaches in football', Scandanavian Journal of Medical Sci Sports, Vol. 19, No. 1: 129–141.

Maslow, A.H. (1943) 'A theory of human motivation', Psychological review, Vol. 50, No. 4: 370–396.

——(1987) Motivation and Personality, 3rd edition, New York: Harper & Row.

Mason, V. (1995) Young People and Sport in England, 1994: A National Survey, London: Sports Council.

McDermott, L. (2000) 'A Qualitative Assessment of Significance of Body Perception to Women's Physical Activity Experiences: Revisiting Discussions of Physicalities', Sociology of Sport Journal, Vol. 17: 331–363.

McNeill, F. (2009) '"Condoms cause AIDS": Poison, prevention and denial in Venda, South Africa', African Affairs, Advance Access: 1–18.

Mellanby, A., Newcombe, R., Rees, J. and Tripp, J. (2001) 'A comparative study of peer-led and adult-led sex education', Health Education Research: Theory and Practice, Vol. 16, No. 4: 481–492.

Merton, R.K. (1968) Social Theory and Social Structure, New York: Free Press.

Michielsen, K., Chersich, M., Luchters, S., De Koker, P., Van Rossem, R. and Temmerman, M. (2010) 'Effectiveness of HIV prevention for youth in sub-Saharan Africa: systematic review and meta-analysis of randomised and nonrandomised trials', AIDS, Vol. 24, No. 8: 1193–1202.

Morris, L., Sallybanks, J., Willis, K. and Makkai, T. (2003) Sport, Physical Activity and Anti-Social Behaviour, Research and Public Policy Series 49, Canberra: Australian Institute of Criminology.

Moynihan, D (nd) The Moynihan Challenge: 5 Years Late, http://jaypgreene.com/tag/national-review-online (accessed 22 December 2012).

Moyo, D. (2010) Dead Aid: Why aid is not working and how there is another way for Africa, London: Penguin Books.

Munro, B. (2005) 'Role Models: Is Anything More Important for Future Development?', Role Models Retreat, Laureus Sport for Good Foundation, 23–24 November, Pretoria, South Africa.

——(2006) 'Greed vs Good Governance: The Fight for Corruption-Free Football in Kenya', a paper presented at Play the Game 2005 – Governance in Sport: The Good, The Bad and The Ugly, Copenhagen: www.playthegame.org (accessed 22 December 2012).

Mwaanga, O. (2002) Kicking AIDS Out Through Movement Games and Sports Activities, Oslo: NORAD.

——(2003) 'HIV/AIDS At-Risk Adolescent Girls' Empowerment through Participation in Top Level Football and Edusport in Zambia', MSc thesis submitted to the Institute of Social Science at the Norwegian University of Sport and PE, Oslo.

——(2010) 'Sport for addressing HIV/AIDS: explaining our convictions', Leisure Studies Association Newsletter, Vol. 85: 61–67.

New York Times (2005) 'AIDS now compels Africa to challenge widows' "cleansing"', 11 May, www.nytimes.com/2005/05/011/international/africa/11malawi.html (accessed 2 August 2002).

Nicholls, S. (2009) 'On the Backs of Peer Educators: Using Theory to Interrogate the Role of Young People in the Field of Sport-in-development', in R. Levermore and A. Beacom (eds) Sport and International Development, London: Palgrave, pp. 156–175.

Nicholls, S., Giles, A.R. and Sethna, C. (2011) 'Perpetuating the "lack of evidence" discourse in sport for development: Privileged voices, unheard stories and subjugated knowledge', International Review for the Sociology of Sport, Vol. 46, No. 3: 249–264.

Nichols, G. (2007) Sport and Crime Reduction: The role of sports in tacking youth crime, London: Routledge.

Nichols, G. and Crow, I. (2004) 'Measuring the Impact of Crime Reduction Interventions Involving Sports Activities for Young People', Howard Journal of Criminal Justice, Vol. 43, No. 3: 267–283.

Nichols, G. and Taylor, P. (1996) West Yorkshire Sports Counselling: Final Evaluation Report, Sheffield: University of Sheffield, Management Unit.

NORAD (2002) Study of Future Norwegian Support to Civil Society in Mozambique, Oslo: NORAD, www.norad.no/default.asp?V_ITEM_ID=1137 (accessed 3 March 2012).

Norwegian Ministry of Foreign Affairs (2006) Strategy for Norway's culture and sports co-operation with countries in the South, Oslo: Norwegian Ministry of Foreign Affairs.

Norwegian Olympic Committee and Confederation of Sport (NIF) (nd) Sport and Development Cooperation. 1984–2002, unpublished document.

Nutley, S., Walter, I. and Davies, H. (2007) Using Evidence: How research can inform public services, Bristol: Policy Press.

Oettingen, G. and Zosuls, K. (2006) 'Culture and self-effciacy in adolescent', in F. Pajares and Y. Urdan (eds) Self-efficacy Beliefs of Adolescents, Charlotte, Information Age Publishing, pp. 245–265.

Okada, C. and Young, K. (2012) 'Sport and social development: Promise and caution from an incipienrt Cambodian football league', International Review for the Sociology of Sport, Vol. 47, No. 1: 5–26.

Okayasu, I., Kawahara,Y. and Nogawa, H. (2010) 'The relationship between community sports clubs and social capital in Japan: a comparative study between the comprehensive community sports clubs and the traditional community sports clubs', International Review for the Sociology of Sport, Vol. 45, No. 2: 163–186.

Pajares, F. (2002). Overview of social cognitive theory and of self-efficacy, www.emory.edu/EDUCATION/mfp/eff.html (accessed 13 November 2012).

Papacharisis, V., Goudas, M., Danish, S.J. and Theodorakis, Y. (2005) 'The Effectiveness of Teaching a Life Skills Program in a Sport Context', Journal of Applied Sports Psychology, Vol. 17: 247–254.

Patriksson, M. (1995) 'Scientific Review Part 2', in The Significance of Sport for Society – Health, Socialisation, Economy: A Scientific Review, prepared for the 8th Conference of European Ministers responsible for Sport, Lisbon, 17–18 May, Strasbourg: Council of Europe Press.

Pawson, R. (2001a) Evidence Based Policy, vol. 1, In Search of a Method, ESRC UK Centre for Evidence Based Policy and Practice, Working Paper, 3, London: University of London.

——(2001b) Evidence Based Policy: vol II, The Promise of 'Realist Synthesis', ESRC UK Centre for Evidence Based Policy and Practice. London: University of London.

——(2006) Evidence-Based Policy: A Realist Perspective, London: Sage.

Pawson, R. and Tilley, N. (2000) Realistic Evaluation, London: Sage.

——(2004) 'Realist Evaluation', paper prepared for the British Cabinet Office, www.community matters.com.au/RE_chapter.pdf (20 November 2011).

Pawson, R., Greenhalgh, T., Harvey, G. and Walshe, K. (2004) Realist synthesis: an introduction, ESRC Research Methods Programme University of Manchester, RMP Methods Paper 2/2004.

Payne, W., Reynolds, M., Brown, S. and Fleming, A. (2003) Sports Role Models and their Impact on Participation in Physical Activity: A Literature Review, Victoria: VicHealth.

Pelak, C.F. (2006) 'Local–Global Processes: Linking Globalisation, Democratisation and the Development of Women's Football in South Africa', Afrika Spectrum, Vol. 41, No. 3: 371–392.

Pearlman, D., Camberg, L., Wallace, L., Symons, P. and Finison, L. (2002) 'Tapping youth as agents for change: Evaluation of a peer leadership HIV/AIDS intervention', Journal of Adolescent Health, Vol. 31: 31–39.

Pisani, E. (2008) The Wisdom of Whores: bureaucrats, brothels and the business of AIDS, London: Granta Books.

Plummer, M., Wight, D., Obasi, A., Wamovi, J., Mshana, G., Todd, J., Mazige, B., Makokha, M., Hayes, R. and Ross, D. (2007). 'A process evaluation of a school-based adolescent sexual health intervention in rural Tanzania: the MEMA kwa Vijana programme', Health Education Research, Vol. 22, No. 4: 500–512.

Pollard, A. and Court, J. (2005) How Civil Society Organisations Use Evidence to Influence Policy Processes: A Literature Review, Working Paper, 249, London: Overseas Development Institute.

Portes, A. (1998) 'Social Capital: Its Origins and Applications in Modern Sociology', Annual Review of Sociology, Vol. 24: 1–24.

——(2000) 'The Hidden Abode: Sociology as analysis of the unexpected. 1999 Presidential Address', American Sociological Review, Vol. 65: 1–18.

Portes, A. and Landolt, P. (2000) 'Social Capital: Promise and Pitfalls of its Role in Development', Journal of Latin American Studies, Vol. 32: 529–547.

President's Council on Physical Fitness and Sports (2006) Sports and Character Development, Research Digest Series, 7/1, Washington, DC: President's Council on Physical Fitness and Sports.

Prochaska, J. and Velicer, W. (1997) 'The transtheoretical model of health behaviour change', American Journal of Health Promotion, 12: 38–48.

Putnam, R. (2000) Bowling Alone: The Collapse and Revival of the American Community, New York: Simon & Schuster.

Reasoner, R. (nd) Extending self-esteem theory and research, www.self-esteem-international. org/Research/Extending%20research.htm (accessed 22 December 2012).

Renard, R. (2006) The Cracks in the New Aid Paradigm, Discussion Paper, Antwerpen: Institute of Development Policy and Management.

Right to Play (nd) 'Sport for development', www.righttoplay.com/International/our-impact/ Pages/SportforDevelopmentcont%27d.aspx (accessed 22 December 2012).

Rogers, E.M. (1983) Diffusion of Innovations, New York: Free Press.

Rosenberg, M. (1965) Society and the Adolescent Self-image, Princeton, NJ: Princeton University Press.

Rossi, P.H., Lipsey, M.W. and Freeman, H.E. (2004) Evaluation: A Systematic Approach, 7th edition, Thousand Oaks, CA: Sage.

Saavedra, M. (2005) Women, Sport and Development, Sport and Development International Platform, www.sportanddev.org/data/document/document/148.pdf (accessed 3 August 2011).

——(2007) Some Dilemmas and Opportunities in Gender, Sport and Development, Chicago, IL: International Studies Association.

Saga, S., Boardley, I. and Kavussanu, M. (2011) 'Fear of failure and student athletes' interpersonal antisocial behaviour in education and sport', British Journal of Educational Psychology, Vol. 81: 391–408.

Sandford, R.A., Armour, K.M. and Warmington, P.C. (2006) 'Re-engaging disaffected youth through physical activity programmes', British Educational Research Journal, Vol. 32, No. 2: 251–271.

Scheff, T.J., Retzinger, S.M. and Ryan, M.T. (1989) 'Crime, Violence and Self-Esteem: Review and Proposals', in A.M. Mecca, N.J. Smelser and J. Vasconcellos (eds) The Social Importance Importance of Self Esteem, Berkeley, CA: University of California Press.

Scriven, M. (1994) 'The Fine Line between Evaluation and Explanation', Evaluation Practice, Vol. 15: 75–77.

Seippel, O. (2006) 'Sport and Social Capital', Acta Sociologica, Vol. 49, No. 2: 169–183.

Shah, M.K., Kambou, S., Goparaju, L., Adams, M.K. and Matarazzo, J.M. (eds) (2004) Participatory Monitoring and Evaluation of Community- and Faith-Based Programs: A Step-by-Step Guide for People Who Want to Make HIV and AIDS Services and Activities More Effective in their Community, Washington, DC: Core Initiative.

Shephard, R.J. (1997) 'Curricular Physical Activity and Academic Performance', Pediatric Exercise Science, Vol. 9: 113–126.

Sherer, M., Maddux, J.E., Mercandante, B., Prentice-Dunn, S., Jacobs, B. and Rogers, R.W. (1982) 'The Self-Efficacy Scale: Construction and validation', Psychological Reports, Vol. 51: 663–671.

Silverman, D. (1985) Qualitative Methodology and Sociology, London: Gower.

Skidmore, P., Bound, K. and Lownsborough, H. (2006) Community Participation: Who Benefits? York: Joseph Rowntree Foundation.

Smith, T.L. (1999) Decolonising methodologies: Research and indigenous people. Dunedin: University of Otago Press.

Smith, A. and Waddington, I. (2004) 'Using sport in the community schemes to tackle crime and drug use among young people: Some policy issues and problems', European Physical Education Review, Vol. 10: 279–297.

Solesbury, W. (2001) Evidence Based Policy: Whence it Came and Where it's Going, ESRC UK Centre for Evidence Based Policy and Practice, Working Paper, 1, London: University of London, http://kcl.ac.uk/content/1/c6/03/45/84/wp1.pdf (accessed 22 December 2012).

Sonstroem, R.J. (1988) 'Psychological models', in R.K. Dishman (ed.) Exercise Adherence, Champaign, IL: Human Kinetics, pp. 124–154.

Sonstroem, R.J. and Morgan, W.P. (1989) 'Exercise and Self-Esteem: Rationale and Model', Medicine and Science in Sport and Exercise, Vol. 21, No. 3: 329–337.

Spaaij, R. (2011) 'Sport as a vehicle for social mobility and regulation of disadvantaged urban youth', International Review for the Sociology of Sport, Vol. 44, No. 2: 247–264.

——(2012) 'Beyond the playing field: experiences of sport, social capital and integration among Somalis in Australia', Ethnic and Racial Studies, Vol. 35, No. 6: 1519–1538.

Spady, W. (1970) 'Lament for the Letterman: Effects of Peer Status and Extracurricular Activities on Goals and Achievement', American Journal of Sociology, January: 680–702.

Spence, J.C., McGannon, K.R. and Poon, P. (2005) 'The Effect of Exercise on Global Self-Esteem: A Quantitative Review', Journal of Sport and Exercise Psychology, Vol. 27, No. 3: 311–334.

Sport for Development International Working Group (SDPIWG) (2008) Harnessing the Power of Sport for Development and Peace, Toronto: Right to Play.

Stephenson, J., Strange, V., Oakley, A., Copas, A., Allen, E., Babiker, A., Black, S., Ali, M., Montieri, H. and Johnson, A. (2005) 'Peer-led sex education did not reduce the proportion of pupils having unprotected first intercourse before age 16', Evidence-based Obstretics and Gynecology, Vol. 7: 72–73.

Sugden, J. (2010) 'Critical left-realism and sport interventions in divided societies', International Review for the Sociology of Sport, Vol. 45, No. 3: 258–272.

Sugden, J. and Yiannakis, A. (1982) 'Sport and Juvenile Delinquency: A Theoretical Base', Journal of Sport and Social Issues, Vol. 6, No. 1: 22–30.

Svoboda, B. (1994) Sport and Physical Activity as a Socialisation Environment, Scientific Review Part 1, Strasbourg: Council of Europe, Committee for the Development of Sport (CDDS).

Szreter, S. (1998) A New Political Economy for New Labour: The Importance of Social Capital, Policy Paper, 15, Sheffield: Political Economy Research Centre.

Tacon, R. (2007) 'Football and Social Inclusion: Evaluating Social Policy', Managing Leisure: An International Journal, Vol. 12, No. 1: 1–23.

Taylor, P. (1999) 'External Benefits of Leisure: Measurement and Policy Implications'. Presentation to Tolern Seminar DCMS, London.

Taylor, P., Crow, I., Irvine, D. and Nichols, G. (1999) Demanding Physical Activity Programmes for Young Offenders under Probation Supervision, London: Home Office.

Tonts, M. (2005) 'Competitive sport and social capital in rural Australia', Journal of Rural Studies, Vol. 21: 137–149.

Turner, G. and Shepherd, J. (1999) 'A method in search of a theory: peer education and health promotion', Health Education Research: Theory and Practice, Vol. 14, No. 2: 235–247.

UK Sport (nd) Inspirational Inspiration, www.uksport.gov.uk/pages/internationalinspiration programme/ (accessed 22 December 2012).

Ungar, M. (2006) 'Resilience across Cultures', British Journal of Social Work, Vol. 38, No. 2: 218–235.

UNAIDS (1999) Peer education and HIV/AIDS: Concepts, uses and challenges, Geneva: UNAIDS.

UNICEF (2006) Monitoring and Evaluation for Sport-Based Programming for Development: Sport Recreation and Play, Workshop Report, New York: UNICEF.

——(nd) Preventing HIV with young people: the key to tackling the epidemic, London: UNICEF.

United Nations (2003) Sport for Development and Peace: Towards Achieving the Millennium Development Goals, Report from the United Nations Inter-Agency Task Force on Sport for Development and Peace, Geneva: United Nations.

——(2005) Final Report on International Year of Sport and Physical Education, New York: United Nations.

——(2005a) Business Plan International Year of Sport and Physical Education, New York: United Nations.

——(2005b) Sport for Development and Peace: Towards Achieving the Millennium Development Goals, New York: United Nations.

Value of Sport Monitor (nd) http://www.sportengland.org/research/value_of_sport_monitor. aspx (4 January 2013).

van Kampen, H. (ed.) (2003) A report on the expert meeting 'The Next Step' on Sport and Development, Amsterdam: NCDO, www.toolkitsportdevelopment.org/html/resources/ 0E/0E00BE53–2C02–46EA-8AC5-A139AC4363DC/Report%20of%20Next%20Step% 20Amsterdam.pdf (accessed 20 August 2011).

Van Rooy, A. (ed.) (2004) Global Legitimacy Game: Civil Society, Globalisation and Protest, London: Palgrave Macmillan.

Wagner, H.L. (1964) 'Displacement of Scope: A Problem of the Relationship Between Small-Scale and Large-Scale Sociological Theories', The American Journal of Sociology, Vol. 69, No. 6: 571–584.

Warwick, I. and Aggleton, P. (2004) 'Building on Experience: a formative evaluation of a peer education sexual health project in South Africa', London Review of Education, Vol. 2, No. 2: 137–153.

Weiss, C.H. (1980) 'Knowledge Creep and Decision Accretion', Knowledge: Creation, Diffusion, Utilisation, Vol. 1, No. 3: 381–404.

——(1986) 'The many meanings of research utilisation', in R. Bulmer (ed.) Social Science and Social Policy, London: Allen and Unwin.

——(1993) 'Where Politics and Evaluation Research Meet', Evaluation Practice, Vol. 14, No. 1: 93–106.

——(1997) 'How Can Theory-based Evaluation Make Greater Headway?', Evaluation Review, Vol. 21, No. 4: 501–524.

West, S.T. and Crompton, J.L. (2001) 'A Review of the Impact of Adventure Programs on At-Risk Youth', Journal of Park and Recreation Administration, Vol. 19, No. 2: 113–140.

Wight, D. (1999) 'Limits to empowerment-based sex education', Health Education, No 6: 233–243.

——(2005) 'Peer-led sex education did not reduce the proportion of pupils having unprotected first intercourse before age 16: A review', Evidence-based Obstetrics & Gynecology, Vol. 7: 72–73.

——(2007) 'Theoretical bases for teacher- and peer-delivered sexual health promotion', Health Education, Vol. 108, No. 1: 10–28.

Williams, T. and Williams, K. (2010) 'Self-efficacy and performance in mathematics: Reciprocal determinism in 33 nations', Journal of Educational Psychology, Vol. 102, No. 2: 453–466.

Willis, O. (2000) 'Sport and Development: The Significance of Mathare Youth Sports Association', Canadian Journal of Development Studies, Vol. 21, No. 3: 825–849.

Witt, P.A. and Crompton, J.L. (1997) 'The Protective Factors Framework: A Key to Programming for Benefits and Evaluating Results', Journal of Parks and Recreation Administration, Vol. 15, No. 3:1–18.

Wood, P., Hillman, S. and Sawilowsky, S. (1995) 'Comparison of self-esteem scores: American and Indian adolescents', Psychological Reports, Vol. 76, No. 2: 367–370.

Woodcock, A., Cronin, O. and Forde, S. (2012) 'Quantitative evidence for the benefits of Moving the Goalposts, a Sport for Development project in rural Kenya', Evaluation and Program Planning, Vol. 35: 370–381.

Woolcock, M. (2001) 'The Place of Social Capital in Understanding Social and Economic Outcomes', ISUMA Canadian Journal of Policy Research, Vol. 2, No. 1: 11–17.

Woolcock, M. and Narayan, D. (2000) 'Social Capital: Implications for Development Theory, Research, and Policy', The World Bank Research Observer, Vol. 15, No. 2: 225–249.

World Bank (nd) Social Capital and Civil Society, http://web.worldbank.org/wbsite/external/topics/extsocialdevelopment (accessed 22 December 2012).

——(nd) Civil Society, http://web.worldbank.org/ (accessed 22 December 2012).

——(2004) Monitoring and Evaluation: Some Tools, Methods and Approaches, Washington, DC: World Bank.

——(2010) Social capital, http://web.worldbank.org/ (accessed 22 December 2012).

World Commission on Culture and Development (1995) Our Creative Diversity: A Report of the World Commission for Culture and Development, UNESCO: www.unesco.org/culture/policies/ocd/index.shtml (accessed 20 August 2011).

World Health Organisation (WHO) (2006) Preventing HIV/AIDS in young people: A systematic review of the evidence from developing countries, Geneva: World Health Organisation.

YouthNet (2005) From Theory to Practice in Peer Education, New York: United Nations Population Fund and Youth Peer Education Network.

Zaharopoulos, E. and Hodge, K.P. (1991) 'Self-Concept and Sport Participation', New Zealand Journal of Psychology, Vol. 20: 12–16.

INDEX

Please note: Locators in **bold type** indicate figures or illustrations, those in *italics* indicate tables.